# SOCIAL SCIENCE CONCEPTS
# AND MEASUREMENT

# Social Science Concepts and Measurement

## NEW AND COMPLETELY REVISED EDITION

GARY GOERTZ

PRINCETON UNIVERSITY PRESS

PRINCETON & OXFORD

Requests for permission to reproduce material from this work
should be sent to Permissions, Princeton University Press

Published by Princeton University Press
41 William Street, Princeton, New Jersey 08540

In the United Kingdom: Princeton University Press
6 Oxford Street, Woodstock, Oxfordshire, OX20 1TR

press.princeton.edu

Library of Congress Cataloging-in-Publication Data

Names: Goertz, Gary, 1953– author.
Title: Social science concepts and measurement / Gary Goertz.
Description: New and completely revised edition. | Princeton : Princeton
   University Press, 2020. | Revised edition of the author's Social science
   concepts, c2006. | Includes bibliographical references and index.
Identifiers: LCCN 2019056839 (print) | LCCN 2019056840 (ebook) |
   ISBN 9780691205489 (paperback) | ISBN 9780691205465 (hardback) |
   ISBN 9780691205472 (ebook)
Subjects: LCSH: Social sciences—Research. | Qualitative research. |
   Political science—Research.
Classification: LCC H62 .G575 2020 (print) | LCC H62 (ebook) |
   DDC 300.72–dc23
LC record available at https://lccn.loc.gov/2019056839
LC ebook record available at https://lccn.loc.gov/2019056840

British Library Cataloging-in-Publication Data is available

Editorial: Bridget Flannery-McCoy and Alena Chekanov
Production Editorial: Kathleen Cioffi
Cover Design: Pamela L. Schnitter
Production: Erin Suydam

Cover Credit: Joan Miró, Bleu II, 1961 © Successió Miró / Artists Rights Society
(ARS), New York / ADAGP, Paris 2020

This book has been composed in Arno

Printed on acid-free paper. ∞

Printed in the United States of America

10   9   8   7   6   5   4   3   2   1

# CONTENTS

# TABLES

# FIGURES

# PREFACE

I WOULD LIKE to thank a wide range of individuals, institutions, and universities for feedback during the writing of this book. This volume has been in the works for years so it is impossible to remember all individuals and institutions that have contributed. This is a collective thank you to all.

I would like to thank all the students in my methods classes at Notre Dame over the years who have been subjected to various versions of this manuscript, as well as students at IQMR who have been test subjects for much of this material.

Particular thanks go to those who read the whole manuscript, including Barry Cooper, Séverine Deneulin, Carsten Schneider, and Richard Swedberg.

As always, thanks to Charles Ragin and Jim Mahoney for methodological inspiration and discussions over the years.

Various chapters of this manuscript in more final forms have been presented at several workshops and colloquia: thanks go to Simon Hug and Keith Krause at the University of Geneva; Zach Elkins, Pam Paxton, and John Gerring at UT-Austin; the QCA workshop in Antwerp 2019; James Copestake for organizing a couple of talks and a keynote at the University of Bath; and Ezequiel Gonzalez-Ocantos for organizing a talk at Oxford, as well as Colin Elman for a mini book workshop at IQMR in 2019.

Discussions with Eric Crahan at Princeton University Press got things going on the new edition of the book. Thanks to Bridget Flannery-McCoy and Alena Chekanov for managing the job in excellent fashion. Special thanks go to Alison Durham, who as copy-editor turned the raw materials—text, figures, and tables—into a refined and polished product.

# SOCIAL SCIENCE CONCEPTS
# AND MEASUREMENT

# 1

# Introduction

AN ONTOLOGICAL-SEMANTIC
APPROACH TO CONCEPTUALIZATION
AND MEASUREMENT

To define a thing, is to select from among the whole of its properties those which shall be understood to be designated and declared by its name; the properties must be very well known to us before we can be competent to determine which of them are fittest to be chosen for this purpose.

The essence of a thing ... is that without which the thing could neither be, nor be conceived to be.

Every proposition consists of two names [concepts]: and every proposition affirms or denies one of these names, of the other.... Here, therefore, we find a new reason why the signification of names, and the relation generally, between names and the things signified by them, must occupy the preliminary stage of the inquiry we are engaged in.

J. S. MILL

JOHN STUART MILL began his *System of logic* with a "book" devoted to concepts. Starting with concepts was a logical choice since they are key building blocks for constructing theoretical propositions. Propositional logic involves the proper manipulation of symbols. For this to have usefulness in science, these symbols need substantive and empirical content.

1

Concepts are measured en route to statistical and empirical evaluations of theoretical propositions. So concepts must be quantified and measured in many social science applications. However, as Lazarsfeld and Barton state, one must conceptualize before moving to empirical analyses:

> Before we can investigate the presence or absence of some attribute ... or before we can rank objects or measure them in terms of some variable, *we must form the concept of that variable.* (Lazarsfeld and Barton 1951, 155; emphasis is mine)

Philosophers, lawyers, political and social theorists debate normative concepts such as democracy, justice, and human rights. Concepts are fundamental to description. For anthropology, ethnography, grounded theory, and similar methodologies, developing concepts is a core theoretical and empirical activity. Concepts are thus core in causal theories, normative philosophy, and empirical description.

This book provides a unified framework for working with, constructing, and evaluating concepts that applies in these different domains. These domains often overlap. To use an example dear to my heart, which will appear as an ongoing example, "peace" is normative, descriptive, and a domain of causal theories and empirical testing of those theories (Goertz, Diehl, and Balas 2016).

Concepts are fundamentally about meaning, semantics, and ontology. Thus a methodology of concepts must to a significant degree be about semantics and ontology (which is a theory of being):

> Concepts are an answer to "what is" questions.

To ask *what* democracy *is*, or *what* poverty *is*, etc., is to inquire about ontology and definition. Concepts are about meaning and semantics.

As such, this volume uses terminology rarely seen in the literature on indicators, measurement, etc. Concepts are about definitions, semantics, ontology, meaning, and the like. *Downstream* we often want to have numeric, quantitative measures of these concepts—the so-called indicators. J. S. Mill started with "names" in his *System of logic*, not indicators of names.

It should be stressed that this ontology can vary and be contested on various grounds. For example, gender analyses of concepts contest the bias of their traditional ontologies, be it democracy, the welfare state, etc. This is closely related to normative issues that underlie many concepts. The concept and data for transitional justice are inherently normative. The ontology might vary depending on purpose and use. Finally, I'm personally working on the concept of civil or intrastate negative peace (Goertz et al. 2019), which has different versions depending on whether I'm focusing more on it as a dependent variable or as an independent and causal variable. This becomes quite evident in the guidelines regarding independent and dependent variables at the end of chapter 3.

The basic framework, described in detail in the next chapter, provides a methodology for analyzing, critiquing, and creating complex concepts (which might be given quantitative expression). *Complex concepts are multidimensional and multilevel.* Multidimensional appears semantically in definitions that include multiple attributes and features. They appear in data sets with multiple coding rules. Multidimensional is typically quite obvious; for example, in the next chapter see the analysis of the *Multidimensional* Poverty Index (MPI; Alkire et al. 2015).

The multilevel character of concepts in contrast has received almost no explicit attention. As discussed in the next chapter, the logic varies as one moves up and down the different levels. The logic of definitions is one of completeness and nonredundancy. Going back to Aristotle—and in philosophy in general—a good definition gives the set of necessary and jointly sufficient conditions for a concept. The logic of the data level is usually *multiple indicators of one defining dimension*. This is a logic of redundancy with no real need for completeness. One wants many—or enough—indicators of a one-dimensional concept: indicators are good when they are redundant.

This implies that the mathematics of the levels tends to differ significantly, which then means that final quantitative expression of the complex concept should typically incorporate different logics and the appropriate mathematics when generating the final numeric value.

In spite of the primordial importance of concepts, they have received relatively little methodological attention. At the same time there is a booming industry in complex *indicator* and *index* construction, such as the Multidimensional Poverty *Index*. International institutions such as the World Bank, the United Nations, OECD, and the EU— not to forget many prominent NGOs—generate hundreds of complex indicators. There has been a surge of books on indicators, such as Merry (2016) and Laurent (2018). Kelley and Simmons have an ongoing project examining dozens of "Global Performance Indicators" (2015); see also the Broome et al. project, e.g., 2018, for another long list of global indicators, as well as Weaver's global indices project.[1] All of these indicators are complex multilevel and multidimensional concepts.

An equally long list, and perhaps an even bigger industry, involves measures of physical and mental health or, more accurately, measures of illness, sickness, and disability. For example, I will refer on occasion to the DSM manual, which is the bible for clinical psychology and psychiatry (American Psychiatric Association, various years). It consists of a set of concepts, aka mental illnesses, along with sets of symptoms or indicators of the illnesses. Governments generate and use for crucial policy decisions many health indicators. For children there is the US Department of Health and Human Services Children's Bureau's child well-being measure, UNICEF's State of the World's Children measure, and Stirling Children's Wellbeing Scale, among others (see Alexandrova 2017 and Hausman 2015 for nice discussions of health concepts and scales). These are all very complex—multidimensional and multilevel—indices.

The terms "index" and "indicator" come from the idea of pointing, for example with one's index finger. These are all indicators of *something*. This book focuses on that "something," which is a concept.

1. http://www.ipdutexas.org/global-indices-project.html

One core feature of the basic framework is that conceptually it works top down. It asks for definitions which then connect downward to empirical indicators and data. Quantitative measures work from the bottom up: one starts with the data–indicators and then moves up to the top level. There is no real separation between conceptualization and measurement: they are fused.

In the appendix to the next chapter I contrast this ontological-semantic approach to conceptualization and measurement with latent variable models. These present a radically different approach, focused much more on indicators and measurement and much less on ontology and semantics. *Latent variables are cause indicators.* The ontological-semantic approach does not have causal relationships within the basic framework. The core criteria of completeness and nonredundancy for concepts make no sense in the latent variable framework. In the basic framework the focus is first and above all on the definitions and concept structure and then secondarily on the empirical indicators; for latent variables the focus is on "measurement models."

More generally, *all data sets rest on concepts.* It is hard to imagine the data being good if the underlying conceptualization is problematic, as is the case for example with terrorism. It is not uncommon for there to be disconnects between conceptualization and measurement, as we will see for the Polity democracy concept-measure. In short, this volume provides a methodology for the analysis of data sets of all sorts. The basic framework sees "coding rules" as conceptualizations with a certain aggregation structure. To understand data sets one needs a semantic and conceptual interpretation of the coding rules. "Coding rules"—always in the plural—implies multidimensional concepts.

Mill in the epigraph starts with "to define" and he continues with "its properties": this is about semantics, meaning, and ontology. He follows with "a thing" that is something in the real world, identifying and locating those "things" in the world. He then moves to "propositions," which are causal claims about the world. This volume focuses on the central role that concepts play in description and causal hypotheses as well as in normative analyses.

# The Conceptual Juggling Act

My notion would be, that anything which possesses any sort of power
to affect another, or to be affected by another, if only for a single
moment, however trifling the cause and however slight the effect, has
real existence; and I hold that the definition of being is simply power.

PLATO

A property carries its [causal] capacities with it, from situation to
situation.

NANCY CARTWRIGHT

The failure to explain is caused by a failure to describe.

BENOÎT MANDELBROT

Developing valid concepts for social science involves the juggling of
multiple conceptual balls. I use the juggling metaphor because typically
the focus is on one or two of the balls and the others are left to fall to the
ground. Some people focus on one or two balls in their research, while
others focus on other balls. This volume argues that one needs to keep
all of the balls in the air in one's mind when thinking about concepts,
and eventually downstream for measurement.

Figure 1.1 illustrates the nature of the juggling problem. All these
aspects of concept development and analysis will appear prominently
in the chapters to come. Given the emphasis on measurement in many
contexts, it is worth noting that these balls typically do not appear in
research design or measurement books. In contrast, the first three chapters of this volume focus in particular on these conceptual balls and
it is only in later chapters that measurement appears. This does not
mean that measurement will not be implicitly, or sometimes explicitly, present in the discussion, because one of the key issues is linking
conceptualization with measurement.

In the middle of the figure lies the semantic ball. A core question is
what does one mean by a concept? This means that conceptualization
is about definitions. For example, in some areas, such as political and

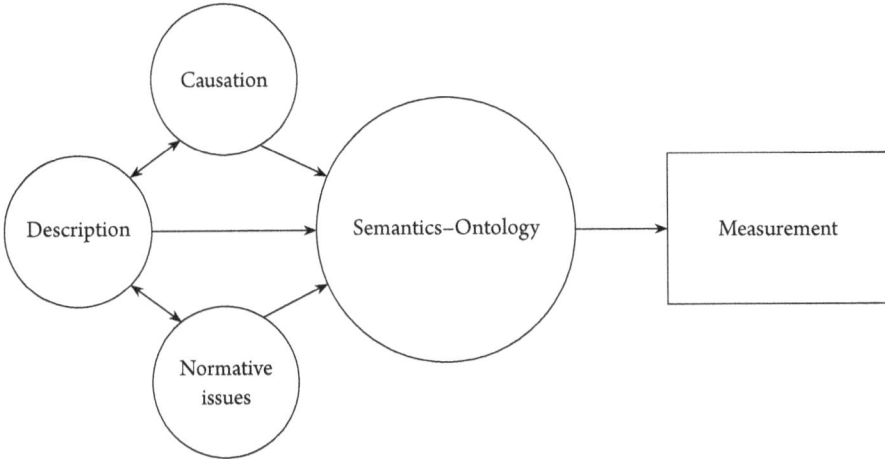

FIGURE 1.1. Juggling conceptual balls.

moral philosophy, the majority of the analysis is about the definition of some key political concept.

If one focuses exclusively on definitions, one risks getting a completely nominal view of concepts and their ontology. Hence it is absolutely critical to keep the three balls to the left of semantics in the air when discussing semantics. How does one determine what one should put into the semantics of concepts? As the arrows in figure 1.1 illustrate, there are three important factors or issues that should determine the semantic content of concepts in social science.

At the core of the methodology of concepts is the connection between the semantics of concepts and real-world phenomena. One dimension of this is the degree to which concepts and measures correctly capture and describe the world. For example, the degree to which Central American countries were democracies in the early 20th century is very debatable (Bowman et al. 2005). These debates combine the various possible conceptualizations of democracy with an application of those concepts to the reality of these countries in that time period. In general these are *both* conceptual and empirical questions.

Hence one conceptual ball is descriptive validity or what might be called empirical validity. A core goal of all sciences—natural and social—is to accurately describe the world. This means that this book rejects a nominalist view of concepts and, in contrast, takes a realist view of them. Good concepts accurately describe the world.

Often in psychology one hears about "constructs," which leaves the ontological character of the concept ambiguous. Remaining with psychology, depression is a real thing and the goal of the researcher is to conceptualize and describe depression accurately. In short, concepts have descriptive purposes and can be evaluated in terms of their empirical accuracy. One of my core examples will be concepts and measures of poverty: perhaps the central goal of these indices is to accurately describe the level of poverty in the world.

Figure 1.1 indicates via the arrow that descriptive validity influences the semantics of concepts. Hence, empirical accuracy should be a factor in determining semantics. The real world should influence definitions, because concepts are about ontologies in the world.

Concepts and numeric measures often lie at the beginning of the process of causal analysis. This was Mill's reason for beginning with a discussion of names. Causal inference depends critically on getting concepts and measurement right.

Figure 1.1 includes an arrow from causation to semantics. To state the obvious, concepts and measures are used in causal mechanisms, hypotheses, and theories. Issues of causation must, or at least should, play a role in determining the semantics of concepts. For example, in chapter 3 a guideline states that one should use features of causal mechanisms to conceptualize and define concepts. Not surprisingly, this also makes the methodology presented here a realist one. Concepts need to tap into the workings of the world; that needs to inform conceptualization. Hence it is completely appropriate to use the epigraph from Nancy Cartwright to begin this section. Valid concepts identify causal features of the world that constitute their causal powers.

Causation and causal inference appear at various points in this volume. Causal mechanisms play a key role in deciding upon defining dimensions when the concept in question is an explanatory factor. Normally the researcher will choose attributes that are parts of causal mechanisms and that have significant causal capacities. This is the point that Cartwright is making: core constitutive features of the phenomenon travel with their causal powers. Those causal powers are key to the conceptualization.

It is useful to distinguish causal relationships within concepts from causal relationships between concepts. Causal relationships between concepts are when they function as independent or dependent variables in some theory or causal mechanism. Causation is also an important feature of analysis *within* concepts. Figure 1.1 is about causal relationships within concepts.

Causal relationships within concepts lie at the core of the latent variable approach to measurement. Typically, the unobserved latent variable causes the indicators. I like to call this the disease–symptom model, since diseases cause symptoms. One *infers* diseases based on symptoms. But one would be wrong to confuse the symptoms with the disease: the disease *is not*—an ontological claim—the symptoms.

One might also argue that there are causal relationships between defining dimensions of concepts. This comes up quite often in the literature on poverty and human well-being:

> Development consists of the removal of various types of unfreedoms that leave people with little choice and little opportunity of exercising their reasoned agency. The removal of substantial unfreedoms, it is argued here, is *constitutive* of development.... The intrinsic importance of human freedom, in general, as the preeminent objective of development is strongly supplemented by the instrumental effectiveness of freedoms of particular kinds to promote freedoms of other kinds. The linkages between different types of freedoms are empirical and causal, rather than constitutive and compositional. (Sen 1999, xii)

Sen illustrates how ontological, aka constitutive, dimensions may have causal relationships between them. At the end Sen is making strong causal claims about the relationships between the constitutive elements of "development as freedom."

On the dependent variable side the defining dimensions influence causal hypotheses because they are part of what is being explained. For example, if one includes women's suffrage as part of democracy then one might need to think about the causes of women's suffrage on the independent variable side of things.

Issues of causal inference lie at the core of many aspects of concept construction because of the various roles that concepts play in constructing and evaluating causal hypotheses.

Figure 1.1 includes a normative ball being juggled as well. Obviously, political and moral philosophies focus on the relationship between normative issues, semantics, and conceptualization. But many other research questions implicitly or explicitly involve normative issues. The whole area of international indicators and indices usually has normative dimensions: for example, one should increase transparency, one is concerned with the very poor, one wants to understand peace.

Unsurprisingly, social scientists have tended to avoid, dance around, and not explicitly address normative issues in conceptualization. It has really been philosophers of social science who have seriously explored the connection between normative issues and the various other conceptual balls. Yet these connections are fundamental in both the social as well as health sciences.

Much of the capability approach to human well-being has been normative as well as descriptive. What is frequently absent is how this can be linked to causal questions of various sorts. For example Robeyns discusses the linkage between the capability approach and explanatory issues:

> Nevertheless, the notions of functionings and capabilities in themselves can be employed as elements in explanations of social phenomena, or one can use these notions in descriptions of poverty, inequality, quality of life and social change.... This raises the question of whether the capability approach should aspire to do this kind of explanatory capabilitarian analysis. Another very important task of the capability approach is to reach out to those disciplines in order to make bridges between the normative and the explanatory analyses—one valuable element of the truly post-disciplinary agenda to which the capability approach aims to contribute. (Robeyns 2017, 142–43)

The huge literature and industry on physical and mental health indicators illustrates the importance of normative considerations. For example, in the history of the DSM, homosexuality was for decades considered a mental disorder. DSM-I (American Psychiatric Association 1952) defined homosexuality as a disorder as follows:

OOQ-x63 Sexual deviation:
This diagnosis is reserved for deviant sexuality which is not symptomatic of more extensive syndromes, such as schizophrenic and obsessional reactions. The term includes most of the cases formerly classed as "psychopathic personality with pathologic sexuality." The diagnosis will specify the type of the pathologic behavior, such as homosexuality, transvestism, pedophilia, fetishism and sexual sadism (including rape, sexual assault, mutilation). (DSM-I, 39–40)

Obviously, today such a claim would not be widely accepted. This is also highly problematic from a normative perspective. In retrospect—and even at the time—it seems amazing that homosexuality is in a list together with rape and mutilation. It took Stonewall and gay activism in the 1970s to finally incite the DSM to remove homosexuality as a mental disorder in the DSM-III supplement (American Psychiatric Association 1987).

Similar issues arise when deafness and other "handicaps" are considered illness or not-healthy. For example, "according to the HUI(3), the value of the health state of being deaf and having no other health deficiencies on a 0–1 scale is .465. According to the HUI(3), two years of life for someone who is deaf produces fewer QALYs [quality of life years] than one year of life for someone in full health. In contrast, many in the deaf community deny that deafness is a disability at all. This assertion is not sour grapes: many in the deaf community decline the partial restoration of hearing made possible by a cochlear implant, thereby showing an effective preference for deafness over partial hearing" (Hausman 2015, 90–91).

The concept and literature on "transitional justice" deals directly with normative issues of "crime," "wrongdoing," and the like. The

During Conflict Justice data set focuses exclusively on "justice" as crimes or wrongdoings related to the events of a particular conflict. The data set includes information on six forms of addressing wrongdoing: trials, truth commissions and commissions of inquiry, reparations, amnesties, purges, and exiles (Loyle and Binningsbø 2018, 445). It is not at all obvious that amnesty is justice, even though it is included in data sets on transitional justice. Typically, amnesty means that justice is not being served. So to include amnesty in the concept of transitional justice is to make a clear—and in my opinion completely invalid—normative decision. The United Nations takes the same stance in refusing to include amnesty in its list of standard and approved transitional justice mechanisms (United Nations Secretary General 2010).

The philosophy of social science literature has dealt with the connect between normative and empirical issues within conceptualization using the concept of "mixed hypotheses." Alexandrova defines them in this way: "A hypothesis is mixed if and only if (1) It is an empirical claim about a putative causal or statistical relation. (2) At least one of the variables in this claim is defined in a way that presupposes a moral, prudential, or political value judgement about the nature of this variable" (Alexandrova 2017, 82). Tiberius signals the importance of "mixed" claims:

> Without identifying them as mixed claims, philosophers have noted normative content in concepts of efficiency, rape, spousal abuse, unemployment, divorce, inflation, aggression, health and specific diseases, and, of course, well-being. My notion of a mixed claim captures these examples. What has not been done is to settle whether mixed claims should be part of science and if so what rules they should obey. (Tiberius 2004)

Most of the concepts discussed in this volume are mixed in this philosophical sense. The normative ball is often present, if most often not in the air but rather left on the ground.

One should be suspicious of any claim that says a social science concept has no normative underpinnings or dimensions. For example,

Rotberg argues that his influential indicator of governance is not very normative:

> My work on governance (here and earlier), in contrast, has been predicated on governance—and hence good governance—being defined as the performance of national, provincial, municipal, and other governments in delivering specific articulated political goods. The designation of such political goods is much more descriptive than normative; the political goods in question are those that citizens everywhere—in every culture, in every political jurisdiction—expect their governments (and their political leaders) to provide. (Rotberg 2018, 35)

Whether many or few people demand a political good does not make it more or less normative in character. One should be wary of claims about "no normative judgement." Some describe the concept of democracy as a decision-making procedure. This is true, but there is a significant set of normative values about individual liberties, rights, etc. that underlie democracy as a decision-making procedure.

In summary, figure 1.1 argues that semantics should be driven by considerations other than just pure meaning. Because concepts are used to describe the world, to explain the world, and to evaluate the world, these criteria need to feed into the semantics of the concept.

Also in the figure is an arrow from the semantics–ontology ball to the measurement square. The methodology of this arrow constitutes a very large part of this volume. A central methodological question is the connection of all of these aspects of concept construction to numeric measures. Numeric measurement appears in data sets as well as in variables in statistical hypotheses, essentially anything which receives numeric values (this includes dichotomous presence–absence as measurement). In short, connecting conceptualization with numeric variables and the construction of data sets forms a core part of the methodology of concepts.

Once one places concepts in the larger social science research enterprise, the nature of conceptual juggling becomes clearer. Concepts–measurement plays four core roles in the research enterprise:

- They are used in descriptive inference. One often asks questions about the evolution of poverty or peace in the world; the answer requires concepts and corresponding measures.
- One uses concepts as independent and explanatory factors. Thus the features that constitute independent variables must in general play some role in causal mechanisms and causal explanations, otherwise why would one include features that have no causal relevance in the concept?
- Concepts and measures appear as dependent variables. Thus to explain the level, occurrence, or changes in those dependent variables one must be explaining the attributes that constitute the concept.
- Concepts are used in case selection and scope decisions. These are not fundamentally different from independent or dependent variables. One cannot have a complete causal inference research design without making important case selection decisions that apply concepts.

These uses of concepts and measures naturally align with the concept juggling balls. They are important in conceptualization because they play core roles in social science research.

## Concept Semantics and Measurement: Aggregation, Scaling, and Transformations

The questions "What counts as a measurement of (physical quantity) X?" and "What is (that physical quantity) X?" cannot be answered independently of each other.

BAS VAN FRAASSEN

Unlike most "methodological" treatments, which focus more on the statistics and mathematics of measurement, my treatment starts with meaning, conceptualization, and ontology. Later chapters in the book explore in detail mathematical, operational, and measurement issues, but this chapter and the next two focus on meaning, semantics, and ontology. The mathematically inclined will already see much of what is coming down the pike in later chapters because the mathematics of concept structure already implies *classes* of mathematical procedures for measurement. I stress "classes" because the mean, OR, AND really form classes of options and not a specific mathematical function.

One of the most important and hard methodological, conceptual, and measurement challenges lies in connecting semantics and ontology with aggregation, scaling, and measurement. Concepts are about definitions, ontology, and semantics. At the same time we want quantitative measures for these concepts. How can one make the connection closely and smoothly so that measurement reflects as much as possible meaning and ontology? Various chapters in this volume address aspects of this challenge, in particular issues of making data–indicators commensurable (i.e., scaling) and aggregating numeric data–indicators, as well as defining attributes. This must all remain as faithful as possible to the meaning and semantics of the concept.

Aggregation becomes critical when it comes to quantification and measurement. Many researchers want a numeric value for a concept for each observation for some population or scope. The UN wants HDI data for all countries for as many years as possible. The same is true for democracy data sets.

Core to concept structure is the problem of aggregation. The continuum of aggregation involves *degrees of substitutability*. To analyze this substitutability continuum I use a combination of fuzzy logic and public goods economics, i.e., production and utility functions. The three aggregation classes below are not a free-floating typology, but rather constitute alternatives along a continuum of substitutability. There are three zones of the substitutability continuum, but it is still a continuum. It is useful to consider the logics that underlie the three zones:

- Weakest link: the minimum is the core aggregating principle, along with functions that produce smaller values than the minimum, no substitutability.
- Mean: the mean is typically used for "indicators of," moderate substitutability.

- Best shot: the maximum or sum of the defining features, extensive substitutability.

The metaphor of weakest link comes from the literature on the production of public goods (e.g., Sandler 1992), which uses the idea that the strength of a chain is the value of the weakest link. In mathematical logic this is the minimum aggregation rule used in fuzzy logic as well as QCA. The best shot comes also from the literature on public goods, and signals that what really matters is the best of the dimensions. Economics examples often involve technology: what matters is not the average technology or product but the best one. In the fuzzy-logic context this is the maximum or OR aggregation function.

For economists the standard way to address aggregation is via utility and production functions. For example, consumption poverty analyses rely on some utility function. Some utility functions are weakest link (including the classic Cobb–Douglas production function), others are mean (e.g., the generalized mean, known to economists as the constant elasticity of substitution function), and others are best shot. They vary in the degree of substitutability between dimensions or indicators. Fuzzy logic is clearer on this because it formalizes the three zones and includes aggregation procedures smaller than the minimum and larger than the maximum.

Chapter 6 explores some of the core issues surrounding concept structure and aggregation choices. One of the tensions is that between the definitions and the mathematical operations used in aggregation. For example, it is quite common for the semantics of the concept to invoke necessary and sufficient conditions while the aggregation operation uses sums and means (see the Polity example in the next chapter). It is also quite possible to use different aggregation schemes for different levels of the basic framework. As discussed at length in the next chapter, the logic of aggregation often varies between levels.

Creating numeric measures in complex concepts means deciding on aggregation rules and the structure of the concept. This is unavoidable. Even in purely conceptual, philosophical, and moral philosophy discussions one must take—usually implicitly—a position on concept structure (aka aggregation). For example, Kantian moral philosophy typically invokes weakest link procedures while utilitarianism allows for high levels of substitutability.

Chapter 7 on hybrid concepts continues the discussion of chapter 6 on aggregation. It introduces hybrid structures, particularly those where instead of using the same aggregation procedure across a level, one uses a mixture of logical AND and logical OR. Hybrid structures are also those that use different aggregation procedures at different levels. Chapter 10 focuses on a popular hybrid where the secondary level uses logical AND while the data-indicator level uses logical OR. Hybrids seem particularly appropriate for gray zone concepts where often one requires that the gray zone not be at either end of the spectrum, i.e., two necessary conditions, but then uses different aggregation procedures—logical OR or family resemblance—for the middle, gray zone. Hybrid concept structures are a critical part of any conceptual and measurement toolbox.

Concept structure is also key factor in the discussion of intension–extension, where intension is the ontology of the concept and extension is empirical coverage. Chapter 9 analyses how concepts can be looser or stronger in terms of the number of cases that they cover, i.e., cases that score high in terms of their membership in the concept. The intension–extension distinction was imported into political science by Sartori (1970) and then discussed by Collier and his students (e.g., Collier and Mahon 1993). The key fact is that by removing necessary defining features, the empirical coverage of the concept increases. Chapter 9 discusses how concept structure in general, including best shot and weakest link, relates to empirical extension. Family resemblance was the philosophers response to requirements of necessary defining features: conceptualization without any necessary conditions at all. Family resemblance is another way to think about concept structure ranging from weakest link to best shot depending on the family resemblance rule. The relationship between intension and extension is illustrated concretely using the Democracy–Dictatorship data set (Cheibub et al. 2010).

In practice, for a variety of reasons—philosophical, practical, policy, theoretical, and causal—one must aggregate. To do this aggregation requires some important decisions about the common scale. Aggregation across dimensions is required to move up to the next level. For example, one popular option is to convert all measures to the standard deviation scale; latent variable measurement models usually do this.[2] So the question in general is not *whether* to aggregate but *how* to aggregate. One needs a framework for thinking about aggregation decisions. This is a core goal of this volume.

In a more philosophical vein, scholars argue that dimensions are incommensurate. For example, in *Disadvantage*, Wolff and De-Shalit argue vigorously against reducing all the elements of lives to a single numerical scale. They argue that aggregation across the diverse elements of lives is bound to miss things of vital importance. For example, Sen describes "non-commensurability" as "a much-used philosophical concept that seems to arouse anxiety and panic" (2009, 240). In philosophy, incommensurability is used as an argument against aggregation at all (e.g., Chang 1998). In practice a complex concept or definition involves putting together different components. So at some important semantic level one cannot even construct a definition if one is strict about the noncommensurability of defining features.

To aggregate across dimensions requires a common scale. However, it might well be the case that different dimensions, data, or indicators are of different scale types. From psychology one has the classic typology of scales, including nominal, ordinal, interval, and ratio. Very common in research design textbooks is the conventional wisdom (dating to the 1950s) about these scales. Aggregation procedures usually minimally require interval data, and most often require ratio or real numbers. Ideally one needs methods of converting dichotomous, ordinal, and interval data into ratio variables, which are required for most mathematical operations.

Some approaches, e.g., economics, virtually assume ratio or real numbers. This is because to do virtually any complex mathematical

2. It appears to be common among experimenters to evaluate causal effects in terms of standard deviations.

operation one needs ratio variables. One frequently sees nominal variables converted into interval ones with no justification, e.g., adding up a bunch of 0–1 nominal indicators. It is sometimes not clear whether a quantitative measure is interval or ratio. Chapter 5 addresses some of the generally ignored issues and common problems of scaling. One advantage of the fuzzy-logic approach is the provision of a methodology for converting various scale types into real-valued numbers.

Aggregation across different dimensions or indicators is often routinized. However, it cannot be stressed enough how important the semantic issues involved are. Extremely common for example is to standardize via linear transformation of each dimension so that the minimum is 1 and the maximum is 100 (or something equivalent). The core semantic equivalence question lies in what constitutes "high" or "low" for each dimension. To assess this, one must explore the connection between the numeric measures and meaning. To use my canonical example, how much GDP per capita does it take for a country to be wealthy or poor? Creating common scales for dimensions or indicators is a central semantic operation.

Chapter 4 introduces a core methodological device, the "semantic transformation." One can connect semantics, meaning, and definitions with some related quantitative measures or indices. A principal example is how one could connect concepts such as poverty, wealth, and economic development with data such as GDP per capita. Chapter 4 is devoted to exploring the relationship between indicators such as GDP per capita and concepts such as poor country. It provides a methodology for tightening the connection between what we mean in practice by such concepts as poor country and common measures of poverty. The methodology of semantic transformations also provides a framework for thinking about standard default transformations such as dichotomizing and linear relationships between quantitative measures and meaning. The semantic transformation methodology also proves critical in thinking about how to transform ordinal data to ratio which is essential to aggregation operations.

The semantic transformation methodology allows one to compare and contrast different options. A common tension is between concepts that include thresholds versus linear transformations. One option is to use straight GDP per capita as a measure of poverty. Often one uses logged GDP per capita. Almost all poverty measures, such as MPI and Sen–Nussbaum, use thresholds. Dichotomization is in fact a threshold operation.

There is really an underlying continuum here as well, which might be called "degree of thresholdness." Linear transforms have no threshold. S-curve relationships have varying degrees of thresholdness depending on how sharp the S-curve is. Dichotomous transformations are the extreme threshold where there is a vertical threshold leap. For example, typically poverty measures are linear from zero until the threshold (poverty line) and then flat above that. Headcount measures of poverty use the extreme dichotomization threshold transformation.

The methodological issue is how to link semantics with numeric measures. For social science and social policy to move together it means that this linkage needs to be made explicit and justified. Fuzzy logic provides a framework for linking data-indices and concepts. I encourage researchers to take existing data and use them to the extent possible to incorporate what they mean by the concept in question.[3] I will take GDP per capita data and see how one might semantically transform them to fit better with concepts such as poverty and wealth.

## Sets of Concepts, Concept Pairs, Bipolar Concepts, and Typologies

Concepts in this introduction focus on what the next chapter calls the "positive pole," such as human well-being, poverty, and peace. In fact, concepts often come in pairs, one of which is seen as the "negation" or "opposite" of the other. Examples appearing frequently in this volume include democracy–autocracy, peace–war, and poverty–wealth. To give them a name I refer to them as concept pairs or "bipolar concepts." For example, the Polity measure of democracy–autocracy is

---

3. In the previous edition of this book (a chapter cut for space reasons in this edition) I took the Polity measure of democracy and reworked it to conform better with the concept of democracy of the Polity researchers.

literally "democracy minus autocracy," where there is an autocracy concept as well as a democracy concept. Finally, concepts often come in sets under the rubric of typologies. For example, there are a variety of typologies of autocracy. All of these options raise the question of the relationship *between* connected concepts.

The position defended here is that the negation of a positive pole concept such as democracy is literally "not-democracy." The conceptual claim—which as we will see has huge causal implications—is that autocracy is not the same as not-democracy. One can see this often in semantic practice when people state that "peace is not just the absence of war." A person making this statement is rejecting the idea that peace = not-war.

Bipolar concepts are often fundamentally incomplete. A core example from the next chapter deals with the World Bank's conceptualization of poverty using individual or household consumption data. Poverty is conceived of as low levels of consumption. However, consumption by itself runs from low to high as a concept. One must apply additional criteria to consumption to get to the concept of interest, which is poverty. Many social science concepts have this feature. For example, "education" as years of schooling is typically incomplete. The linkage to theories and hypotheses is critical: one does not have hypotheses about education *tout court* but rather about "educated" or "uneducated." Similarly, one has hypotheses about democracy, not the bipolar democracy–autocracy.

In addition to bipolar concepts where one is the "opposite" of the other, one often sees sets of concepts. Scholars usually refer to these sets as typologies. In chapter 8 I define a typology as a set of concepts, typically more than two.[4]

A set of concepts can—and often does—contain bipolar pairs. For example, Schmitter's (1974) very influential typology focused on the positive pole of corporatism, with its opposite of pluralism, along with the additional two types "monist" (e.g., USSR) and "syndicalist."

---

4. I do not treat the separate issue of typologies of causal relationships.

Chapter 8 argues that typologies created following standard advice are fraught with problems in multiple ways. The standard advice is to make typologies that are (1) mutually exclusive and (2) exhaustive. Following this advice leads to major methodological, empirical, and causal problems. I use Geddes's (Geddes et al. 2014) influential typology of autocratic regimes as my main example; however, these problems are inherent in standard typology methodology, i.e., anyone following these methodological rules is going to run up against the same problems as Geddes.

While this volume focuses mostly on individual concepts, one cannot ignore the issue of bipolar concepts. In addition, scholars love typologies—sets of concepts—which may or may not include bipolar pairs, and which may or may not be somewhat ordered (i.e., not a nominal set of concepts).

In short, there are sets of concepts that have various kinds of relationships with each other, as bipolar pairs or as members of typologies. My methodology of concepts provides a framework for analyzing these common conceptual situations.

## Complex Concepts Producing Complex Theories

J. S. Mill started his *System of logic* with a "book" on concepts because they are used as components of scientific propositions. Chapter 10 looks at how multilevel concepts appear in theories. The basic framework—presented in the next chapter—is about one concept. What happens when you begin to put complex concepts together into a theoretical model that makes causal claims about the world?

Chapter 10 outlines what I call two-level theories. Complex concepts are multidimensional and multilevel. When you begin to put them together into theories, those theories then also become complex. In particular, theories become multilevel: I focus on theories that have two theoretical levels, which not surprisingly I call two-level theories. The multidimensionality feature of these complex theories is less novel and interesting. People are completely used to multivariate analyses.

However, the multilevel nature of theories is much less present in research.[5]

One can construct a large variety of two-level theories with differing concept structures and causal relationships. Chapter 10 focuses on a very common one illustrated by Skocpol's famous *States and social revolutions*. It turns out that many famous scholars have independently arrived at this two-level theoretical structure. I use a variety of examples to explore the key variants on the basic model, including Skocpol's theory of social revolutions, Ostrom's work on common pool resource institutions, Kingdon's influential model of agenda setting, and Hick's study of the causes of the welfare state. With these various examples we will see different ways to build concepts, as well as several kinds of causal and noncausal relationships within and among dimensions and levels.

## Conclusion

Concepts are theories about ontology: they are theories about the fundamental constitutive elements of a phenomenon. While many quantitative scholars may find the term "ontological" provocative and many interpretivists may object to my usage, I use the term in a straightforward way to designate the core characteristics of a phenomenon and their interrelationships. For example, we can ask about what constitutes a welfare state. Typically, these are states that provide goods and services like unemployment insurance, medical services, and retirement benefits. To *be* a welfare state *is* to provide these goods and services.

Good concepts pick out the causally relevant factors in phenomena. To use Cartwright's nice terminology (1989), defining features of concepts pick out the causal capabilities of phenomena. For example, a good conceptualization of democracy includes those features that are relevant in causal mechanisms about the impact of democracy.

---

5. There exists a huge literature on "hierarchical models" (e.g., Gilman and Hill 2007), which is quite different from what I present. The variables–concepts in these models are still treated in a single-level way.

As such, this volume rejects a strong nominalist, Red Queen, *Alice in Wonderland,* view of concepts.[6]

Good concepts accurately describe the world. Many people want to know whether poverty is increasing or decreasing in the world (Alkire et al. 2015; Ravallion 2016), or whether the world is getting more peaceful and less violent (Pinker 2011; 2018). To answer these questions requires good empirically descriptive concepts.

Good concepts often require serious normative justification. One's conceptualization of human well-being must be at least partially normative.

Because concepts serve various purposes, like causal analysis, description, and normative analysis, their ontology can and should vary according to purpose.

In terms of social science, I propose a causal, ontological, and realist view of concepts. It is an ontological view because it focuses on what constitutes a phenomenon. It is causal because it identifies ontological attributes that have causal capacities and that play a key role in causal hypotheses, explanations, and mechanisms. It is realist because it involves a descriptive analysis of the phenomenon. My approach stresses that concept analysis involves ascertaining the constitutive characteristics of a phenomenon that have central causal capacities. These causal powers and their related causal mechanisms play a role in our theories. A purely semantic analysis of concepts, words, and their definitions is never adequate by itself, at least in social science, and probably not in moral and political philosophy either.

Thus this volume embraces a realist philosophy of science like that described by Kitcher:

> Minimal realism holds that there are objects independent of human cognition. Strong realism adds the thesis that, independently of us, these objects are assorted into natural kinds and that there are causal processes in which they participate. The task of

---

6. It is notable that Lewis Carroll was also a prominent logician, and that informs many great parts of *Alice.*

science is to expose the causal structure of the world, by delineating the pre-existent natural kinds and uncovering the mechanisms that underlie causal dependencies. (Kitcher 1992, 104)

Concepts are about these "natural kinds" that participate in causal mechanisms and causal explanations.

Most important concepts we use are *multidimensional* and *multilevel* in nature. Many, if not most, of the core social science concepts are complex in this sense. This volume provides a systematic methodology for analyzing and constructing complex concepts along with the appropriate corresponding quantitative measures.

# 2

# The Basic Framework for Conceptualization and Measurement

## Introduction

The basic framework presented in this chapter serves as the fundamental methodological framework for this whole volume. It is a framework that privileges semantics and ontology in terms of conceptualization. This chapter and the next have relatively little to say about measurement and quantification. When they do appear, it is in a clearly secondary role. Chapters 4–6 deal extensively with issues of scaling, aggregation, and measurement. But they are subordinate to the issues of conceptualization, semantics, and definitions.

The basic framework provides a methodology for thinking about concept structure as well as the mathematics of aggregation within complex concepts. There needs to be a link between the semantic structure of concepts and the mathematics of aggregation that produces final numeric measures of concepts.

In summary, the basic framework provides a way to think about and analyze concepts in terms of both their semantic structure and how that ends up in the mathematics of aggregation resulting in numeric measures of the concept.

The basic framework confronts the basic fact of social science and philosophy that many concepts of great importance are *complex* in the sense that they are *multidimensional* and *multilevel*. The methodological question is how to deal with the vertical and horizontal dimensions of complexity simultaneously.

One of the core challenges in a book on concepts and measurement is linking the two. As a rough generalization, scholars tend to focus on one or the other. Most research design textbooks have a chapter on measurement, but no chapter on the methodology of concepts. Many qualitative or philosophical discussions of concepts have no linkage to measurement. One central goal of the basic framework presented in this section and used throughout the book is to provide a framework for linking the two.

Figure 2.1 provides the basic framework used in this volume to analyze concepts, measurement, scaling, typologies, etc., emphasizing that they are multilevel and multidimensional.

The *basic level* in figure 2.1 is the concept as used in causal hypotheses or as the focus of theoretical, normative, or descriptive analysis. This term comes from cognitive psychology and people's preference to work at a certain level of abstraction. For instance, core examples in this volume consist of concepts important in international politics, comparative politics, economics, and philosophy, such as human development, poverty, and well-being. The basic level is the top level of hundreds of international indices. Other important examples in this volume include peace, democracy, and the welfare state. One simple way to locate the basic level is in the variables of the statistical analysis or core hypotheses.

The *secondary level* (SL in figure 2.1) refers to the multidimensionality of these concepts. In terms of semantics and definitions, concepts have multiple defining features or attributes. For many complicated concepts, much of the debate is about the content as well as the inclusion of a given defining feature. What is the substantive content, for example, of "peace" between states?

The *data–indicator level* (DIL in figure 2.1) is where one includes numeric data and indicators. The term "indicator" itself suggests

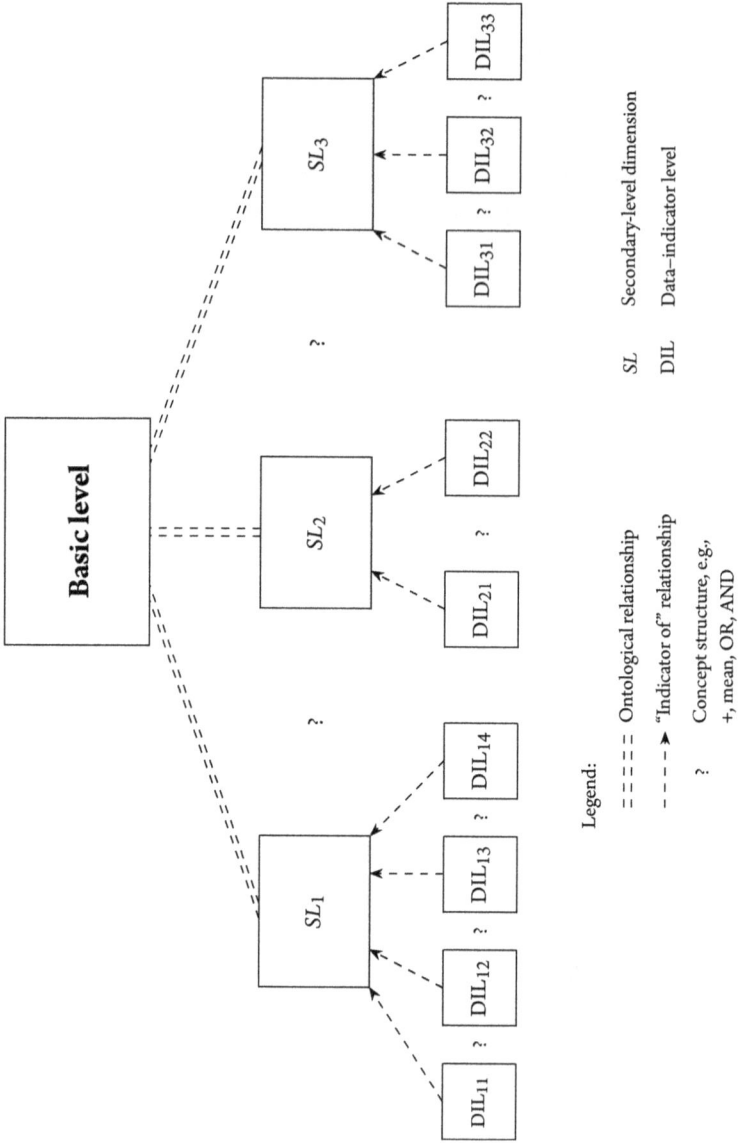

Legend:

= = = = =  Ontological relationship

– – – –▸  "Indicator of" relationship

?  Concept structure, e.g.,
   +, mean, OR, AND

SL   Secondary-level dimension

DIL   Data–indicator level

FIGURE 2.1. The basic three-level framework.

quantitative data (including presence–absence as ordinal 0–1 data). Typically, each secondary level has multiple indicators or quantitative data. The convention adopted here for all concept figures is that the basic level be in boldface, the secondary-level dimensions in italics, and the indicator level in regular font.

My approach to concepts and measurement starts with ontology and definitions. Another term for the secondary-level dimensions is "defining or constitutive features or attributes." As such, figure 2.1 uses dashed equal signs to indicate an ontological relationship between the basic-level concept and its defining characteristics.

Typically there are multiple (quantitative) "indicators of" each defining dimension. These are shown by a dashed arrow, which signals an "indicator of" relationship between the data–indicator level and the secondary level.

Of importance is the absence in figure 2.1 of any causal arrows, i.e., →. At the end of this chapter, I will contrast the basic framework with latent variable models where causation is absolutely central, linking indicators as causal effects of latent variables. In contrast, the basic framework is a semantic and ontological one. One can think of figures like 2.1 as a semantic mapping that connects definitions, meaning, and ontology with data and measurement.

There are numerous "?" throughout figure 2.1. These indicate concept structure or aggregation decisions. These aggregation decisions constitute a large part of the methodology and semantics of complex concepts. One must determine how the concept is structured: How do the secondary-level dimensions combine to form the basic level? Similarly, how do the numeric indicators combine to form the secondary-level attributes? These structure and aggregation decisions tend to differentiate approaches to conceptualization and measurement and I will devote a whole chapter to the mathematics and logic of aggregation within and across levels.

Figure 2.1 is also a very useful description of how numeric indices of concepts are actually constructed. One of the most useful guidelines of this volume uses figure 2.1 to help researchers analyze indices, variables, data sets, and concepts:

Concept Mapping Guideline: For any given concept, index, or data set, draw the semantic and measurement map corresponding to figure 2.1.[1]

From years of personal experience I can testify that drawing these figures reveals numerous issues, problems, and unexamined or unjustified assumptions.

Fuzzy logic provides a philosophy, methodology, and mathematics for thinking about semantics, ontology, quantification, and aggregation. Fuzzy logic is, among other things, a mathematical theory of semantics. For example, it has a methodology for dealing with the situation where one has adjectives modifying concepts. One might want to describe and have causal theories about "very poor" countries. What are the semantics of connecting the basic concept of "poor" with the adjective "very"? As an example I will explore how the World Bank implicitly has constructed a concept of "poor" countries and how that relates to the data–indicator, GDP per capita. One can then use that concept of poor to develop the concept of "very poor." Fuzzy logic will prove central in linking quantitative indicators to meaning, as well as providing a framework for aggregation decisions.

I will discuss two general mathematical ways to think about concept structure and aggregation. I use fuzzy logic in particular, and mathematical or philosophical logic in general, as one way to structure or aggregate concepts and to perform measurement. A parallel set of operations exist using the resources of linear algebra and statistics. One of the features of qualitative and philosophical discussions of concepts is the use of mathematical logic as the fundamental tool for conceptualization. In contrast, much measurement and indicator construction uses the resources of linear algebra, utility functions, and calculus, as well as statistics. The key point here is not that one is better than the other but

---

1. It is not uncommon for important methodological details—or even central issues—of a global index to be not completely public. Drawing the figure will bring out dramatically how much is kept private; see for example the failed state index www.fundforpeace.org. One is supposed to trust the institution that generates the index, but one should always be skeptical when core methodological details are secret.

rather that they constitute different approaches. I've heard innumerable times that mathematical logic can be represented using linear algebra. It is a mathematical fact that mathematical logic and Boolean algebra are different from linear algebra and statistics. At the same time there are clear parallels and analogies between the two approaches. This creates the opportunity for dialogue but also confusion.

A key part of this framework is the use of various symbols and what they mean in terms of mathematical operations. A useful conceptual framework must—sometimes at least—end with a quantitative measure that can be used in causal-statistical analysis and description. This means that the "?" in figure 2.1 must be connected to mathematical operations. A key requirement is that the mathematical operations match the semantics of the concept. For example, if the concept states that a given feature is necessary for the concept then the mathematics involving that feature must be faithful to the idea of a necessary condition.

While the basic framework is relatively complex—many global indices are significantly more complicated than that—it has a basic fractal kind of character. The essential building block of the framework consists of two levels with one box at the higher level and two indicators or boxes at the lower level. The fractal metaphor illustrates that one can take a microscope to the basic structure and see most of the basic conceptual, methodological, scaling, and structural decisions in the micro simplest case. Almost all the issues discussed in this volume can be brought back to this simple building block from which the whole basic framework is constructed. For example, almost all the aggregation and structural decisions can be discussed using only two lower-level boxes. Almost always, adding more boxes does not change anything. This means that the discussion in many instances can be much simpler than that implied by the basic framework. It can be conducted using the simple fractal, building-block figure with two levels, one item at the higher level and two at the lower.

One interesting and essential feature of the basic framework is that conceptualization and semantics work from the top down, while measurement and numeric measures work from the bottom up. The data–indicator level is where one starts the process of aggregation, which ends up with numeric measures at the basic level. Conceptualization and semantics start at the top and work their way down. This up-and-down feature of the basic framework helps to integrate semantics with measurement.

A central claim of this volume is that the basic framework allows one to explore the key methodological issues of conceptualization and how conceptualization connects with numeric data and indicators. The framework is complex enough to capture the core methodologies of conceptualization and measurement and how they work in social science and philosophy. At the same time it is not so complex as to become unmanageable. In fact, this basic framework underlies a very large amount of applied concept and measurement work. It provides a valuable tool for the analysis of data sets, descriptions, and normative discussions. The 100+ exercises I have developed over the years (available via request at ggoertz@nd.edu) have convinced me of the usefulness of the basic framework in many varied settings. This volume is devoted to working out various standard (i.e., popular) conceptual frameworks and basic decisions in concept creation and measurement.

## Quality of Life, OECD

The easiest way to get a feel for how the basic framework works is with examples. The various examples in this chapter illustrate some of the key design decisions that one must make when constructing concepts and eventually performing measurement. They also illustrate some standard and common practices in concept design. The abstract structure of figure 2.1 is filled in with substantive content and design decisions about the structure and aggregation of the concept. One can see also how the number of dimensions varies, as well as the number of levels. These examples are also ones that reappear in various guises throughout the volume, such as alternative concepts of democracy, poverty, or well-being.

A core set of examples in this volume comes from the global performance indicators industry. In particular, concepts, indicators, and measures of things like poverty, wealth, human well-being, health, and illness form a massive number of complex concepts and measures. As a first short illustration of how nicely the basic framework works, I use the OECD's concept of "quality of life." It is in fact a subconcept of their concept of "individual well-being." The OECD over the last eight to ten years has issued an annual report on the quality of life in OECD countries. They link this closely to other concepts of human well-being, in particular the Sen–Nussbaum capability approach which dominates most of this literature as well as the Sustainable Development Goals articulated by the United Nations (see below).

OECD includes the following eight different secondary-level dimensions: health status, work–life balance, education, social connections, civic engagement, environment, security, and subjective well-being. These eight dimensions constitute what quality of life *is*. They are the ontological, normative, conceptual core of the concept. I have chosen in figure 2.2 three of the eight dimensions—(1) personal security, (2) work–life balance, and (3) health—some of which are less common (work–life balance) in this literature, as well as those which are virtually universal, such as health. These three secondary-level dimensions illustrate all of the issues involved, which remain more or less constant over all of the dimensions.[2]

In the basic framework these definitional–ontological elements are indicated by dashed equal signs. The indicators used by the OECD appear at the bottom at the data–indicator level. These are "indicators of" these conceptual dimensions. The dashed arrow indicates that these are indicating something in the conceptualization. Obviously, one could have other indicators as well. Indicator decisions are typically pragmatic ones about the quality and comparability of data across the OECD countries. Indicators can be included or excluded without much problem. In contrast, the defining dimensions cannot

2. The OECD distinguishes between "quality of life" and "material conditions" as two higher-level dimensions which themselves constitute "human well-being." So well-being is a four-level concept (see OECD 2015, figure 1.1, "The OECD framework for measuring well-being"). Four levels or more is not uncommon for these big concepts; for another example see the discussion of the Multidimensional Poverty Index (MPI) below.

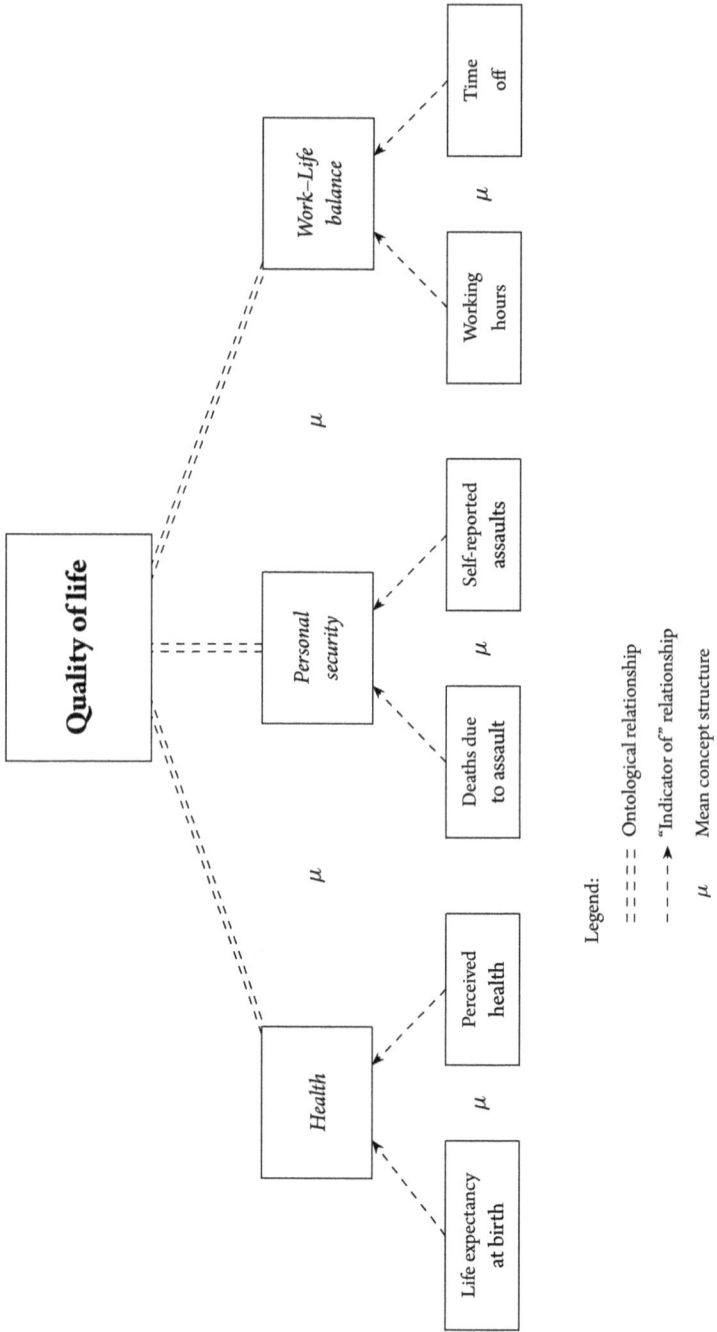

FIGURE 2.2. Quality of life, OECD.

Legend:

= = = = =  Ontological relationship

- - - - ▶  "Indicator of" relationship

μ          Mean concept structure

just be changed, but require significant conceptual, normative, and philosophical defense. This is a different matter altogether.

The framework uses the Greek letter $\mu$ to signal that in mathematical practice the OECD is taking the average across factors at the same level. It averages at the data–indicator level as well as at the secondary level. This illustrates a typical default used in a number of, but far from all, global indicators.

A key methodological issue involves the fact that one starts from the bottom with the indicators and aggregates upward to get the final numeric value for the concept. This means taking a variety of indicators with different scales and different features and then normalizing or standardizing them onto the same scale; here it will always be $[0, 1]$. This is a hugely critical operation that is often done without much reflection. Chapters 4 and 5 deal with this major methodological issue.

## Completeness Guideline

To be a man, or of the species man, and have the *essence* of a man, is the same thing.

JOHN LOCKE

The issue of the completeness of conceptualization arises most clearly and visibly in the philosophical approach to conceptualization. Going all the way back to Aristotle, a good definition is complete in that it provides all the necessary conditions that are jointly sufficient for the concept. It is complete because there are no missing important, necessary dimensions. It is complete in the sense that together they are jointly sufficient.

This philosophical approach to concepts and definitions then directly raises the question of completeness, which produces the core Completeness Guideline:

Completeness Guideline: The concept definition should ideally be complete, i.e., not missing any essential or important dimensions.

To illustrate completeness and how it works from a philosophical perspective, I use what I call the Sen–Nussbaum concept of human well-being, Nussbaum's account (e.g., 1992; 2011) being based on Sen's work. Nussbaum presents a complex, multilevel, multidimensional view of human well-being.

Sen and Nussbaum have both been very involved in international debates about poverty and have edited influential volumes (e.g., 1993) devoted to the topic. In addition, both Sen and Nussbaum are prominent philosophers and so nicely represent how completeness and concept structures work using mathematical logic. Human well-being is a nice example because it cuts across moral philosophy, development economics, political science, sociology, and anthropology. It is connected to concepts that are important in international politics, such as the Human Development Index (HDI), the Gender Development Index (GDI), poverty–wealth, and other concepts that play a large role in international fora such as the UN, the World Bank, the EU, NGOs, IGOs, and international law.

It is an interesting concept because it is both a normative and empirical concept as discussed in the previous chapter: it is meant to help evaluate development policies as well as describe the situation of people around the world. Human well-being is not only a definitional debate, but one about the reality of human lives in various cultures around the world. It is ontological because it is about being human. Here we see the descriptive and normative dimensions of conceptualization at the forefront.

Nussbaum clearly sees the concept of human well-being in ontological terms: "Here, then, is a sketch of an internal-essentialist proposal, an account of the most important functions of the human being, in terms of which human life is defined" (Nussbaum 1992, 214). She is defining or conceptualizing what it means to be human. She wants to know empirically how human beings and their lives are constituted. She does not want a series of indicators of what it is to be human, but rather a description of the essence of human well-being. Sen makes the same ontological claim: "The claim is that functionings are *constitutive* of a

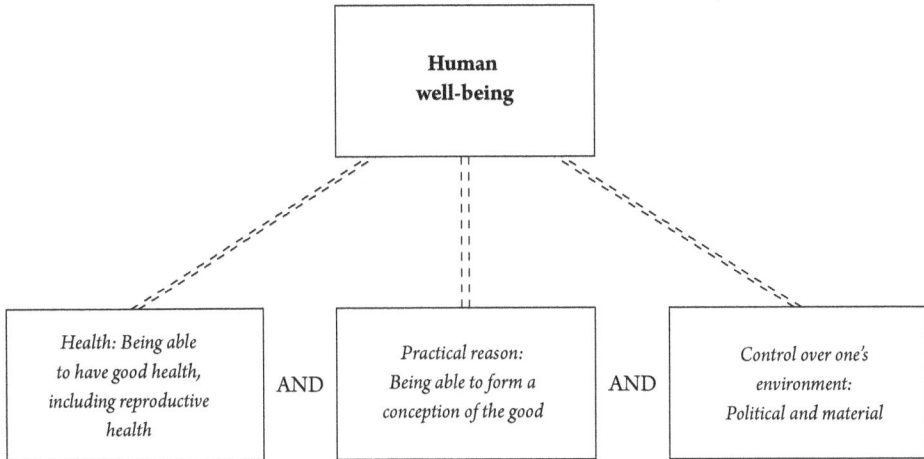

FIGURE 2.3. Human well-being: Sen–Nussbaum concept, basic and secondary-dimension levels.

person's being, and an evaluation of well-being has to take the form of these constitutive elements" (Sen 1992, 39). Hence it is a nice example of the ontological approach proposed in this volume.

A key feature of the Nussbaum concept is that she wants her conceptualization to be *complete*. When approaching concepts via definitions, a reasonable requirement is that the definition be relatively complete. This means that no important or essential component is left out. This is a nontrivial requirement. It is very tempting to give partial or minimal definitions. Nussbaum (2011) has criticized Sen for his unwillingness to provide a complete list. Laurent (2018) explicitly states that his list of indicators is incomplete. In the next chapter we will see that often researchers argue for "minimal" concepts, which implies that they are not complete.

Figure 2.3 gives the structure and content of the Sen–Nussbaum concept of human well-being at the conceptual levels, i.e., the basic level and the secondary-dimension level. Since we are in the realm of logic, the structure and aggregation operations used are those of mathematical logic. Hence AND means the logical AND, while the dashed equal signs mean, as usual, an ontological relationship.

Nussbaum describes the functions and capabilities, aspects of what it means to live a good human life. Here is her list of ten:

1. Life. Being able to live to the end of a human life of normal length; not dying prematurely, or before one's life is so reduced as to be not worth living.

2. Health. Being able to have good health, including reproductive health; to be adequately nourished; to have adequate shelter.

3. Bodily integrity. Being able to move freely from place to place; to be secure against violent assault, including sexual assault and domestic violence; having opportunities for sexual satisfaction and for choice in matters of reproduction.

4. Senses, imagination, and thought. Being able to use the senses, to imagine, think, and reason—and to do these things in a "truly human" way, a way informed and cultivated by an adequate education, including, but by no means limited to, literacy and basic mathematical and scientific training. Being able to use imagination and thought in connection with experiencing and producing works and events of one's own choice, religious, literary, musical, and so forth. Being able to use one's mind in ways protected by guarantees of freedom of expression with respect to both political and artistic speech, and freedom of religious exercise. Being able to have pleasurable experiences and to avoid nonbeneficial pain.

5. Emotions. Being able to have attachments to things and people outside ourselves; to love those who love and care for us, to grieve at their absence; in general, to love, to grieve, to experience longing, gratitude, and justified anger. Not having one's emotional development blighted

by fear and anxiety. (Supporting this capability means supporting forms of human association that can be shown to be crucial in their development.)

6. Practical reason. Being able to form a conception of the good and to engage in critical reflection about the planning of one's life. (This entails protection for the liberty of conscience and religious observance.)

7. Affiliation. (A) Being able to live with and toward others, to recognize and show concern for other human beings, to engage in various forms of social interaction; to be able to imagine the situation of another. (Protecting this capability means protecting institutions that constitute and nourish such forms of affiliation, and also protecting the freedom of assembly and political speech.) (B) Having the social bases of self-respect and nonhumiliation; being able to be treated as a dignified being whose worth is equal to that of others. This entails provisions of nondiscrimination on the basis of race, sex, sexual orientation, ethnicity, caste, religion, national origin.

8. Other species. Being able to live with concern for and in relation to animals, plants, and the world of nature.

9. Being able to laugh, to play, to enjoy recreational activities.

10. Control over one's environment. (A) Political. Being able to participate effectively in political choices that govern one's life; having the right of political participation, protections of free speech and association. (B) Material. Being able to hold property (both land and movable goods), and having property rights on an equal basis with others; having the right to seek employment on an equal basis with others; having the freedom from unwarranted search and seizure. In work, being able to work as a human being, exercising practical reason and entering into meaningful relationships of mutual recognition with other workers.

(Nussbaum 2011, epub 73–80)

These functions are the secondary-level dimensions of her concept. Having these capabilities is what it means to live a rich and fulfilling life, it is what it means to be fully human.

Nussbaum suggests that this is a complete list in the sense of including all the core, essential, necessary components for high levels of human well-being. She implies also that these are jointly sufficient for high levels. This seems quite reasonable since if one has all these capabilities and functionings then it seems like a good life.

The subtitle of one article—"In defense of Aristotelian essentialism"—suggests that she is using a standard approach to concepts, the mathematical logic of necessary and sufficient conditions. An intimate bond links the necessary and sufficient condition structure to essentialism. If some characteristic is essential to be a human being, then that characteristic is a necessary condition for being human. She is quite clear that the various dimensions she discusses are necessary:

> As far as [secondary-level] capabilities go, to call them part of humanness is to make a very basic sort of evaluation. It is to say that a life without this item would be too lacking, too impoverished, to be human at all. (Nussbaum 1992, 220)

> In general, then, the Capabilities Approach, in my version, focuses on the protection of areas of freedom so central that their removal makes a life not worthy of human dignity. (Nussbaum 2011, epub 71)

Core to the basic conceptual framework are issues of structure and aggregation. How does one aggregate between and within levels. Absolutely central is the degree of substitutability across dimensions or indicators. The classic Aristotelian logic approach to concepts allows no substitutability (chapter 6 qualifies this).

The OECD example illustrated the common use of the mean to connect the various secondary-level dimensions. Here we see a very common option, which is to use the logical AND to structure concepts at the secondary level. This implements the notion that each dimension is necessary and essential. As we will see in detail in the chapter on aggregation, it also means that there are no substitutes for that dimension. So the Sen–Nussbaum concept nicely illustrates how the logical AND is a common structural principle. In fact, for philosophers it is the default. For example, in the literature on "natural kinds" (e.g., Khalidi 2013) the mathematical logic of necessary and sufficient conditions underlies the whole discussion.

The challenge to the logical AND came from the philosopher Wittgenstein who proposed the family resemblance approach to conceptualization and definitions. The key feature of this was that it denied the necessary condition aspect of the structure. It still maintains typically some kind of sufficiency criteria, discussed at some length in chapter 9. For the purposes of this section, one can replace the logical AND with the logical OR. Once one moves to social science, it is not hard to find examples of this structure. Typically the OR connects various different manifestations of the basic-level concept. This often occurs when there are substitutes: as long as one of the substitutes is present then that is sufficient. For example, this is how the standard data set on constitutions works:

> We identify written constitutions by invoking a set of three conditions. The first is sufficient to qualify the document(s) as a constitution, whereas the others are applied as supplementary tests if the first is not met. Constitutions consist of those documents that either: (1) are identified explicitly as the Constitution, Fundamental Law, or Basic Law of a country; OR (2) contain explicit provisions that establish the documents as highest law, either through entrenchment or limits on future law; OR (3) define the basic pattern of authority by establishing or suspending an executive or legislative branch of government. (Elkins et al. 2009, 48–49)

Thus any legal structure that functions as the "fundamental, basic law of the land" counts as a constitution.

The logic of completeness still applies. They want all legal documents that function as the fundamental law of the land. Depending on the country, this might not be called the constitution, or it might have slightly different forms than the standard constitution. Completeness means capturing all the different variations on this theme, at least those that appear in real-world practice. The motivation is still completeness, but the structuring principle is the logical OR instead of the logical AND.

The topic of gender quotas, which has generated a massive literature, illustrates nicely the use of the logical OR conceptualization and measurement. Basically, there are three main ways in which countries have implemented gender quotas. At the basic level one has a "gender quota" via three substitutable means to implement gender quotes: (1) party quota, adopted voluntarily by political parties, OR (2) legislative quota, mandated by the national parliament, OR (3) reserved seats, usually written into the constitution. Any of these mechanisms counts as a gender quota for statistical or other analysis (see Krook 2009 for an extensive analysis).

In summary, one should always inquire about the completeness of a conceptualization. For example, in the OECD quality of life concept discussed above, is it complete? Are there important dimensions missing? It can well be that for practical reasons, such as data availability, a concept is not complete; the Multidimensional Poverty Index discussed below is incomplete. This is recognized by its authors as an issue, and they have discussed various ways in which that indicator could become more complete. So while it might not always be possible to have a complete conceptualization, it should always be a goal.

## Redundancy Guideline

The philosophical approach to conceptualization via necessary and sufficient conditions along with the logical AND raises a second key issue in concept design: Should secondary-level dimensions be redundant or not?

The Sen–Nussbaum example of the previous section, using necessary and sufficient conditions, suggested that redundancy is not a good idea. This makes sense in terms of concepts as definitions with multiple dimensions. High levels of redundancy would be using synonyms to define something. The addition of synonyms is not really adding anything semantically to the definition; they can be removed at little cost. The reason that one includes attributes as *separate dimensions* already suggests that they should be nonredundant. If dimensions are redundant then they are probably not necessary because the absence of one can be replaced by another. In short, the classic philosophical approach to conceptualization implies or assumes nonredundancy.

However, in the secondary level one can certainly use the logical OR to connect the secondary-level dimensions as illustrated above. This suggests that redundancy is quite possible and perhaps even desirable. We have just seen it, in the previous section, where the logical OR replaced the logical AND.

One needs to be clear about whether one wants and desires redundancy or whether in fact it should be avoided. So the Redundancy Guideline is not a simple do or not do:

> Redundancy Guideline: Decide whether redundancy is desirable. Typically, using the logical AND or addition suggests not, while the logical OR suggests it is.

One way to think about redundancy is via the metaphor of double counting. If double counting is to be avoided then redundancy is bad.

This comes up already in the OECD's of quality of life concept where the concern is about multicollinearity among indicators in constructing complex indicators:

> When using equal weights, it may happen that—by combining variables with a high degree of correlation—an element of double counting may be introduced into the index: if two collinear indicators are included in the composite index with a weight of $w_1$ and $w_2$, the unique dimension that the two indicators measure would have weight $(w_1 + w_2)$ in the composite. The response has often been to test indicators for statistical correlation—for example using the Pearson correlation coefficient—and to choose only

indicators which exhibit a low degree of correlation or to adjust weights correspondingly, e.g. giving less weight to correlated indicators. (OECD 2008, 32)

To illustrate the redundancy issue I use the concept of poverty. I focus on what might be called "consumption poverty." For development economists, poverty falls in many theoretical and methodological ways into the larger field of consumer behavior: poor people are people who do not consume much (Ravallion 2016).

If one examines the consumption surveys conducted by governments and the World Bank they are quite detailed. The ideal is to capture *all* relevant consumption. This matches with Nussbaum's desire to include all important and essential capabilities in her list. So ideally, consumption poverty follows the Completeness Guideline.

Figure 2.4 uses the basic framework to model consumption poverty. At the basic level one has consumption poverty. At the secondary level there are basic categories of consumption. Clearly, food has received a lot of attention. An average family (which is typically the unit of analysis in international poverty surveys) consumes food, clothing, housing, etc. A typical survey by the World Bank has a basket of goods in each category and asks about a family's consumption of these goods.

Included in figure 2.4 is just a sample from the list of things that fall under "food." These range from food bought in stores, to food raised by the family, to food purchased in restaurants. There will be controversial categories such as alcohol, which strictly speaking also provides calories.

I include non-market consumption items because they are very important in measuring poverty. Figure 2.4 includes examples of this for each secondary-level dimension, such as home-grown food, self-made housing, or self-transportation in bicycling. These must be converted into dollars for aggregation purposes. Poor people tend to have much less recourse to the market for many goods, and often produce these goods themselves. I can remember as a child the massive garden that my grandparents had as a result of the depression; there is a home video of my father and uncle building the house I grew up in.

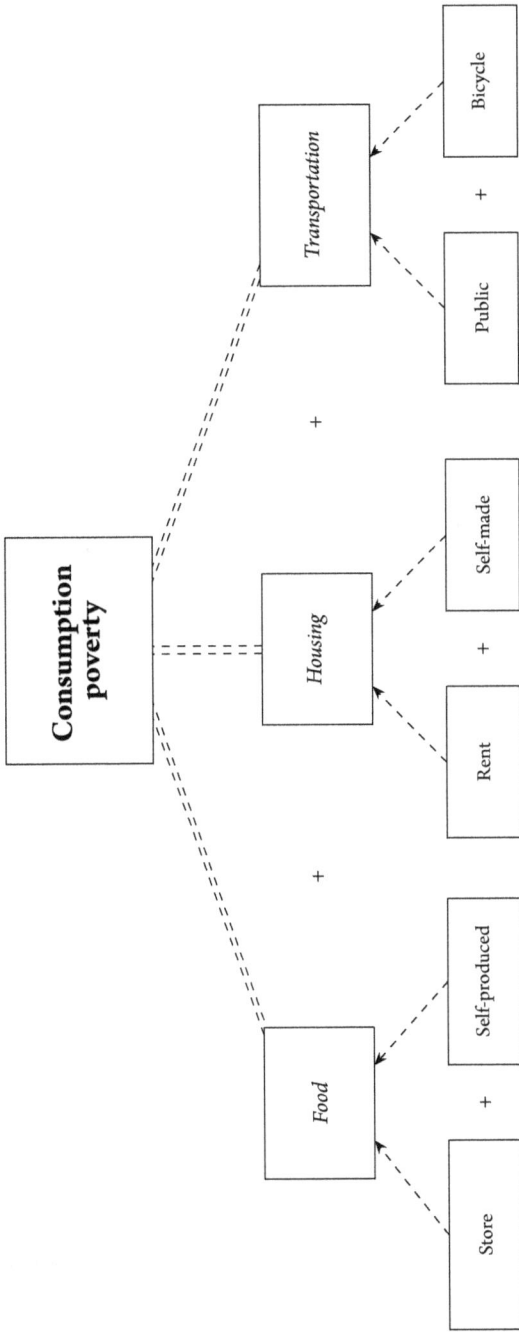

Legend:

==== Ontological relationship

– – –▸ "Indicator of" relationship

+ Sum concept structure

FIGURE 2.4. Consumption poverty.

All these different baskets of goods are converted into a common money (a complicated and tricky methodological issue in itself) to permit interpersonal and international comparisons.

In terms of conceptual structure and aggregation, one is literally adding up consumption to get the final poverty measure. As such, in figure 2.3 there are +'s at the data–indicator level as well as at the secondary level.

The Completeness and Redundancy Guidelines appear in discussions of World Bank consumption surveys:

> To measure welfare accurately, the consumption concept must be *comprehensive*. *All* goods and services that contribute to people's standard of living need to be included in the measure, which can be thought of as a practical approximation to an indirect utility function or money-metric measure of welfare. (Deaton and Grosh 2000, 102; emphasis is mine)

> Double-Counting: It may sometimes be useful to create a cross-check by gathering data on the same items in more than one place in the questionnaire. In these cases, the questions should be worded carefully so that the analyst knows how to exclude one or the other *to avoid double counting* these data in the estimate of total consumption. (Deaton and Grosh 2000, 124; emphasis is mine)

Redundancy should be kept separate from empirical collinearity. Dimensions might be more or less correlated in the real world, but conceptually they constitute different dimensions.

As a rule of thumb, if the secondary-level dimensions are connected by the logical AND or via addition then one should worry about redundancy at the conceptual level.

## Data–Indicator Level: Mean, OR, Thresholds

The basic framework is not only multidimensional but also multilevel. The multilevel feature of these complex concepts has not been clearly recognized and the implications of it are not always followed up on. The multilevel characteristic of these complex concepts is often critical because the logic of the concept structure is often quite different between the secondary level and the data–indicator level. This is compounded by the fact that often the secondary level is dealt with in terms of semantics, definitions, and ontology while standard mathematical reflexes kick in at the data–indicator level, which are not necessarily clearly connected to the semantics and ontology of the secondary level. Both this section and the next deal with the critical importance of understanding the logics of these two levels in some standard situations and how they are likely to differ.

The OECD quality of life concept and measure illustrates perhaps the canonical way to think about the data–indicator level and how it connects to a single secondary-level dimension. A key feature here is that we are in basically a unidimensional mode. In principle, these are indicators of a single secondary-level dimension. Here the logic of the mean applies with full force. In the history of statistics and measurement one often has multiple measurements of one value, say, the position of a star. The arguments for taking the mean of these independent observations lie at the core of statistics. Ideally, because they are measurements or indicators of the same thing they should be highly correlated, since they are all being driven by a single external stimulus.

So it makes complete sense to take the mean if one has multiple indicators of a concept that is unidimensional. The latent variable models discussed in the appendix to this chapter implement complex versions of this basic idea.

It is useful then to consider this standard use of the mean at the data–indicator level with the Completeness and Redundancy Guidelines:

Indicators are ideally redundant.

The possible list of indicators has no end: there is no need to have a complete list of indicators.

These two facts about concept construction dramatically illustrate that how to think about the secondary level differs from the data–indicator level. Sometimes they match, as we have seen in the case of consumption poverty. But this is much more the exception than the rule. Typically, the logics of the two levels differ in important ways, as illustrated by the application of these two guidelines.

Normally this means that the indicators should be highly correlated. In fact the OECD indicators of quality of life are frequently not very highly correlated (see OECD 2011, table 1.A.1, "Correlations between the headline indicators included in *How's life?*"). The conceptual and methodological question is what to do when these indicators of the same thing significantly disagree: Does that mean that they are not indicators of one secondary-level dimension? The OECD uses them anyway in spite of low correlations.

The Multidimensional Poverty Index (MPI; Alkire et al. 2015) illustrates another potential approach to the data–indicator level. The MPI has clear theoretical and conceptual linkages to the United Nations Human Development Index (HDI), and has become an official measure of poverty for the United Nations (see the next chapter for the competing concept and measure coming from the World Bank). It is useful for exploring how it does the various indicators at the data level.

Table 2.1 gives the basic content of the MPI along with its four levels, where the basic level is MPI, followed by "secondary level," "indicator," and "data." "Data aggregation" indicates how the raw data are aggregated into the indicators. The whole MPI is generated bottom up from these dichotomous data. Measurement starts with the data column and then one uses various aggregation procedures to get to the top, single MPI number for each country.

As noted above, ideally indicators of one secondary-level dimension should be redundant because they are measures of one thing. So concept structures that incorporate redundancy naturally work at this level. As we saw above, the logical OR implements redundancy. It is thus not surprising to see logical OR used frequently at the data–indicator level.

The MPI illustrates nicely how the logical OR makes a lot of sense at the data level. In the data aggregation column of table 2.1, a number of the indicators use the logical OR. Each of these indicators is dichotomous, but as we will see in chapters down the road, the logic works just as nicely for continuous variables. For example, the cooking fuel

TABLE 2.1. Concept structure and aggregation at the data level: MPI

| Secondary level | Indicator | Data | Data aggregation |
|---|---|---|---|
| Education | Schooling | No household member has completed 5 years of schooling | If $(\max(S_i) < 5)$ then Deprivation=1; $S_i$ is the Schooling of member $i$ |
| | Attendance | Any school-age child in the household is not attending school up to class 8 | If $\min(A_i) \leq 8$ then Deprivation=1; $A_i$ is the Attendance of school-age child $i$ |
| Health | Nutrition | Any person in the household is malnourished | If $\max(N_i < \text{Body Mass Index}_i)$ $= 1$ then Deprivation=1; $N_i$ is household member weight |
| | Mortality | Any child has died | If $(\max(M_i) = 1)$ then Deprivation=1; $M_i$ is death of child $i$ |
| Standard of living | Electricity | Household has no electricity | If $E = 0$ then Deprivation $= 1$ |
| | Sanitation | Sanitation facility is not improved or is shared with other households | If $(I = 0 \text{ OR } S = 1)$ then Deprivation $= 1$ |
| | Water | No access to safe water or more than 30 min walk | If $(A = 0 \text{ OR } W > 30)$ then Deprivation $= 1$ |
| | Floor | Household has a dirt, sand, or dung floor | If $(DI = 1 \text{ OR } S = 1 \text{ OR } DU = 1)$ then Deprivation $= 1$ |
| | Cooking fuel | Household cooks with dung, wood, or charcoal | If $(D = 1 \text{ OR } W = 1 \text{ OR } C = 1)$ then Deprivation $= 1$ |
| | Assets | Household owns at most one of (radio, telephone, TV, bike, motorbike, refrigerator) and does not own (car or truck) | If $\sum(R, T, TV, B, MB) \leq 1$ AND $\neg(C \text{ OR } T)$ then Deprivation $= 1$ |

*Source:* Based on Alkire et al. (2015, table 5.5).

indicator consists of cooking with dung OR wood OR charcoal, each coded dichotomously. If the household uses any one or any combination of these three it is considered deprived. If there were other, similar fuels used for cooking then they would be added to the list. This is following the Completeness Guideline for the logical OR.

Thresholds feature often in the data aggregation of the MPI. The indicators are combined and if they achieve a certain threshold then the household is deprived on that indicator. It is not surprising that they use the terminology of "cutoffs." If one achieves a certain level then one is deprived on that particular indicator. It is clearly an important design decision to determine what those cutoffs are going to be for each individual indicator. For example, the schooling indicator uses a standard threshold structure where if $(\max(S_i) < 5 \text{ years})$ then Deprivation $= 1$, where $S_i$ is the Schooling of member $i$ of the household.

The sum is a very common concept structure principle that is often associated with thresholds. Poverty consumption is a threshold concept (as are virtually all poverty measures since there is a poverty line): if $(\sum_{i=1}^{N} C_i < \text{poverty threshold})$ then the person is in poverty, where $i$ represents the consumption categories in figure 2.4. Basically, one adds up consumption and when it reaches the poverty threshold then one is out of poverty.

The assets indicator is quite interesting because it involves what I call a hybrid concept structure involving logical ORs, logical AND, and negations: if $\sum(R, T, TV, B, MB) \leq 1 \text{ AND } \neg(C \text{ OR } T)$ then Deprived-in-Assets. Chapter 7 is devoted to an extensive analysis of hybrid concept structures, which are particularly relevant for gray zone concepts. The standard hybrid structure is very similar to this asset one, but in a very different conceptual context.

This use of the logical OR and the maximum—what I will define as best shot concept structures or aggregation in chapter 6—constitutes the second most popular fashion to think about the data–indicator level. Most of the MPI indicators use some form of maximum as seen in table 2.1. I have purposefully used the more cumbersome mathematical notation in addition to the simpler English to emphasize the frequent use of best shot concept structures at the data level of the MPI. With one exception, all the data–indicators involve some kind of aggregation over individuals in the household or options for some function, such as the flooring of the habitation, that fall into the best shot aggregation class.

Thus the logical OR, thresholds, maximum, and similar kinds of logics very naturally appear at the data–indicator level as well as the mean. They all implement redundancy in various ways. Often completeness is an issue as well with the logical OR: one wants to include all alternatives that satisfy the concept, e.g., all kinds of flooring that suggest deprivation. The same concern for completeness often applies to addition aggregation, as we saw for consumption poverty.

## Importance of Levels: Democracy, Polity Concept, and Measure

A key feature of the basic framework is that it includes a semantic, definitional, ontological level along with a separate measurement, data level. It is not uncommon to find ambiguity and confusion about the semantic versus the data levels. The basic framework separates the two but it is often not clear in practice because one moves directly from the indicators to the basic level. In my terms, it is not a multilevel concept.

A key thing to note is that the mean is the dominant and most obvious structural principal at the data–indicator level. Conversely, it usually does not make much sense at the secondary, semantic level. Principles of completeness and nonredundancy make the mean an inappropriate choice. This makes the levels very important in the analysis and construction of concepts, because they often embody different principles of concept construction. Failure to recognize the levels in concepts can easily lead to problematic conceptualization and measurement.

Aggregation and concept structure can vary from level to level. One of the core motivations for the first edition of this book was the tension and contrast between the semantic and ontological level vis-à-vis the data–indicator level. The Polity measure and concept of democracy illustrates this very nicely. In the previous edition this was a whole chapter, which is here condensed into a couple of pages.

The conceptual, qualitative, and philosophical literature on democracy virtually always discusses democracy in terms of secondary-level dimensions that are necessary and jointly sufficient for democracy. In political science, Dahl is a good place to start for a tradition that continues still through almost all conceptualizations of democracy. However, when it comes to numeric measurement, almost no one follows through on the implications of this necessary condition conceptualization of democracy. In short, the measurement model is fundamentally inconsistent with the conceptual model. In the previous edition, as an example I reformulated the measurement model of the Polity data to match the conceptual model and then illustrated the systematic differences in the final democracy scores.

The Polity indicator or measure of democracy (Jaggers and Gurr 1995) illustrates some of the tensions involved. If there is no semantic, secondary-dimension level, then the content of the concept of democracy lies in the indicator list. One takes the five indicators of democracy in the Polity data set and aggregates them using addition to get the basic Polity measure of democracy. However, if one includes the conceptualization of democracy given by Polity then one has a multilevel concept and measure. Here is the core conceptualization of democracy according to Polity:

> At its theoretical core, we argue that there are three essential interdependent elements of democracy as it is conceived of in Western liberal philosophy. The first is the presence of institutions and procedures through which citizens can express effective preferences about alternative political policies and leaders. This is accomplished through the establishment of regular and meaningful elections.... a second component of Western-conceived democracy is the existence of institutionalized constraints on the exercise of executive power.... The third dimension ... is the guarantee of civil liberties to all citizens in their daily lives and their acts of political participation. (Jaggers and Gurr 1995, 471; this repeats almost verbatim Gurr et al. 1990, 83).

Notice that Polity talks about "essential" and "interdependent elements" between these constitutive features of democracy. This terminology means using the logical AND, and conversely that the mean or sum is not appropriate.

Figure 2.5 illustrates what a multilevel view of democracy looks like according to Polity. Notice the top-down nature of figure 2.5. I've taken the defining features of democracy and associated the various Polity indicators with them. In terms of concept structure and aggregation at the indicator level, Polity is a weighted sum. However, at the constitutive secondary level the language of Polity means that one should be using the logical AND. This is indicated by the language of essentialism and interdependence. So in terms of the final measure one would aggregate up from the indicators and then choose some appropriate mathematical operation for the logical AND which then would generate the final quantitative measure.

The previous edition of this book devotes a whole chapter to analyzing the difference between the non-multilevel measure of Polity and one that includes the defining dimensions and appropriate aggregation. For more details and a comparison of this version of the Polity concept-measure and the original, see chapter 4 of the previous edition of this book.

This example illustrates an extremely common situation, where the structure of the concept or aggregation differs according to the level. This is why the multilevel aspect is critical. Unless one has mapped out the concept and appropriately identified the aggregation implied or concretely given in the conceptualization, one will not get a final numeric measure that accurately reflects the content of the concept.

## Conclusion

Absolutely central to this volume is the semantics and ontology of concepts. As illustrated in the basic framework in figure 2.1, the goal is to develop a methodology of complex and multidimensional concepts and *then* deal with quantification, aggregation, and measurement. Fuzzy logic provides a means for thinking about linking semantics and ontology with indicators, data, and aggregation. It provides the theoretical and mathematical tools needed for exploring the various

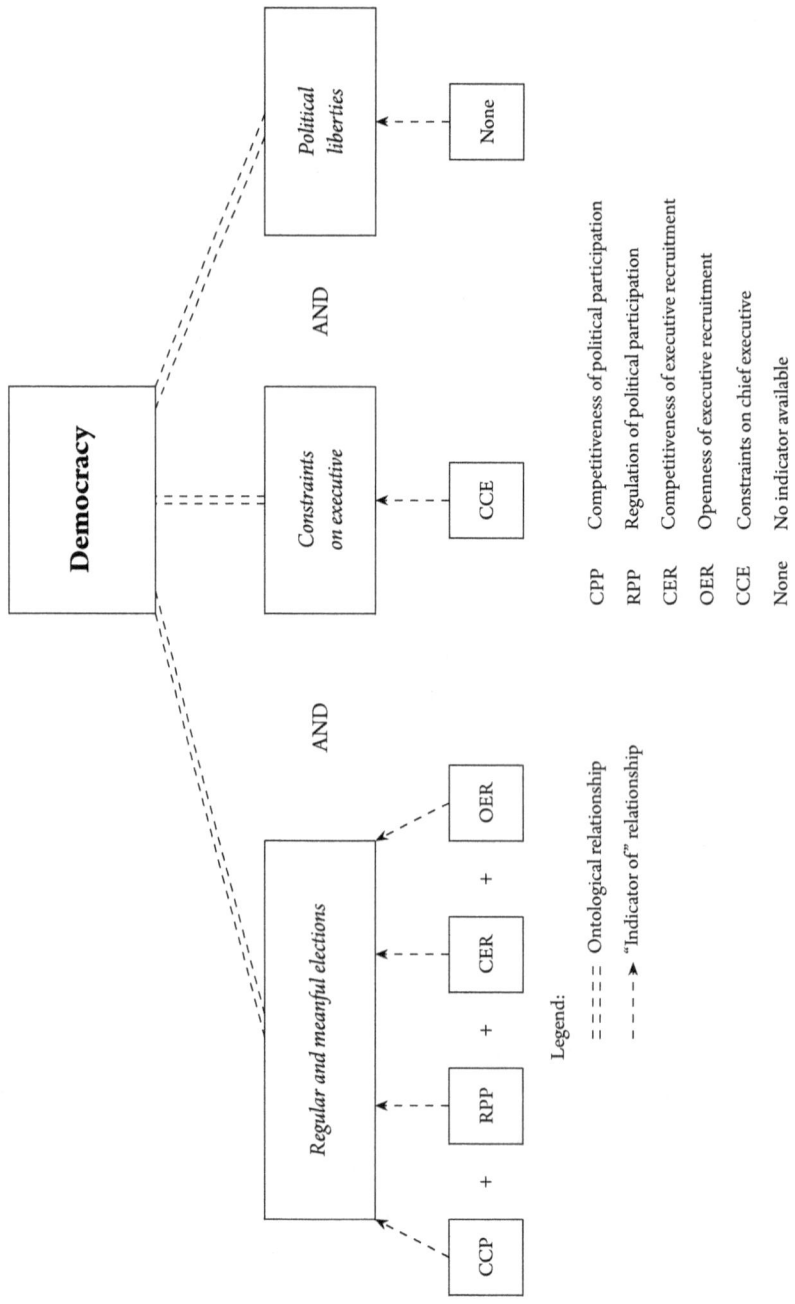

FIGURE 2.5. Polity concept and measure of democracy.

Legend:

= = = = Ontological relationship

– – – ▶ "Indicator of" relationship

| | |
|---|---|
| CPP | Competitiveness of political participation |
| RPP | Regulation of political participation |
| CER | Competitiveness of executive recruitment |
| OER | Openness of executive recruitment |
| CCE | Constraints on chief executive |
| None | No indicator available |

issues raised by the basic framework of figure 2.1. The various figures in this chapter illustrate ways in which scholars have given and can give specific content to the basic framework. These various options constitute by far the most popular way to conceptualize and measure in the various social sciences and philosophy. One goal of this volume is to encourage researchers to go beyond, be creative, and produce concept-measurement models that reflect their substantive interests, ontologies, and causal hypotheses.

If one were talking just about concepts—and not numeric indices—the Completeness and Redundancy Guidelines would not be too controversial. We naturally want definitions to be complete and not missing central elements, as well as nonredundant. This is the core of the Aristotelian requirement that a definition give the necessary and sufficient conditions.

The discussion of this chapter provides insights and a methodology for analyzing data sets. As part of my interest in concepts I have become an avid reader of coding manuals. It is often there, and often only there, that one gets the complete conceptualization along with measurement, aggregation, and structure discussed. Typically, coding rules follow the Completeness Guideline and use the necessary and sufficient condition concept structure. In addition, one usually does not want redundant coding rules.

It is common that one must infer the concept structure at both the basic and secondary levels because it must be interpreted from the text. Often the default interpretation follows philosophy and one should assume the necessary and sufficient condition structure. Frequently the philosophy concept structure is just taken for granted. For example, the concept of "semipresidential" political regimes appears several times in this volume. Here is the original definition:

> The concept of a semi-presidential form of government, as used here, is defined only by the content of the constitution. A political regime is considered as semi-presidential if the constitution which established it, combines three elements: (1) the president of the republic is elected by universal suffrage, (2) he possesses

quite considerable powers; (3) he has opposite him, however, a prime minister and ministers who possess executive and governmental power and can stay in office only if the parliament does not show its opposition to them. (Duverger 1980, 166)

The assumption given the context is that each of these factors is necessary and they are jointly sufficient. However, it is not explicit in that quote or elsewhere. It is really a matter of textual interpretation and analysis along with examples and counterfactuals that justify this as the correct interpretation.

When there is a quantitative measure then of course one can get the structure of the concept from the mathematics of the indicator construction. Here the most common problems are those illustrated by the Polity democracy measure, where the semantics of the concept at the secondary level do not match the mathematics of the quantitative measure. It is not uncommon to see the logical AND at the definitional level with the use of addition or the mean at the data–indicator level. This is a signal of confusion about the concept. This is yet another reason why drawing the basic framework figure is critical: it forces one to be explicit about everything.

A key point is that complex concepts normally have at least three levels. Confusing the ontological secondary-level dimensions with the data–indicators almost always leads to problems. Core to the basic framework is that *both* the semantic as well as the indicator levels need to be present. A focus exclusively on the indicators means a stress on measurement and less attention to the substantive content of the concept.

The basic framework is quite useful for exploring purely conceptual and definitional analyses such as those that appear in many qualitative works, as well as in political and moral philosophy. Mapping out the content, the levels, and the structure of the concept makes clear many aspects of the conceptualization that would be hidden in purely linguistic discussions. To describe the content and structure of a concept without the basic framework figure is very likely to produce confusion and ambiguity.

# Appendix: Latent Variable Approaches to Conceptualization and Measurement

It is useful to contrast the basic semantic and ontological framework outlined here with the dominant approach to measurement using latent variable models of various sorts. There are hundreds of textbooks devoted to measurement using this statistical framework. These are the core of methods classes in psychology and education, and are also commonly used in political science, sociology, and economics.

The point of this appendix is to illustrate the contrast between the latent variable approach and the one presented in this volume. A few features differ dramatically between the two approaches, summarized here and discussed in more detail below:

- Causal versus semantic–ontological as the core framing of the conceptual–measurement model.
- Conceptualization really occurs at the indicator level in latent variable models: that is where one sees the semantic content of the concept. The semantic and definitional content of these models appears in the indicators. So instead of appearing at the top, as in the basic framework, they are at the bottom.
- Latent variables are constructed bottom up from the indicators, in contrast to the basic framework which is conceptually top down.
- Concept-structure measurement fundamentally uses the mean. The numeric measures of the latent variables are weighted means of the indicators. The weakest link or the best shot concept structures are virtually never used. In contrast, in the basic framework these are common and often the default for secondary-level dimensions.
- Basically, latent variables are unidimensional and two level in nature. One can get multiple latent variables from the indicators when they fail to correlate highly, but each is usually treated as a separate concept. Models with three or more levels are very rare (though possible).

- The Completeness Guideline does not apply.
- The Redundancy Guideline is fundamental and the logic is often the same as at the data–indicator level of the basic framework.

———

The central problem in the history of psychology is that of "unobserved" or "latent" variables. Many psychological concepts are not directly measurable, e.g., "intelligence." One tries to get at them via questionnaires, surveys, and tests. The answers to these questionnaires then become the indicators of the latent variables. These techniques are widely used in political science in order to construct measures of ideology for members of Congress or Supreme Court justices. Votes in Congress become the indicators and left-right measures of ideology are constructed using them.

Lazarsfeld and Blalock were among the key players in importing the factor analytic approach to concepts into political science and sociology. Lazarsfeld (1966) provides a nice history of how he and others took the basic insights of psychological methodologies and applied them to social and political phenomena. Blalock's 1982 volume *Conceptualization and measurement in the social sciences* expresses very well the factor analytic approach to concepts and measurement (see also Bollen 1989).

Democracy is an important ongoing example in this volume. The meaning and content of the concept of democracy have been debated over the centuries by a wide variety of social scientists and philosophers. There are probably dozens of democracy data sets that are an excellent source of examples for issues of conceptualization, quantification, and aggregation. Figure 2.6 illustrates the latent variable approach using the V-Dem (Varieties of Democracy) model of democracy (Coppedge and Gerring 2011).

Immediately, a core difference is evident from the basic framework in figure 2.1: there are no secondary-level dimensions. In the latent variable approach there are only latent variables and indicators. The V-Dem project includes data on hundreds of indicators of democracy.

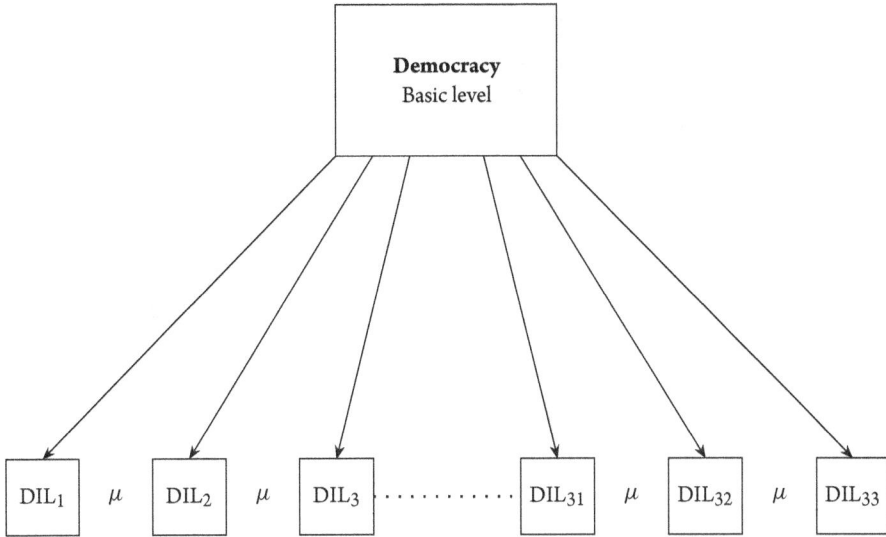

FIGURE 2.6. Latent variable models: democracy.
*Source:* Based on Coppedge and Gerring (2011).

Figure 2.5 includes the first three on the Coppedge and Gerring list, as well as the last three (2011, 255–56).

I like to refer to the latent variable methodology as the disease–symptom approach to concepts and measurement. The indicators are *of* democracy. Symptoms are *of* diseases. We do not confuse, in principle at least, the symptoms with the disease itself. If the indicators are pretty distant from the concepts, one often hears of "proxy" indicators or variables. The following point is key:

Indicators are *neither* about definitions *nor* about ontology.

The unmeasured variable is the "something" these are indicators of: they are the symptoms not the disease.

One very large ambiguity floats around latent variable approaches to concepts like democracy:

Are the indicators defining features or indicators of?

In the classic uses in education and psychology it is pretty clear that the test questions are not ontology. Correct answers on IQ tests are an effect of intelligence not intelligence itself. Votes in Congress are a reflection of ideology not the ideology of the individual. In contrast, for the concept of consumption poverty one is trying to measure actual consumption, not indicators of consumption. In the case of human well-being, infant mortality might be a good indicator of the quality of healthcare in a country. In short, the basic framework of figure 2.1 clearly differentiates between defining ontological features and (quantitative) indicators of those features.

Democracy is a good example where one sees the semantic–ontological approach coexisting with the latent variable approach. What happens in practice is that the defining features of the semantic approach become the indicators of the latent variable.

Above I introduced the Completeness and Redundancy Guidelines:

Indicators are ideally redundant.

The possible list of indicators has no end: there is no need to have a complete list of indicators.

As illustrated in figure 2.5, the number of indicators is indeterminate and pretty arbitrary. One can add or subtract without fundamentally changing anything. For V-Dem, the goal is to be inclusive in the list of features that scholars have included in their conceptualizations of democracy.

Also very distinctive of this approach is the causal nature of the relationship between variable and indicator. Signaled by the causal arrow →, the latent variable *causes* the indicator. This causal view of latent variables is probably the standard in psychology and education. One can find innumerable textbooks and handbooks that provide a causal interpretation of latent variable models. For example, Borsboom has forcefully made this argument:

> Latent variables are viewed as the unobserved determinants of a set of observed scores; specifically, latent variables are considered to be the common cause of the observed variables. (Borsboom 2005, 4)

> The only thing that all measurement procedures have in common is the either implicit or explicit assumption that there is an attribute out there that, somewhere in the long and complicated chain of events leading up to the measurement outcome, is playing a causal role in determining what values the measurements will take.... The crucial mistake is the view that validity is about correlation. Validity concerns measurement, and measurement has a clear direction. The direction goes from the world to our instruments. It is very difficult not to construct this relation as causal.... Now, measurement is a causal concept, not a correlational one, and validity is so too. (Borsboom 2005, 153, 160)

Numerous other examples of the causal interpretation in psychology can be found. For example, the chapter on latent variables in the *The Oxford handbook of quantitative methods* starts:

> The intent of latent variable measurement models (i.e., factor analysis) is to establish the number and nature of latent variables or factors that account for the variation and covariation among a set of observed measures, commonly referred to as indicators. Specifically, a factor is an unobservable variable that *influences* more than one observed measure and which *accounts for* the correlations among these observed measures. In other words, the observed measures are intercorrelated because they share a common *cause*. (Brown 2013, 257; emphasis is mine)

There are various reasons why this is a plausible interpretation. One speaks of "effect" models, which suggests that the indicators are the effects of causes. The latent variables are independent variables in the causal model while the indicator variables are the dependent variables.[3]

If these arrows are not given their usual causal interpretation it is not exactly clear how to interpret them. Presumably they would be interpreted as correlational but not causal. Nevertheless, how this correlational interpretation is to be explained in terms of the phenomena under consideration is left to be determined. This is one reason why the basic framework uses dashed arrows to symbolize the "indicator of" relationship. These dashed arrows explicitly suggest a noncausal relationship.

Causal measurement models are very common. For example, thermometers are based on a causal model of heat expansion. The use of measuring instruments in the natural sciences often requires a causal mode of measurement.

In most circumstances one does not end up with just one, but in fact multiple, latent variables, as in figure 2.2. These multiple latent variables can thus play the role of secondary-level dimensions in the basic framework. This is illustrated in figure 2.2 in the case of democracy. Typically, when one has multiple indicators of democracy and applies latent variable methodologies, one ends up with at least two, if not more, latent variables (e.g., Coppedge 2012).

Figure 2.2 gives an influential latent variable model by one of the leading methodologists in this field. So while one starts with something like figure 2.3, there are in fact often *multiple* dimensions to the indicators that the statistical analysis generates. In the case of Bollen's analysis of democracy there are two latent factors. Coppedge (2012) in his analysis of democracy ends up with two factors of democracy. In another analysis, Treier and Jackman (2008) have only one latent variable of democracy.

---

3. The causal interpretation appears to be quite controversial in political science. In my modest experience, describing these models in causal terms provokes a strong, usually negative, reaction in political science audiences.

The statistical model together with the data usually produces multiple latent factors (the number is often a matter of convention, i.e., eigenvalues greater than 1 get included, but those less than 1 are dropped). In terms of the basic framework, the statistical analysis generates multiple secondary-level dimensions of democracy, as indicated in figure 2.2. Each has its own set of indicators, which are highly correlated (ideally at least) with the unmeasured latent variable and not correlated with other latent variables generated from the list of indicators.

With regard to the Completeness Guideline, this list of all latent variables thus might be seen as being a complete conceptualization. While some latent variables will be excluded, the grounds for exclusion are statistical in nature not substantive. Given the inductive, data-based nature of the methodology, it is clear that a different set of indicators or a different population might generate a different list of latent factors.

Each of these latent variables can be considered a secondary-level dimension. For example, the V-Dem project has generated a number of secondary-level latent variables of democracy. These latent variables use many, often 10 or more, indicators. Figure 2.5 gives a partial list of a partial list: the project has over 200 indicators of democracy.

The latent variable approach is virtually, by construction, a unidimensional approach. This is a function of the statistical methodology used. The core requirement of the latent variable approach is that the indicators be of one thing, and hence highly correlated with each other. In contrast, in definitions there is no requirement at all that the defining features be highly correlated. In fact, we have seen that typically they should be separate and nonredundant attributes.

So while one might start out with dozens of indicators of democracy, one might end up using significantly fewer. They will be dropped because of low correlations or other statistical requirements. For example, Treier and Jackman (2008) start with 5 indicators and end up with only 3 meeting their statistical requirements.

The origins of statistics and measurement lie in the situation where one had multiple measurements of the same physical phenomenon, e.g., the position of a planet. The true position is unobserved, but we do have multiple measurements. The natural thing to do, following the central limit theorem of statistics (and assuming random errors), is to take the mean as the estimate of the position of the planet.

The mean makes sense because these are multiple observations of one thing. Typically, the more observations the better. One does not worry about multidimensionality because it is unidimensional. There are no defining features that constitute the secondary-level dimensions. It is the model of figure 2.5.

What happens in practice is that the defining features of the concept often become the indicators in the latent variable model. One person's defining feature is another's indicator. How did the V-Dem project come up with its list of indicators? They explored various conceptualizations of democracy and used them to develop quantitative indicators.

Typically, the analysis ends when one has arrived at the final list of latent variables. This is illustrated in figure 2.7 (the $\epsilon$ are error terms). Most often the various latent factors are then used separately in various statistical or descriptive analyses.

One can take the arrows in figure 2.5 and flip them around. This changes the causal direction so that the indicators are causing the latent variable. These are often called "formative" models. If one looks at the acronym for them, MIMIC (multiple indicators and multiple causes), a causal interpretation is given to the arrows. A nice example comes from Paxton's work on social capital, reproduced as figure 2.8, where "associations" is one of the core dimensions of the basic-level social capital concept.

MIMIC, or formative latent variables, are not too common in political science and sociology. Doing a Google search for the acronym does not produce many examples from the social sciences (they seem more popular in the health sciences).

This appendix does not discuss the methodology of latent variable estimation and construction. This is a huge topic, well treated in many (text)books (e.g., Bollen 1989) and forms a very important part of methods training in psychology, sociology, and political science.

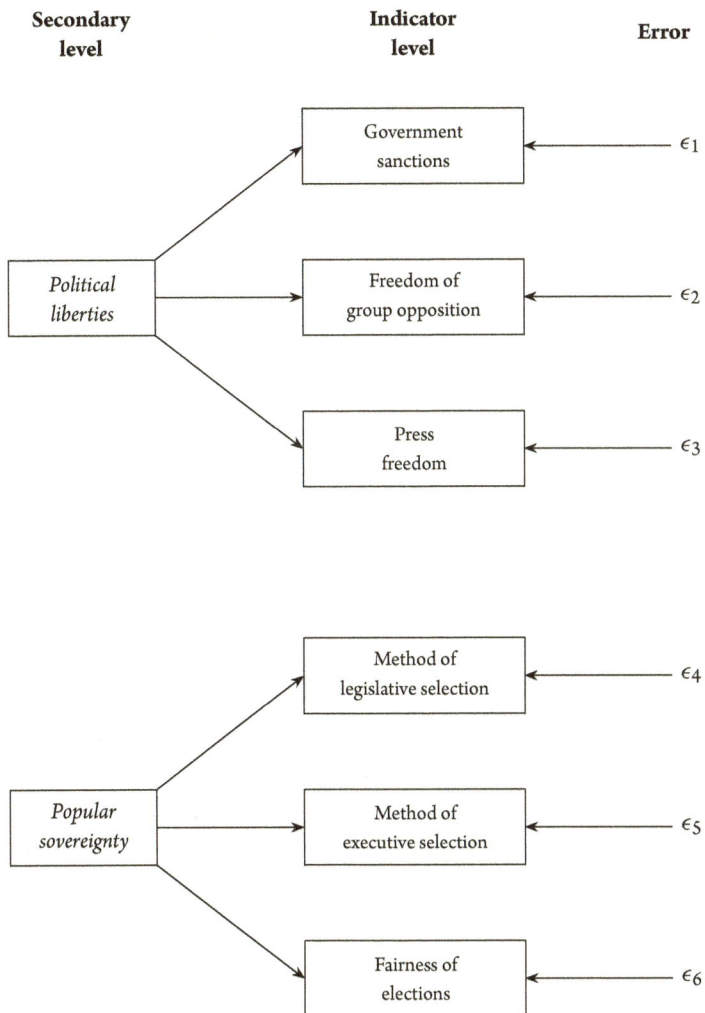

| Secondary<br>level | Indicator<br>level | Error |
|---|---|---|

Government
sanctions — $\epsilon_1$

Political
liberties

Freedom of
group opposition — $\epsilon_2$

Press
freedom — $\epsilon_3$

Method of
legislative selection — $\epsilon_4$

Popular
sovereignty

Method of
executive selection — $\epsilon_5$

Fairness of
elections — $\epsilon_6$

FIGURE 2.7. Two latent variable model of democracy.
*Source:* Based on Bollen and Grandjean (1981).

| **Cause indicators** | **Secondary level** | **Effect indicators** |

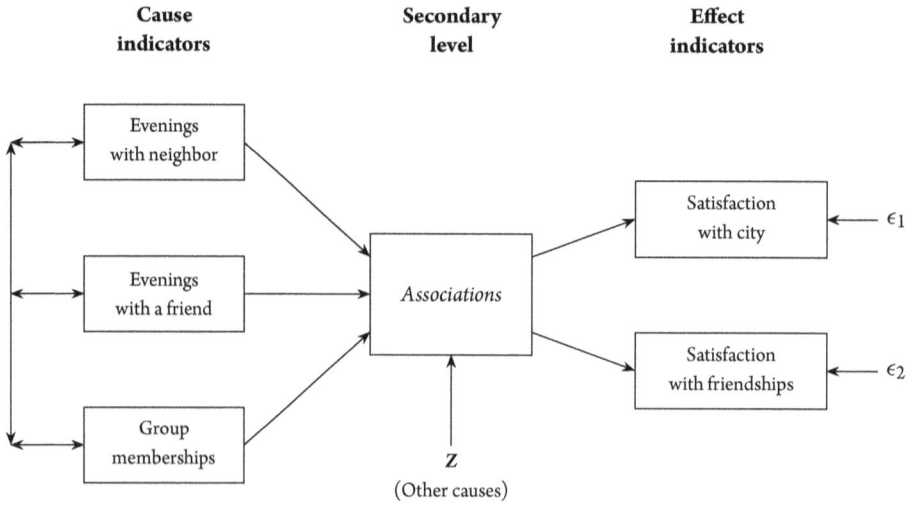

FIGURE 2.8. Indicators causing factors, MIMIC models: associations dimension of social capital. *Source:* Based on Paxton (1999, 274). *Note:* Other secondary-level dimensions for social capital include two trust dimensions.

Importantly, for the purposes of this volume, latent variable models clearly raise the question of causation within conceptualization and measurement. One of the main motivations for developing a separate set of symbols is to make clear the contrast between causal relationships and other kinds of relationships, such as definitional or ontological.

# 3

# Guidelines for Creating Concepts

ONTOLOGY, SEMANTICS, AND DEFINITIONS

> While I proposed to myself nothing more than to improve the chemical
> language, my work transformed itself by degrees, without my being able
> to prevent it, into a treatise on the Elements of Chemistry.
>
> ANTOINE LAVOISIER[1]

## Introduction

Concepts are about definitions, meaning, ontology. They are a response to "What is?", "What do you mean?", and similar sorts of questions. This chapter presents a series of guidelines for the creation, analysis, and understanding of concepts. These guidelines constitute a checklist of issues, principles, and considerations that should guide concept construction and analysis.

This chapter rests at the basic and the secondary levels of the three-level concept–measurement structure outlined in the previous chapter. The first half of the chapter remains at the basic level, while the second half dips down to the secondary level. The chapter does not discuss measurement, data, indicators, quantification, and issues related to numeric measures. Of course, decisions made at the basic and the secondary levels should influence decisions made about measurement.

---

1. Quoted by Goodfield and Toulmin (1962, 218).

In fact, a key point in the following chapters is that measurement should be faithful to ontology. The next chapter presents a first discussion of the connection between semantics–meaning and quantitative measures.

These guidelines present a set of decisions and issues that are absolutely central to the development of good concepts. Some are quite controversial in the sense of recommendations that go against much current practice.

My list of guidelines starts with those implicit in the previous edition of this book (2006), and then builds on the couple of hundred exercises dealing with concepts that I have developed over the years.[2] They represent problems and issues that I have repeatedly seen in articles, books, and PhD dissertations. As guidelines, they do not apply universally, but certainly very widely. Going against a guideline requires some serious justification.

## Terminology

The analysis of terminology is central to understanding concepts. The *words* that people use for concepts often have varied meanings. There is significant variation in terminology for the "same" concept. Sometimes the word does not describe very well what is going on in the definition.

Terminological problems are already present in the methodological language of this volume. What is an "indicator"? First of all, indicators are indicators *of something*. This "something" is usually a concept. Second, my usage—which reflects the way the word is usually used—is that indicators are numeric. This is why I use the expression "data–indicator" in the three-level framework. "Numeric" includes absence–presence, typically coded as 0–1, usually on an underlying continuum. Therefore, an expression like "qualitative indicator" makes little sense. I will use terms like indicator, measure, data as all

---

2. Exercises for all my methods books are updated and expanded roughly every summer. A copy can be obtained by emailing a request to me at ggoertz@nd.edu.

being numeric values given to entities that fall within the scope of the concept.[3]

"Variable" often means concept in the context of this book. Standard usage in statistical analyses uses expressions like "indicator of a variable." Since variables in empirical analyses, models, theories, and hypotheses typically lie at the basic level, that means variable = concept for the purposes of this volume.[4]

Terminology is often very normatively loaded. To call an action "terrorist" is a normative evaluation. Terrorism is notoriously a problematic concept, in part because of these normative loadings. Because

3. "We define 'indicator' as follows: An indicator is a named collection of rank-ordered data that purports to represent the past or projected performance of different units. The data are generated through a process that simplifies raw data about a complex social phenomenon. The data, in this simplified and processed form, are capable of being used to compare particular units of analysis (such as countries or institutions or corporations), synchronically or over time, and to evaluate their performance by reference to one or more standards. This definition includes composite or mash-up indicators that are themselves compiled by aggregating and weighting other indicators. Some indicators are numerical, some qualitative (producing information that may or may not be rendered numerically), and some mix quantitative and qualitative information" (Davis et al. 2015, 4).

4. "To equate concepts with variables also seems to be characteristic of the first sustained attempt in U.S. sociology to explore the process of theorizing, the so-called theory construction movement that emerged in the 1960s and 1970s. In *Constructing social theories* by Arthur Stinchcombe, concepts are equated with variables in an unproblematic manner. 'A "variable" in science is a concept which can have various values, and which is defined in such a way that one can tell by means of observations which value it has in a particular occurrence' (Stinchcombe 1968, 28–29, 38). The same tendency can also be found in *Theoretical sociology: from verbal to mathematical formulations* by Hubert Blalock which refers to 'concepts or variables.' This is similarly true for Blalock's presidential address at ASA in 1978, which was devoted to 'measurement and conceptualization problems', and in which the author refers to what he calls 'theoretical variable' (Blalock 1979, 881). Finally, the discussion of indicators that was central to Lazarsfeld's approach to concepts has continued till today and is still very much alive, both when it comes to how to locate the indicators and how to handle them. A student who is interested in learning the technique of how to construct indicators can, for example, easily find good instructions for how to proceed. There also exists a number of works on various types of validity which have as their goal to ensure that the chosen indicators capture what they are supposed to capture. There exists little discussion, in contrast, of the fact that the move from concept-to-variable-to indicator (1-2-3) is often reduced to a move from variable-to-indicator (2–3)." (Swedberg 2015, 12)

terrorism is such a problematic concept it makes data sets problematic, and then downstream causal analyses problematic.

People often distinguish between "objective" indicators and "subjective" ones. Here subjective typically implies not good, because these indicators are based on individual perceptions. For example, this means that objective measures of poverty are better than subjective measures of happiness. When Ravallion (2016) uses the term "mash-up" to describe how some do concept measurement, this clearly has a negative connotation.

Often, uncertainty about terminology reflects conceptual problems. I use the term autocracy in the concept pair democracy–autocracy. However, there are a variety of other possibilities, e.g., "totalitarian," "authoritarianism," "dictatorship" (this is quite popular); in the 19th century the opposite of democracy was "monarchy." These all have somewhat different meanings and suggest different definitions. In contrast, there is widespread consensus on the term "democracy." This suggests that scholars are much clearer about the concept of democracy than the concept of autocracy (chapter 5 presents some statistical evidence that supports this claim).

Another set of issues relates to what I call "hyphenated concepts." This includes actually hyphenated terms such as competitive–authoritarian, but also concepts that have multiple parts such two or more nouns or adjectives and nouns. For example, "transitional justice" invokes the huge concept "justice" plus the term "transitional." Sometimes the adjective modifies the root concept. For example, the next chapter discusses the concept of a "very poor" state. So how does "very" modify the meaning of "poor"? Would it be better to talk about "extreme poverty" or "destitution" rather than "very poor"? Some of these issues will be discussed in chapter 4 and in chapter 7 on hybrids, which use multiple words, but one needs to be particularly careful when using concepts with multiple words.

As such, there are a number of guidelines relating to terminology:

Connotation Guideline: If the terminology involves very negative or positive connotations then one needs to explore how that affects all aspects of the concept and its use (e.g., scope, coding). This is often closely connected to normative issues of conceptualization.

Multiple Word Guideline: Does the concept use multiple words? If so, how do the two or more concepts interact?

Multiple Terminological Options Guideline: Are there various alternative terminological choices for a concept? What are the implications of choosing one over the others?

## Scope Guideline

The Scope Guideline requires that one determine the scope of application of the concept:

Scope Guideline: Give the scope where the concept can be applied (and eventually not applied).

Pragmatically this means determining the population of observations in the data set of the concept. Typically, the scope of application of the concept of democracy is states. The scope of poverty is often individuals, but sometimes households. As one can see, scope itself can easily involve problematic and tricky concepts, e.g., "state" or "household."

While this guideline might seem obvious, chapter 8 discusses common methodologies for typologies of *something*, where the core example is typologies of autocratic regimes. Typically, the scope of these typologies is autocratic regimes (a dichotomization procedure), not all states. So not all states are coded on their degree of monarchy, only autocratic states. However, the various regime types in the typology have as a scope all states since that is the basic unit of analysis. If one wants a data set on "monarchy" the scope is all states. Hence there is a choice between the scope being all states versus all autocratic states. Chapter 8 argues that the correct scope choice is all states, not all autocratic states.

This is different from the number of positive instances of the concept. For example, it is a separate question how many countries will score above zero on the monarchy concept; obviously a lot of countries will have zero membership in the set of monarchies. However, the number of zero or nonzero cases is a separate empirical and causal question (see chapter 9).

There is a debate in the literature on democracy about how to code or not code certain situations. For example, if the central government has completely collapsed (i.e., anarchy), can one code regime type? If the country is under foreign occupation, can one code regime type? What about transitional periods? Practice with the Polity data set of democracy has varied over time regarding these problematic situations. It is not so obvious what to do. For example, a country under foreign occupation has a government; it is not a democracy. Polity historically coded these cases as missing, and now many code these cases in the gray zone as competitive–authoritarian regimes (i.e., 0 on the $-10$ to 10 Polity democracy scale).

The Scope Guideline requires that one be able to code *all* observations within the scope, and ideally in data gathering one does exactly that. As democracy illustrates, there may be a variety of borderline cases that may or may not fall within the scope; these need explicit discussion and justification.

## The Underlying Continuum of Concepts

One of the most important guidelines is always to think about concepts as having an underlying continuum, to think of them as continuous variables. The positive pole constitutes one extreme of the continuum. A corollary of this guideline is that one should not conceptualize in dichotomies (see below):

> Continuum Guideline: Concepts should always be thought of as a continuum with the positive pole at one end.

Concept pairs are very common and they virtually assume, by definition, some underlying continuum between them. My standard examples such as peace–war, democracy–autocracy, poverty–wealth all assume some continuum.

One of the core reasons to think of concepts in continuous terms is that it allows for the existence of the gray zone. This is such an important issue that chapter 7 is devoted to it.

A second reason for having a continuous view of concepts is that it allows semantically neighboring concepts to overlap with each other. Using democracy as the positive pole, the concept of competitive–authoritarian overlaps with democracy. This central idea will be discussed in the next chapter.

The Continuum Guideline has a potentially controversial corollary. One often hears something like "It is difference in kind, not a difference in degree," or "It is qualitatively different." With continuous concepts there is no qualitative difference along the continuum, it is always a difference in degree. If one looks at the many figures of concepts in the next chapter, they all illustrate difference in degree (except dichotomous ones). Conceptualization should allow for a smooth transition (which *does not necessarily mean slow*; the slope—or derivative—can be quite large at points) from an object not being a member of the concept to partial membership to full. To use democracy, there is a smooth conceptual transition from not being a democracy to being somewhat democratic.

The way to formulate this claim of "difference in kind, not degree" is to ask "How different is object $A$ from object $B$ vis-à-vis concept $Z$?," where $A$ and $B$ are members of the scope of application of the concept.[5] It might be the case that $A$ scores 1.0 (maximum) on the concept while $B$ scores 0.0 (minimum): they are very different from each other. Another object $C$ might be close to $A$ scoring 0.9, while object $D$ is close to $B$ with value 0.1. As such, "qualitatively different" actually means "very different." For example, poor people are not qualitatively different from wealthy, nor are autocratic regimes qualitatively different from democratic ones: they are "very different."

It is the Scope Guideline that defines the universe of the phenomenon. Within that scope, objects range from 0 to 1 (according to

---

5. The question is whether "apples" and "oranges" fall within the scope of the concept; they might if the concept is caloric value of food.

the convention adopted in this volume). Whether two concepts are qualitatively different is a separate question. They may or may not be, depending on their definitions and ontologies. The DSM disorders illustrate this in a big way (DSM is the bible for defining mental disorders, the current version is DSM-5 2013). Many symptoms appear for various different mental disorders. Thus these disorders overlap and are not "qualitatively different."[6]

Core to concepts is the goal of description. For almost all social, political, and economic phenomena there exist gray zones and variation. As such, the Continuum Guideline encourages more accurate representations of social phenomena, i.e., descriptive inference.

The Continuum Guideline also reflects widespread semantic usage. It is completely natural to say that something is more, less, or somewhat C. There are all kinds of other expressions that indicate degree. Shades of gray, white, and black are almost impossible to avoid in describing the world.

## Dichotomization Is Problematic

One way to rephrase the Continuum Guideline is via a guideline regarding dichotomization:

Dichotomization Guideline: Do not conceptualize in dichotomies.

Indicators and measures of poverty illustrate how ingrained the dichotomization reflex is. Standard practice is that the first order of business in assessing how much poverty there is in a country is to establish a poverty line. This poverty line often is a dichotomization procedure (and is often closely related to thresholds discussed at length in the next chapter).[7] The World Bank textbook on poverty measures states this very clearly: "Three steps need to be taken in measuring

6. An interesting exercise would be to see whether there are any disorders that do not overlap with other disorders.

7. "It is entirely defensible for an external observer to judge that there is a qualitative difference in welfare at one or more critical levels [poverty lines] in a specific society." (Ravallion 2016, 191–92)

poverty: (1) Defining an indicator of welfare, (2) Establishing a minimum acceptable standard of that indicator to separate the poor from the nonpoor (the poverty line) (3) Generating a summary statistic to aggregate the information from the distribution of this welfare indicator relative to the poverty line" (Haughton and Khandker 2009, 9; see also Ravallion 2016; Alkire et al. 2015). Once the poverty line is established, *then* one evaluates the degree of poverty of those below the line.

The ideal procedure is to have a concept and measure of poverty (or well-being) that applies to all individuals in the country. Total poverty in a country is then some aggregate (e.g., sum) of individual poverty, i.e., one skips completely step (2) in the World Bank procedure.

It appears that many people feel strongly that dichotomization is a good procedure. The Democracy–Dictatorship group (Cheibub et al. 2010) has defended dichotomization for their concept of democracy. It is not clear to me where these ideas come from. From a statistical point of view dichotomization is a loss of information and is less desirable than continuous, ratio, or interval data. The vast majority of the statistical literature discourages dichotomization. So this preference for dichotomization does not come from statistics or calculus.

I suspect that this preference for dichotomization is what one might call an "Aristotelian holdover." Historically, e.g., in Aristotle, logic was dichotomous: something was true or false. To say something is "partially true" was problematic. I suspect that this heritage continues to implicitly inform a lot of thinking about concepts. For example, Sartori, throughout his influential career, argued against "degreeism." He borrowed most of his methodology from the most influential philosophical logic textbook of the 1930s. This philosophical tradition could explain perhaps the preference for dichotomization in political and moral philosophy, as well as qualitative methods more generally.

One must be pragmatic. Often data come only in dichotomized form. There might be other practical compromises one might need to make. But one should not take dichotomization as the preferred option.

There is one situation where dichotomization is almost unavoidable: case selection. It is very hard for a case to be "partially" in the data set: it is in or out. The problem is that there is always a gray zone and one needs to draw a line through it for case selection. For example, one might want to code some concept, e.g., democracy, for all "states" as the scope or population of interest. One needs a list of states. An early and very influential aspect of the Correlates of War project was to develop a list of states of the world. Choices can be contested (e.g., Gleditsch and Ward 1999). Historically, it is not very clear which non-Western political units to include as states, e.g., Tokugawa Japan or traditional African states. Sometimes projects will have a population minimum for a state to be included: Should one consider Andorra, Liechtenstein, Monaco, or the Vatican City as states? There is a gray zone of entities that are almost states, for example, de facto states such as Northern Cyprus or Kosovo. There will be a variety of crucial dichotomization choices about whether or not to include these political entities in the population of states.

In short, case selection involves hard decisions about including or not cases that lie in various gray zones. Here dichotomization is almost unavoidable. Otherwise, it should be avoided if possible.

Chapter 8 returns to dichotomization in the context of typologies, which usually include dichotomization as part of standard practice and advice.

## The Ideal Type Guideline

The terminology of positive pole and the underlying continuum implies itself that there is some extreme end of the continuum. This leads to the guideline that one should explicitly conceptualize the concept at that end of the continuum:

> Ideal Type Guideline: One should conceptualize in terms of ideal types, i.e., the positive pole as the extreme of the underlying continuum.

In preparing the first edition of this book I did an extended search for methodological discussions of Weber's ideal type. That search— which involved consultation with Weber specialists—produced almost

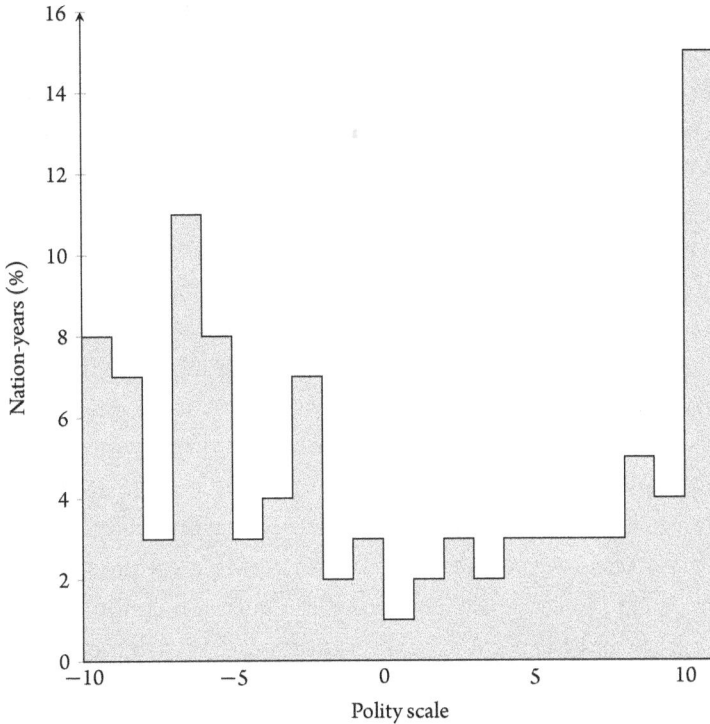

FIGURE 3.1. Concepts and ideal types: Polity democracy measure.

nothing about the methodology of constructing ideal type concepts (Swedberg 2017 confirms this). The clearest point was that there were few if any empirical referents for the ideal type. This is about how often one can find cases in the real world, a topic discussed at length under the rubric of intension–extension of concepts in chapter 9. This depends obviously on the concept and the world. This section focuses on the conceptualization side.[8]

To see how the distribution of cases is a symptom of a failure to observe the Ideal Type Guideline examine figure 3.1, in particular the

8. "The second view … proposes that concepts are ideals—representations of the perfect instances of a class. This view was proposed by Barsalou in the 1980s. Despite a few interesting applications, this view has not become a major approach in the psychology of concepts" (Machery 2009, 108).

positive pole of democracy. The massive spike at Polity $= 10$ indicates that the Polity concept of democracy stopped too soon conceptually.

To see this, imagine what would happen if the scale went to 15 instead of 10. Many of the Polity $= 10$ cases would be located in this higher-quality democracy zone. At 15 we might have very few or no cases of ideal type democracy.

Depending on my mood, I call this the "Lake Wobegon" or "Harvard grading" problem: in Lake Wobegon everyone is above average and at Harvard almost everyone gets an A.[9] The problem is that the concept does not capture all the interesting variation and hence when applied empirically you can get distributions with spikes at the pole.

One can see with examples that Polity stops too soon in its conceptualization of democracy. For example, the USA in 1900—when African-Americans did not have the vote in much of the country—is a Polity $= 10$ case. All you need to be a 10 in terms of voting is adult white males. A big of chunk of America—the South—was not very democratic at all, but the USA gets the maximum Polity democracy score nevertheless.

The Ideal Type Guideline has some important corollaries. The first is that dichotomization is a bad idea because one will almost certainly not have an ideal type conceptualization.

A second, probably controversial, corollary is that contextualization is not a good idea. By contextualization I mean, for example, a conceptualization of democracy relative to a given historical period. It is true that the USA was a very good democracy for the 18th century, but it is also true that it is not a very good democracy in the 21st century.

An absolute or ideal type conceptualization will reveal such claims about historical relativity, because among all countries in the 18th century the USA scores the highest. It will also be the case that no country in the 18th or 19th centuries scores the maximum on democracy.

---

9. Lake Wobegon is the famous town invented by Garrison Keillor for his radio program; the closing words of the monologue of each show were usually "Well, that's the news from Lake Wobegon, where all the women are strong, all the men are good-looking, and all the children are above average." See Wikipedia for more.

Another important corollary deals with "minimal conceptualizations." In the democracy literature, there is a tradition of talking about "minimal" conceptualizations of democracy. Typically this is traced back to Schumpeter's analysis in 1950. This informs the Democracy–Dictatorship group's view of democracy (e.g., Przeworski et al. 2000; Cheibub et al. 2010). Virtually by definition, a minimal conceptualization is not an ideal type. Minimal conceptualizations are not a good idea.

The recourse to minimal definitions often occurs when there is much debate over a concept. Scholars then use—almost always implicitly—Mill's method of agreement to locate those dimensions upon which most agree:

> Defining the term welfare state comes with a number of difficulties. The first and probably most striking difficulty is the huge empirical diversity of welfare states which makes it extremely difficult to identify a common denominator of the term. (Kuhlmann 2018, 1)

> The best way to deal with the contested nature of the term populism is to work with a minimal definition. The great advantage of minimal definitions is that they force us to identify the main characteristics—or to use more a sophisticated jargon, the necessary and sufficient criteria—of the phenomenon under consideration. (Kaltwasser 2019, 64)

This is a great way to start but not a good place to stop. It can give the list of necessary condition dimensions—because it uses Mill's method of agreement—but only problematically gives the sufficient list. Essentially, these minimal definitions are an application of the Usual Suspects Guideline discussed below.

Dasgupta (2001, 54) illustrates the connection between minimal conceptualizations, necessary conditions, and the lack of sufficiency: "A minimal set of indices for spanning a reasonable conception of current well-being in a poor country includes private consumption per head, life expectancy at birth, literacy, and civil and political liberties.

Private consumption is food, shelter, clothing, and basic legal aid. Life expectancy at birth is the best indicator of health, while literacy of basic primary education. Civil and political rights allow people to function independently of the state and their communities. Each of these is necessary. They cannot be reduced to some one item or replaced by a monetary value, for they may be undervalued by the market." This is very typical in that there is clearly a set of minimal necessary conditions, but rarely does the author address the sufficiency question, which is absolutely necessary if one is actually going to code, categorize, or measure well-being.

Often people talk about "typical" or "representative" cases. This usually refers to the empirical distribution of cases. Typical or representative often becomes the mean or median in practice (e.g., Gerring 2017). Semantically, the gray zone is rarely typical or representative. Following the Ideal Type Guideline one rarely has the statistically average case being a *good* case of the concept. Chapter 9 explores the tension between concepts and the empirical distribution of cases.

Figure 3.1 suggests that ideal type means few cases at the positive pole. However, the next chapter focuses on the concept of poverty: there might be quite a few ideal type cases of poverty. In general, if the empirical distribution of data is highly skewed then it is quite possible that there are a lot of cases at the positive pole. Chapter 7 analyses ideal type, hybrid, and gray zone concepts, which may have many instances. So while the problems of figure 3.1 might be quite common, they are certainly not universal.

## Gray Zone

The gray zone is important enough to merit its own extended discussion in chapter 7. The key overall guideline here is to think explicitly about the gray zone. Often the gray zone is an interesting, distinctive phenomenon in its own right. Often it has distinctive terminological issues, notably a tendency to involve hyphenated names, such as competitive–authoritarian for democracy.

Gray Zone Guideline: Conceptualize specifically the gray zone.

Often the gray zone is left unconceptualized as the middle part of the continuum. Often it is chosen in a pretty arbitrary manner, and often symmetrically in the middle.

The Ideal Type Guideline applies to gray zone concepts as well. To continue with the gray metaphor, it is the point exactly between completely white and completely black. Whether there are many or few cases here often constitutes a core theoretical and causal puzzle.

Implicitly it often becomes merely an interpolated middle of the continuum. This linear interpolation might be problematic, as we will see in the next chapter.

## Concept Pairs, Negations, and Opposites

Often concepts come in pairs, where one can be considered the positive pole and the other the negative pole. For some researchers the positive pole is one of the pair and for others it is the negative pole. Research focusing on autocratic regimes uses that as the positive pole while research on democracy takes democracy as the positive pole.

The key guideline in this section is to focus explicitly on the negative pole:

Negative Pole Guideline: Explicitly conceptualize the negative pole.

A common fact is that the negative pole (1) does not have a clear, consensus term and (2) uses a quite different word. Both suggest conceptual issues that need attention.

While an explicit consideration of the negative pole is often not necessary for theory and hypothesis building, when it comes to case selection one will almost always have to choose negative cases.

The next chapter will discuss the difference between the negation of a concept and its opposite. For all positive poles, the negative pole can always be conceptualized as "not" the positive pole. For concept pairs, the "opposite" is the other concept in the pair, where the exact term for the opposite can be up for grabs.

Naturally one will not give the same amount of attention to the negative pole as to the positive. The point of the guideline is to not completely ignore it. The next few sections deal with issues regarding the negative pole.

## Heterogeneity of Negations

It is not uncommon that the positive pole is a pretty focused concept, which has as a consequence that the negative pole can be quite—or even extremely—heterogeneous. This matters most directly because statistical, empirical, and causal analyses depend on comparisons with a control, counterfactual, or non-treatment category. One reason to think about the heterogeneity of the negative pole is that it answers the question "Compared to what?":

Heterogeneity of Negation Guideline: Is the negative pole heterogeneous in ways that make causal inference problematic?

My favorite example of this involves large-$N$ cross-national—often with 100+ countries—statistical analyses where proportional representation is an independent variable. The Heterogeneity of Negation Guideline recommends looking at what is covered by "not–proportional representation." This comparison group usually includes countries such as North Korea and the USA. With such a diverse set of countries, it is not really clear at all how one should interpret the coefficient of the proportional representation variable in the statistical analysis.

This issue arises with additional force for hybrid or gray zone concepts. As discussed in detail in chapter 7, the not-gray comparison category points in two opposing directions simultaneously: toward the positive pole as well as toward the negative pole. One has three general options: choose (1) the positive pole as the comparison group,

(2) the negative pole as the comparison group, or (3) both positive and negative poles.

There are no easy answers to this heterogeneity problem. It depends a great deal on the causal inference goals of the scholar and the kinds of heterogeneity of the negative cases. The stakes are high: by choosing one versus another comparison group, statistical results can flip sign or significance level. It is worth stressing that this is maintaining exactly the same positive pole cases.

## The Concept Asymmetry Guideline

> The opposite of war is not peace, it is creation.... If you are creating you
> are not destroying.
>
> JOYCE DIDONATO[8]

The Negative Pole Guideline raises a question about the extent to which there is symmetry between the positive poles and their opposites in concept pairs. Conceptual symmetry means that the opposite is the strict mirror image or inverse of the positive pole. For example, autocracy is defined completely as "not-democracy." The Concept Asymmetry Guideline suggests that in general the opposite in concept pairs is *not* literally and strictly the negation of the positive pole.

The next chapter discusses and illustrates the idea that the opposite is a different—though related—concept from the strict negation of the positive pole. Of course, my favorite example is the claim that peace is not the absence of war.

This leads to the following guideline:

Concept Asymmetry Guideline: Concept asymmetry should be the default assumption for concept pairs. One must justify that the pair are mirror images, inverses, or complete negations of each other.

10. Interview with Joyce DiDonato for her concert performance of "In war and peace."

There are several ways in which one can see conceptual asymmetry at work. The first is that the defining features of the opposite contain attributes that are not present in the positive pole. Following the List Defining Dimensions Guideline (below) for both the positive pole and its opposite helps make clear whether there is asymmetry or not.

Concept asymmetry naturally leads to causal asymmetry. If the opposite is not identical to the mirror image of the positive pole then it might well have different causes and effects. Conversely, if the causes of the positive pole are different from its opposite, that strongly implies conceptual asymmetry.

A useful recommendation for PhD students and other researchers is to do a literature review of the causes of the positive pole and contrast it with a literature review of the causes of its opposite in the concept pair. In my experience these literature reviews are rarely symmetrical: common theories and hypotheses about the opposite include variables usually absent from theories of the positive pole. Implicitly, scholars claim that the pair is asymmetrical because their explanations of each of them differ.

For example, to explain democracy frequently uses different theoretical frameworks from explanations of autocratic regimes. Theories of peace are asymmetric to theories of war. Explaining wealth or a high level of economic development is not necessarily symmetric with explaining poverty.

Hence there exists a tension between the idea that there is an underlying continuum between the positive pole and its opposite: the opposite concept is not the inverse or mirror image of the positive pole. This is not inherently problematic but does raise key issues for concept construction. The next chapter provides a framework for thinking about this question and provides several concrete examples of the asymmetry of concepts pairs.

In many ways the Conceptual Asymmetry Guideline is one of the most important guidelines. It raises fundamental conceptual, causal, and theoretical questions that must be explicitly addressed when there are concept pairs. The next chapter introduces a methodology for modeling and visualizing concept symmetry and asymmetry. It makes the default symmetry assumptions clear and provides asymmetric alternatives. While concept symmetry is possible and implicit in most statistical analyses, there is a great deal in terminology, semantics, and theories that suggests that in fact the positive pole and its opposite in concept pairs are asymmetric.

## Defining via the Negation Guideline

Ce corps qui s'appelait et qui s'appelle encore le saint empire romain n'était en aucune manière ni saint, ni romain, ni empire. (The Holy Roman Empire is not Holy, not Roman, and not an Empire.)

VOLTAIRE

One feature of some—maybe many—concepts is the use of negations in conceptualizing the positive pole. The Democracy–Dictatorship group conceptualizes autocracy as the absence of democracy. Many in the poverty literature consider poverty as the absence or low levels of basic capabilities. Poverty is the absence of basic capacities and freedoms, e.g., absence of health, eduction, choice. The concept of "civil society" is often defined in large part as "not-government" AND "not-for-profit" (e.g., not businesses).

If one considers the continuum as having three basic segments, positive pole, gray zone, and negative pole, then it is not often clear what to do with the gray zone. We will see in chapter 7 that the gray zone by default uses negation in conceptualizing. To be in the gray zone means not–positive pole AND not–negative pole.

Sometimes one has a choice between a conceptualization that is positive and one that is negative. My favorite example is that "qualitative methods" is best defined as not-statistics, exactly because to give a positive list of qualitative methods would be hard given the heterogeneous methodologies that fall under that rubric.

Given the huge variety of concepts it is hard to make generalizations; nevertheless, in general one might prefer positive conceptualizations to negative ones:

> Defining via Negation Guideline: One should consider carefully when *completely* conceptualizing via negation and in general prefer positive attributes to negative ones.

## Conceptual Overlap Guideline

Semantically, concepts may lie "near" each other. Often this is the relatively explicit division of the underlying continuum into segments, which is very common. For example, the World Bank defines countries as low, lower-middle, higher-middle, and high income. Another way this can happen is that two concepts share some defining features. As such, it is quite common that a given object or observation can fall under multiple concepts simultaneously. This is partial membership in two or more concepts.

> Conceptual Overlap Guideline: Allow for observations to have nonzero membership in semantically close concepts.

The Conceptual Overlap Guideline says that dichotomization decisions should not be forced for observations that have membership in neighboring concepts. So, for example, a country could be partially a member of the set of poor countries as well as partially a member of the set of low-middle-income countries.

This is closely related to problems with typologies. One of the standard rules for creating typologies is that the categories should be mutually exclusive. Mutually exclusive is fundamentally a dichotomization rule. The Conceptual Overlap Guideline rejects this and says that one should allow membership, partial at least, in more than one type in the typology. For example, many people are partial members of different ethnic or religious groups because their parents come from different backgrounds.

The next chapter provides a visual and graphical way to think about conceptual overlap.

## Defining Attributes Guideline

The above guidelines dealt with concepts at the basic level. The fact is that many important concepts are multidimensional and multi-level. The next set of guidelines deals with the multidimensionality of concepts.

The first guideline for dealing with multidimensional concepts is simple:

Defining Attributes Guideline: Give a clear list of the defining attributes.

These defining features or, using my terminology, secondary-level dimensions, specify the key attributes of the concept. For example, Terry Karl gives this list for democracy:

Democracy is a political concept involving several dimensions: (1) contestation over policy and political competition for office; (2) participation of the citizenry through partisan, associational, and other forms of collective action; (3) accountability of rulers to the ruled through mechanism of representation and the rule of law; and (4) civilian control over the military. (Karl 1990, 2)

These four features constitute her concept of democracy.

In the human capabilities approach, Nussbaum has given 10 capabilities that constitute human well-being (discussed in the previous chapter). She takes Sen to task (e.g., Nussbaum 2011) for talking about some capabilities, e.g., education, but being unwilling to give a complete list. However, to do actual empirical description (e.g., measurement) or causal inference one needs a complete list (see below for more). In the previous chapter we also saw that completeness is a core guideline. So the Defining Attributes Guideline naturally goes along with the Completeness Guideline of chapter 2.

If the concept has a data set then one can usually determine what the defining dimensions are via the coding rules. This is, however, complicated by the fact that discussions of data are often more about indicators and less about concepts. Nevertheless, coding rules follow the Completeness Guideline and so at least implicitly give a complete list of defining features.

## Usual Suspects Guideline

Once one has a list of defining attributes then it becomes possible to analyze and discuss the various constitutive features. Typically, some attributes are not controversial while others are debatable. This leads to the Usual Suspects Guideline:

> Usual Suspects Guideline: Which constitutive features are common and uncontroversial—usual suspects—in the literature on the concept? What are unusual suspects?[11]

In Karl's list above, one can ask whether there are defining features that one does not find in other conceptualizations of democracy. In her case the unusual suspect is "civilian control over the military," which is rarely explicitly present as a defining feature of democracy. One can understand why she included this attribute once one knows that she is a Latin Americanist. She is thinking of countries like Chile during its transition to democracy, when Pinochet and the military still had a lot of power. Her proposal to include that feature explicitly is not very controversial because most democratic theorists would require democratically elected leaders to have control over the military.

In many instances the unusual suspects might be controversial exactly because many people's conceptualizations do not include them. It might be a large part of the discussion that one should add some new feature to the list. This is fundamentally what Sen was doing when he

---

11. The term "usual suspects" comes from the end of the movie *Casablanca* where the police captain tells his men to round up the usual suspects.

argued that income was insufficient for conceptualizing human well-being. One needed to add other dimensions such as political freedom, health, and education.

Similarly, one could debate Nussbaum's list of capabilities. Are there things missing? Are there capabilities that are not important enough to be on the list? One can look at alternative lists, e.g., Stiglitz et al. (2009). One can look at Rawls's list of basic goods (1971; 1982) or Fukuda-Parr et al.'s (2015) list of economic and social rights.

If one includes *only* the usual suspects then often one reads of "minimal conceptualizations." Collier in his various writing talked frequently about minimal conceptualizations of democracy. These minimal conceptualizations more or less explicitly include only the usual suspects, i.e., something we can all agree upon. However, minimal conceptualizations are almost always incomplete and they usually violate the Ideal Type Guideline.

The Usual Suspects Guideline challenges the notion that some concepts are "essentially contested." There are parts that are not essentially contested, which constitute the usual suspects. So while complete agreement on a definition may be unlikely, there are key parts that are essentially not contested.

## Complicated Concepts Guideline

Particularly when the conceptual analysis is normative, philosophical, or qualitative, it is easy for conceptualization to become quite long and complicated.

For social science purposes—and often for philosophical and normative purposes—the Complicated Concepts Guideline suggests that too complicated concepts are problematic:

Complicated Concepts Guideline: Consider carefully when constructing complicated concepts with many constitutive features.

Note that this guideline is about secondary-level dimensions, not data–indicators, for which this guideline does not apply.

This can be partially a matter of personal preference, but I find that concepts with a large number (the concept of "large" being greater than 5–7) of defining attributes become too complicated to handle. Juggling more than 7 balls is a tricky business.

A good example is Schmitter's famous definition of "corporatism," which generated a huge literature in comparative politics and was basically the official definition:

> Corporatism can be defined as a system of interest representation in which the constituent units are organized into a limited number of singular, compulsory, noncompetitive, hierarchically ordered and functionally differentiated categories, recognized or licensed (if not created) by the state and granted a deliberate representational monopoly within their respective categories in exchange for observing certain controls on their selection of leaders and articulation of demands and supports. (Schmitter 1974, 13)

If one were to follow the Defining Attributes Guideline it is likely that different people would come up with different lists. For example, the list might include (1) singular, (2) compulsory, (3) noncompetitive, (4) hierarchically ordered, (5) functionally differentiated. This is only the beginning of a complete list.

As discussed below, once these complicated concepts get put into causal mechanisms, theories, and hypotheses, the risk of conceptual tautology increases significantly.

The issue of "too complicated" concepts arises most often in purely conceptual articles. If there are no data-gathering constraints, no constraints of causal analysis, and the only constraint is the number of words, it is easy to increase the number of defining dimensions.

## Causal Powers Guideline

Nancy Cartwright has influentially talked about "causal powers and capacities" (1989). When constructing and evaluating concepts it is always important to keep in mind how they are used in theories, hypotheses, and mechanisms, or in short, in causal relationships of all sorts.

One way to think of this is via the disease–symptom metaphor. The ontological theory focuses on the disease and only secondarily on its symptoms. Core to the conceptualization of the disease is its causal powers to negatively influence health.

For example, we can ask what "copper" *is*. One property of copper is its reddish color. However, we would not consider a definition of copper based on its color very adequate for most purposes; much better would be a conceptualization of copper based on its atomic structure. The atomic structure of copper is a better and more useful basis for thinking about copper than an approach based on qualities like its redness, because its atomic structure explains more about its causal powers and properties, e.g., the ability to conduct electricity. But if one is interested in the role of copper in health as a dietary mineral, then one might focus on different features of copper.[12]

The theoretical ontology of concepts is important because we attribute *causal powers* to the secondary-level dimensions that constitute the concept. Harré and Madden define causal powers as " 'X has the power to A' means 'X will/can do A,' in the appropriate conditions, *in virtue of its intrinsic nature*" (1975, 86). Notice that these causal powers are ontological because they refer to X's "intrinsic nature." Like for Locke and other philosophers (e.g., Mill), the standard analogy is the chemical elements. In short, secondary-level dimensions play key roles in causal mechanisms. Redness does not play a role in most causal explanations using copper; in contrast, the atomic structure of copper is used in many hypotheses and theories about copper.

As Cartwright puts it, "A property carries its capacities with it, from situation to situation" (1989, 146). Cartwright maintains that it is knowledge of capacities that enables one to extrapolate from one

---

12. The choice of important characteristics of a phenomenon depends on theoretical context and purpose. Sometimes the theory focuses on transient characteristics of the object, e.g., its velocity. Sometimes superficial characteristics are important, e.g., the redness of copper matters to a designer.

setting to another (1989, 157–58, 163). To using the ongoing example of democracy, it has features due to its ontology that make democracies function in similar ways in different contexts.

Hence, when one is asked to justify the choice of secondary-level dimensions, particularly for independent variables, one important criterion is to take those that have important causal powers and capacities:

> Causal Powers Guideline: One core justification for the choice of secondary-level dimensions, particularly for independent variables, is the causal powers and capacities of those dimensions.

The Causal Powers Guideline leads naturally to what one might call "causal mismeasurement." Including a potentially irrelevant—because it has no causal influence—dimension in a concept means that the values on that dimension will influence the final numeric value because the multiple dimensions must be aggregated in some fashion to get the final value. Thus each dimension contributes, though perhaps not for every observation, to the final value. If the dimension is causally irrelevant this means that the final value will be causally off because of this irrelevant information. So while there may not be any mismeasurement in the usual descriptive sense, in the causal sense there is.

The Causal Powers Guideline means one should be connecting these powers to causal mechanisms:

> For Cartwright, the capacities of the entities in a mechanism are properties of the entities, not dependent on anything anywhere else in this world or any other. This nicely fits scientific practice since scientists in many domains spend a lot of time figuring out the capacities of the entities in mechanisms underlying the phenomena that are interesting to them. When scientists point to a mechanism and identify it as the mechanism responsible for certain phenomena, on this view they are pointing to something real and really there. (Ilari and Williamson 2011, 886–87)

In short, the Causal Powers Guideline could well be called the Causal Powers and Mechanisms Guideline. The powers are found and explicated in causal mechanisms.

One can see how the causal analysis of a phenomenon can then feedback on conceptualization and ontology. For example, in multimethod and causal mechanism analyses of individual cases one might discover features not in the original hypothesized ontology, or one might find that proposed dimensions did not have the kind of impact implied by theory. The Causal Powers Guideline is critical because it inserts concepts into causal mechanisms.

## Dependent Variable Guideline

The Causal Powers Guideline focused in particular on concepts used as independent variables: the causal powers to influence something. One needs to think how complex concepts enter on the dependent variable side. As discussed throughout this volume, the issue of aggregation is critical: depending on the concept's structure some dimensions might have significantly more weight than others. This becomes critical when these concepts and variables lie on the dependent variable side of the equation.

For example, take the various HDI, GDI, GII, and other concepts that fall roughly into the necessary and sufficient condition family of concept structures. For these kinds of structures, scoring low on one dimension means that one scores low on the overall concept because of the use of weakest link aggregation rules.

This has important implications for the dependent variable side. The causal mechanism and hypotheses must focus on, say, explaining why a country scored low on a given dimension. For example, India usually scores quite low, around 133rd out of 188 in 2016, on the Gender Inequality Index. On two of the three dimensions India scores reasonably well (adolescent birth rate and share of seats in parliament), but on the third (maternal mortality) it does very badly. Thus, explaining why India scores low on GII comes down to explaining why it does poorly on that dimension. Aggregation and concept structure analysis (see chapter 6) are critical because a different concept structure—best shot—could lead to a different explanatory strategy.

In a different way, the content of the secondary-level dimensions can matter a great deal. If one includes women's suffrage in the concept of democracy (it is often not included in democracy measures that extend back to the pre–World War II period, such as Polity or "minimal" conceptions of democracy), the values on the democracy variable can significantly change (e.g., most famously for Switzerland, which gave the vote to women only in the 1970s; see Paxton 2000). As such, one might need to include factors that influence the decision to give the vote to women when explaining how democratic a country is.

The Dependent Variable Guideline stresses that one needs to explore how the content and structure of the dependent variable influence the causal, explanatory strategy:

Dependent Variable Guideline: Explore how the content and structure of the dependent variable influence explanatory strategies.

## Causal Mechanism Overlap Guideline

One feature of the world is that any object or phenomenon has multiple features. Just as individuals have multiple features, e.g., gender, height, weight, education, nationality, and ethnicity, any unit that a concept applies to might fall under the scope of other concepts.

An example from my substantive interests is that some events can be considered "civil wars" as well as "military coups" (Powell and Thyne 2011). This is "semantic overlap." It is defined below more precisely, but it means that various concepts overlap in terms of their empirical referents and one should think about zones where concepts overlap.

Theories of civil wars and theories of military coups can look quite different. If one's theory of civil war is of the classic rebel group in a (remote) area, then including military coups might be problematic.

This leads to a recommendation regarding when quite different causal mechanisms apply to the same event or observation:

Causal Mechanism Overlap Guideline: Do different concepts apply to the same object? If so, does that matter, particularly for causal mechanism hypotheses?

In many instances, multiple mechanisms are not problematic because there are multiple competing mechanisms or causal explanations for a given phenomenon or observation. So if one is asking whether a military coup mechanism or a civil war mechanism better explains a given case then that is quite normal.

Where the guideline kicks in is if the goal is to test a civil war causal mechanism that involves rebel groups in outlying areas (e.g., the (in)famous mountainous terrain variable in civil war studies). The military coup–civil wars might not count as falsifying the civil war theory because the theory does not apply to them. In fact, they are not falsifying cases.

## Conceptual Tautology

It is not uncommon for concepts to be developed in a relative causal vacuum. The literature on poverty indicators and measures often focuses on the conceptualization and measurement of poverty without any real consideration of how poverty enters into causal mechanisms, as either independent or dependent variables.

As concepts increase in dimensionality and breadth, one runs an increased risk of "conceptual tautology." Conceptual tautology occurs when the independent variable has some of the same secondary-level dimensions as the dependent variable. For example, if the dependent variable has four dimensions and the independent variable has three and they have two dimensions in common, there are significant levels of conceptual tautology. The statistical analysis might find a statistically significant relationship; however, the relationship is not causal, but conceptual and definitional.

My canonical example involves human rights and democracy. It is not uncommon to find human rights as a dependent variable where democracy is one of the independent variables. *By definition,* one cannot be a high-quality democracy and extensively violate human rights: respect for human rights is built into the conceptualization of democracy (particularly following the Ideal Type Guideline). Another example is the literature on flawed elections as a cause of democratization (e.g., Morgenbesser and Pepinksy 2019), where the problem of tautology is explicitly recognized.

Because conceptual tautologies are usually partial this means that the overall levels of correlation between human rights and democracy might not be high. A lot depends on the measure of democracy and how large a role low human rights plays in the final democracy score. One can see how concept structure influences the degree of conceptual tautology. If low human-rights scores really drag down the democracy scores then the tautology problem increases (probably higher correlations); if best shot aggregation is used then the tautology problem is less obvious.

The Conceptual Tautology Guideline stresses the following:

Conceptual Tautology Guideline: Examine the extent to which the independent and dependent variables have the same defining attributes.

This is not an empirical correlation in the data, but rather a conceptual, definitional, and ontological relationship.[13]


## Conclusion

This chapter has provided a set of guidelines for constructing and evaluating concepts. Over the last 10+ years I have developed over 200 exercises (available on request) for thinking about concepts and measurement. The guidelines here distill some of the problems

---

13. Note that MIMIC methodologies almost always raise the tautology question because some of the independent variables could easily be on the dependent variable side. For example, Krishnakumar (2007) uses MIMIC techniques where many of the independent variables appear in measures of quality of life.

and issues I have repeatedly seen in how concepts and quantitative measures are created and used in research settings.

I have intentionally avoided mathematical and technical details in order to provide a broad overview. The sections are often quite short: this is in large part because they are really introductions to longer, more detailed, and often more mathematical, treatments in later chapters.

It is worth stressing that this discussion has made very little reference to empirical issues. How concepts relate to the coding of cases and the distribution of those cases will be a key theme in later chapters. My approach to concepts is top down: it is driven by semantics, normative concerns, and causal mechanisms and theories.

The next chapter begins the discussion of linking the semantics of concepts with numeric data–indicators, and a methodology for describing and analyzing this linkage. It is not exactly measurement, but rather how one can think about linking numeric data (e.g., GDP per capita) with concepts such as poverty or wealth. It will remain at the basic level; questions of aggregation and concept structure will be added to the mix in later chapters.

# 4

# Mapping Meaning

## LINKING CONCEPTS WITH DATA–INDICATORS

Bivalent logic is not the right logic for serving as a foundation for human sciences. What is needed for this purpose is fuzzy logic. Essentially, fuzzy logic is the logic of classes [concepts] with unsharp boundaries.

LOTFI A. ZADEH

## Introduction

Core to the basic approach of this book is linking semantics with numbers. There is no consensus on terminology for these numbers because they are referred to as data, measures, indicators, variables, etc. Instead of measurement, what matters is the connection between the semantics of concepts and how they are represented in terms of numbers. Most of the time this can be considered as a form of "measurement" but I prefer to think of it as mapping meaning onto numbers.

As discussed in the introduction, the basic framework is quite fractal in character. Whether one zooms in to the specifics at the data–indicator level or focuses on the basic level, most of the same issues appear. So in terms of this chapter it does not really matter which level of the basic framework we are looking at because the same issues of mapping semantics onto numbers arise. In the next chapter we will see the same fractal issues applying to scaling at all the levels, as well as for aggregation discussed in the following chapter.

To make it easier I will stick typically at the basic level for which there is some data on the basic-level concept, such as democracy, wealth, or poverty. The key issue is how to connect what we mean by these concepts to indicators and data. It is more interesting and useful to remain at the basic level, but it cannot be stressed enough that the same issues apply all the way down.

Thus, this chapter is absolutely crucial because it provides the linkage of the mathematical and technical issues of scaling and aggregation to the semantics and content of concepts.

Fuzzy logic provides a framework for thinking about the connection between data–indicators and meaning. Fuzzy logic at its origins was a mathematical theory of semantics (see Kosko 1993 and McNeill and Freiberger 1994 for accessible introductions). It was designed to solve problems related to mathematical modeling of natural language terms.

Using fuzzy logic I explore the methodology of "semantic transformations." Another appropriate term would be semantic mappings, hence the title "mapping meaning." It is connecting what we mean by concepts to some underlying numeric indicator or data.

In other methods books this might be considered a measurement model, but here it is a semantic model linking concepts with numbers. A semantic transformation occurs when a researcher transforms or modifies an indicator to better capture the concept of interest. Airplane attendants provide a nice example. Often one hears that the plane is "full." The concept of interest is thus "full." This is related to an indicator, which is the number of seats occupied. The semantic transformation is the function mapping the number of seats occupied onto the concept of full, which is a real number in the [0, 1] range. A number in the range [0, 1] represents the extent to which the value on the $X$-axis maps onto the concept of full, i.e., $Y = 1$, down to not-full, i.e., $Y = 0$.[1]

1. In QCA, semantic transformations are called calibrations. For the purposes of this chapter these can be taken as synonyms. I prefer the term "semantic transformations" because it

When an attendant says that the plane is full, it generally does *not* mean that all seats are occupied. It seems that if 90–95 percent of the seats are occupied, that counts as full. If, in fact, all seats are occupied then an attendant will use other expressions like "no empty seats" to mean "completely full." Expressions like "very full" for a literalist make no sense, but almost everyone understands what is meant. At some point, maybe at about 80–90 percent of seats, an attendant would never use the term full at all but instead might say that the plane is "pretty full." Semantic transformations are a mapping between meaning and data–indicators. The convention is that a given plane is a 1.0 member of the concept or set of full planes if it has 90–100 percent of the seats occupied; it is a 0.0 member of the conceptual set if it has, say, 80 percent or fewer seats occupied. So 90+ percent of the seats occupied maps onto $Y = 1$. As such, there are many figures in this and future chapters with the data–indicator on the $X$-axis and the fuzzy-logic [0, 1] transformation on the $Y$-axis.[2]

Semantic transformations are mathematically just variable or indicator transformations. As such, they are no different from popular transformations such as standardization and logging. This leads to one of the most important points of this chapter:

> All indicator or variable transformations are semantic transformations.

There is no neutral transformation. This comes out most clearly when we get the normative implications of various mappings. There is no "neutral" conceptualization of poverty. There are just more or less popular transformations and common default transformations. This leads to the core semantic corollary:

---

emphasizes that it is the semantic content of the concept that is driving the mathematical transformation.

2. Fuzzy logic has been most used in computer, mathematical, expert systems. So, for example, "if the plane is full then do standard procedure $P$" is a production rule triggering certain behaviors when a plane is considered full; for example, one might start checking luggage for free.

*All* variable transformations change the meaning of the underlying concept.

Validity-increasing transformations make the meaning closer to that of the researcher or research community; less valid ones increase the distance to the substantive content of the concept.

We will see many examples of semantic transformations. To continue with the airplane attendants example, some might be close to standard usage, others might not be accurate representations of meaning. As a social science example I will explore the connection between a standard indicator of economic development, GDP per capita, and the concept of a poor–wealthy country as semantically transformed by World Bank publications. One can map how World Bank writers connect terms like low, lower-middle, higher-middle and high income to the countries they use as examples in the text and in tables and their GDP per capita.

I also explore a key methodological issue of adjectives and how they modify the meaning of a concept. One might want to know about the progress of the "very poor" countries of the world. How does that relate to the base concept of "poor"? In other words, how does one semantically transform "poor" to get "very poor?"

As stressed in the previous chapters, concepts often come in pairs. I continue with the convention of hyphenating these common pairs, such as poverty–wealth, democracy–autocracy. A key point is that semantically these are not inverses or mirror images of each other: they have different semantic transformation functions. One can see this already with the airplane example: an "empty" plane is semantically not the mirror image of a "full" plane. In statistical practice, however, these pairs are almost always treated as semantically symmetric. For example, if the causal hypothesis involves poor countries one uses GDP per capita; if the hypothesis is about wealthy countries, GDP per capita is also used.

When one gets to data for these concept pairs it typically runs the whole spectrum from one side of the pair to the other. This chapter starts with this basic practice, using examples such as wealth and democracy and their corresponding opposites in the pair. But then it will be critical to split the pairs apart. As stressed throughout this volume, these concept pairs are in fact asymmetric: one is not the opposite or the negation of the other. So the semantic mapping is of one side of the pair or the other. When one does the mappings it will become very clear that they are in fact asymmetric and that one cannot treat poverty as the absence or negation of wealth.

One way to get at these transformations semantically is to use the categorization schemes that often accompany the concept pair and are, for example, a very traditional and common part of global indicators of all sorts. Often these categories have names like poor, middle income, wealthy, and give some sense of the semantics underlying the categorization, which then maps onto the actual numeric data.

Thus this chapter covers what might be called "categorization" schemes. These involve breaking up the continuum of the numeric indicator, e.g., poverty to wealth, into three to five different categories ordinally ranked along the underlying numeric continuum. It is very common for policy and other reasons to break a continuum into three to five categories. These categorization schemes provide concrete evidence that the semantics of the continuum are not linear. The "obvious" way to break a continuum into three categories is to divide it into equal categories; this does not seem very common. Typically, categorization implies nonlinear semantic transformations (e.g., see the discussion below on how the US military treats its test scores). Kelley and Simmons (2019) report that about one-third of their population of global indicators have categorization schemes.[3]

As far as I can tell, there are no real methodological discussions about how to break continua into various categories, nor even how many categories to use (see chapter 5). My nonsystematic impression is that three to five categories are what people choose, rarely more than seven.

---

3. It would be an interesting and useful exercise to systematically look at a set of global performance indicators such as those in the Broome et al. (2018) or Kelley and Simmons (2019) data sets. One could then get a much more systematic sense of how common or uncommon equal division of categories is, based on some underlying indicator.

We will return to these categorization schemes in the next chapter because they are closely related to ordinal scales. Here I take advantage of the fact that sometimes the categories map onto numeric data of some sort. The next chapter examines ordinal coding schemes where there are no underlying data or indicators to use.

As stressed throughout this volume, concepts are descriptive and normative (and causal, but that will not be a theme of this chapter). As a central example in this chapter I focus on the concept of poor–wealthy with regard to countries. Poverty is a very nice example because it is one of the core concerns of government and society both domestically and internationally. The concept of poverty has very strong normative dimensions, so one must include political and moral philosophy in the discussion of meaning. For example, John Rawls's ideas (1982) about preferences for the poor imply certain kinds of semantic transformations. The international community often asks as a descriptive question whether poverty is increasing or decreasing across the globe or in individual countries.

The other main example will be conceptualizations and data about democracy. It is a nice example in terms of categorization because one can easily find practices where the underlying numeric continuum is broken into two or three categories. This will allow me to discuss the importance of conceptual overlap between adjacent categories and the concepts attached to those categories, such as autocracy, competitive–authoritarian, and democracy.

## Semantic Transformations: Years of Education versus "Educated"

This chapter introduces the basic methodology of mapping numbers onto concepts. The key approach is via mapping numeric data or indicators, for example the Polity indicator of democracy, on the $X$-axis onto what one means by democracy on the $Y$-axis. These mappings are semantic transformations. In the fuzzy-logic world one talks about membership in a set, which here becomes membership in a concept.

The $Y$-axis is the membership-in-the-set concept and the $X$-axis is the original scale of the data–indicator.

The $Y$-axis is always a standardized unit interval $[0, 1]$ while the $X$-axis retains whatever the original units of the data–indicator are. The end result is always a semantic mapping that lies in the $[0, 1]$ interval. From a mathematical point of view, the restriction to $[0, 1]$ is arbitrary because anything in the $-\infty$ to $+\infty$ range can be rescaled into $[0, 1]$. This will be critical in the next chapter on scaling, as well as in the chapter on aggregation, because to aggregate in the basic framework or in any multidimensional concept requires a common scale.

Ragin and Fiss (2017) provide a number of wonderful and interesting examples of how to do the translation between raw data and indicators and the semantics of concepts. Their book is a reinvestigation of the *Bell curve* (Herrnstein and Murray 1994) debate. As such, it describes the semantic transformations between common socioeconomic variables such as education, parental income, poverty, and the key independent variable of test scores.

One can apply the basic example of the full or empty plane to these various kinds of variables. Figure 4.1 shows how they take basic data on years of education[4] and connect that with the concept of "educated."

One might object that this transformation is "arbitrary." Wrong. They are constrained and follow the semantics of these terms used by scholars as well as by most people. If one said that someone with only a primary education was educated, people would say that is an abuse of the term educated. Most would agree that someone with a college degree is educated. In the USA, people with a high-school degree or a couple of years of college or community college would be considered partially educated. So the broad outlines of the semantic transformation are quite constrained by what people mean when they say "educated."

If the purpose of the analysis is to understand the role of education in hiring practices in Kenya, then one could do a different semantic

---

4. It would be more accurate to call this "years of schooling" but I follow Ragin and Fiss's terminology of "education."

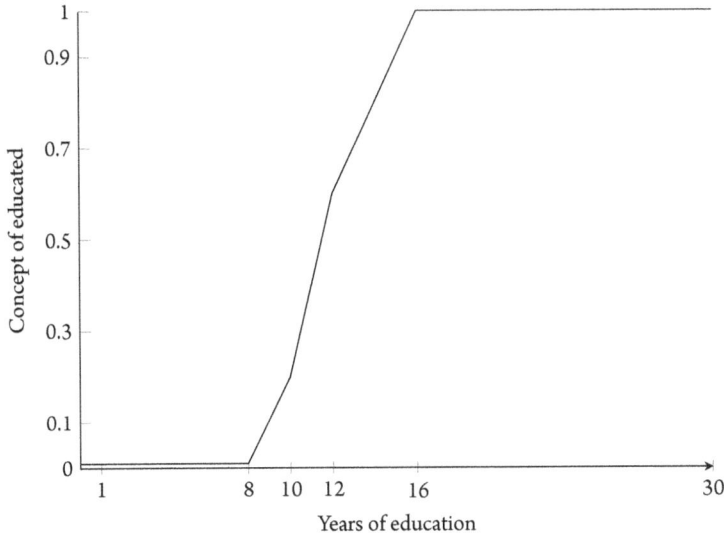

FIGURE 4.1. Semantic transformations: transforming "years of education" to "educated."
*Source:* Based on Ragin and Fiss (2017).

mapping. The concept of a full plane might vary depending on the practical context, e.g., the size of the plane or the kind of emergency. The
semantic mapping needs to reflect the theoretical and empirical context
and purpose.

In a traditional statistical analysis one might use just years of education as an independent variable. But as Ragin and Fiss emphasize, the
concept really of interest is "educated." The semantic transformation is
connecting years of education to these core causal concepts.

This example also illustrates the default S-curve transformation that
seems to reflect well the semantics of many concepts used in the social
sciences (discussed at length below). The key point of this introduc-
tory example is to illustrate the nature of semantic transformations and
the linking of a raw indicator or data such as years of education with the
concept of theoretical importance, which is "educated." Note that theories and hypotheses use the concept of "educated," not the indicator
"years of education." Semantic transformations are ways to link concepts that are used in theories, hypotheses, and causal mechanisms with

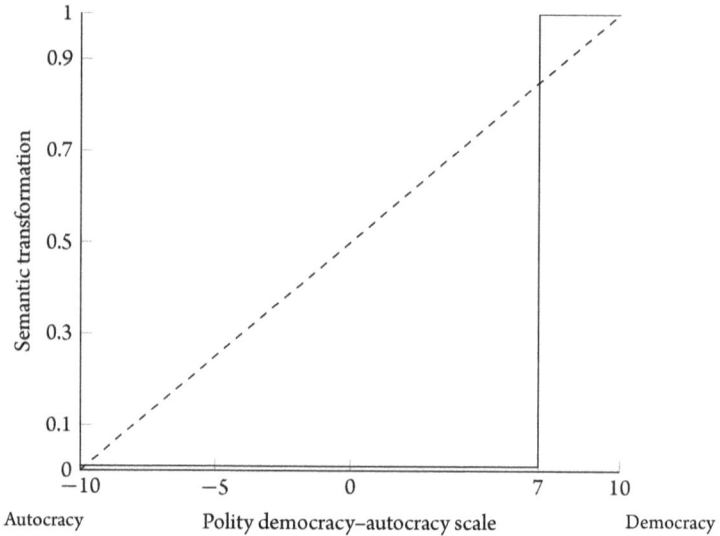

FIGURE 4.2. Standard default semantic transformations: Polity democracy concept and measure.

raw data and indicators that do not themselves appear in the theoretical apparatus.

## Semantic Transformations: The Linear and Dichotomous Defaults

The methodology of semantic transformation leads one to consider the default implicit semantic transformations when raw data or indicators are used instead of the transformed $[0, 1]$ values. One can illustrate this with the Polity democracy data. Figure 4.2 illustrates the two default transformations: the linear (dashed line) and the dichotomous (solid line).

One mapping of the Polity scale into the $[0, 1]$ interval is a simple linear scale translation. This sort of operation is very common when converting to a popular scale, e.g., 1–100. The semantic transformation in figure 4.2 makes this, usually implicit, linear assumption clear.

The dichotomous semantic transformation is also extremely common. With the Polity data, by convention this done at around level 7 of the scale.[5] Usually, dichotomous transformations are seen as information loss vis-à-vis continuous ones. Semantic transformations see this quite differently: it is a very different transformation from the linear one.

The most obvious way to transform continuous data onto a [0, 1] scale is to subtract the minimum value in the data set and then divide the data by the range of the data set (see chapter 5 for more on this). This makes the largest value in the data set 1 and the smallest value 0. Statistically, this is a linear transformation and often has no impact on the statistical results, but there are situations where it does.

Figure 4.2 clearly opens the possibility for other kinds of transformation. For example, the very common log transformation is explored below. The example of the mapping between seats occupied on a plane and the concept of full would be another transformation.

One theoretical and methodological feature of the fuzzy-logic approach is that one is *forced* to transform all data into [0, 1]: *methodologically this is good practice.* At the same time, it has very important implications for conceptualization and measurement.

All multidimensional concepts have the problem of constructing a common scale. The requirement of transformation onto [0, 1] creates a common scale for all dimensions. This issue of a common scale is a major topic of chapter 5.

The key feature of the semantic transformation is justification:

One must justify transformations, be they linear, dichotomous, or any of the many other possible options.

Within the fuzzy-logic framework, the automatic choice of a linear or dichotomous default is no longer noncontroversial. The linear mapping is a semantic one, which can have potentially huge downstream effects on description, causal inference, and normative considerations.

---

5. I have never found the rationale for choosing 6 or 7 as the cutoff.

## The Negation of a Concept

I make a sharp distinction between the "negation" and the "opposite." The negation is signaled by "not-" or the negation symbol ($\neg$) from mathematical logic. The opposite appears in concept pairs, where one concept is seen as the opposite of the other, but it is very different from the negation. The negation of the concept of democracy is illustrated in figure 4.3 where I have done a semantic transformation of the Polity measure democracy that modifies the dichotomous Polity measure in a more nuanced fashion.

For Ragin and Fiss the key dependent variable is "not-in-poverty." Once they have conceptualized poverty they automatically have their dependent variable of "not-in-poverty."

In short, "not" literally means the negation of the concept membership value. There are a variety of circumstances where it would be better to use the literal not, rather than the opposite of the pair. My favorite example is the "democratic peace" which should be called

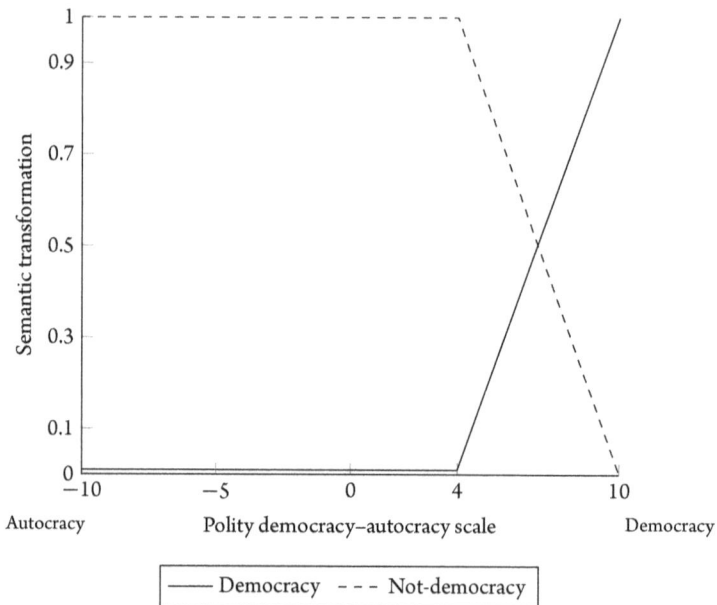

FIGURE 4.3. The semantics of "not" concepts: not-democracy.

the "democratic not-war" because peace is literally defined as not war. Within the fuzzy-logic framework "not" is unambiguous; in general language and writing it is often unclear.

## Concept Pairs: Conceptual Asymmetry and Opposites

Figure 4.4 illustrates what can happen when you split the concept pair and consider each separately. The World Bank is dividing the continuum into parts that have conceptual names, such as poor (i.e., low income), middle income, and wealthy (i.e, high income). The standard data for this consist of GDP per capita, or more exactly in the case of the World Bank, GNI per capita (I use the term GDP per capita to refer to all similar or related measures of national income or production). I use the World Bank's categorization for 2018 of countries into (1) low, (2) lower-middle, (3) higher-middle, and (4) high income to make the semantic transformation. The thresholds are $1,005 or less for "low,"

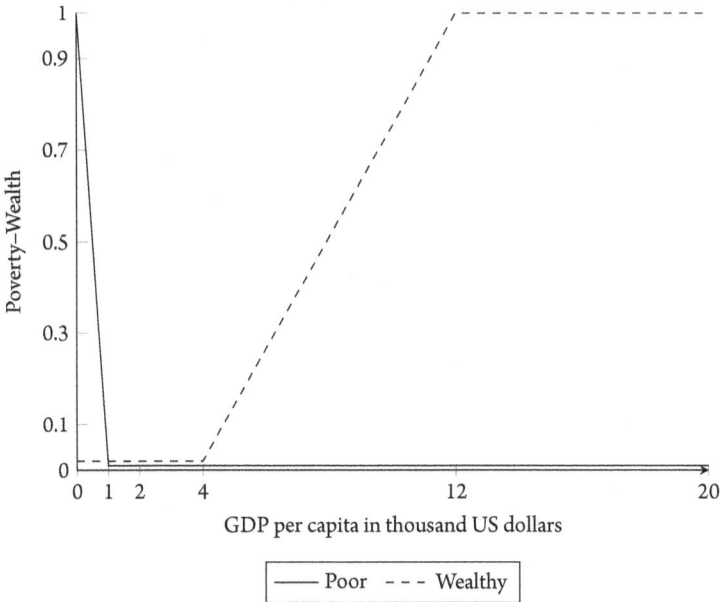

FIGURE 4.4. Poverty and wealth semantic transformations using World Bank categories and GDP per capita.

$1,006–$3,955 for "lower-middle income," (3) $3,956–$12,235 for "higher-middle income," and (4) $12,236 and above for "high income" (World Bank, https://datahelpdesk.worldbank.org/knowledgebase /articles/378833).

As always, terminology is worth noting: here everyone translates "low income" into poverty and "high income" into wealthy. So I follow semantic practice and consider that the concept is wealthy countries. In a different setting it could be high levels of human well-being, or economically developed. Following the Bank I take those above $12,236 as full, i.e., 1.0, members of the club of wealthy countries. Those in the low and lower-middle categories have 0.0 membership in the club. Those in the higher-middle category have partial membership in the club. The top part of the mapping in figure 4.4 is those countries that all would consider wealthy, such as Scandinavian countries, Switzerland, USA, Canada, and so forth.

In determining the semantic transformation for poverty I follow the tradition of thinking in terms of poverty lines, which is completely standard practice. So again I follow the World Bank and draw the poverty line at the end of the first category at $1,005 or less. Also following typical practice, I consider that any country that is above that level has 0.0 membership in the concept "poor"; it is "not-poor."

I also use the implicit notion that poverty is decreasing in linear fashion as GDP per capita is increasing, until it reaches the poverty line. We will change this later in the chapter but it is certainly the most common way in practice—usually implicitly—to think about degrees of poverty.

One can see that the two conceptual mappings are asymmetric: one is not the mirror of the other. They are also definitely nonsymmetric in relation to the underlying GDP per capita data. For purposes of illustration, figure 4.5 gives the standard defaults often automatically applied. One can draw a straight line through the data, which is implicitly how poverty–wealth is considered in many statistical analyses; see the line in figure 4.5. The "middle" of the GDP per capita range is not the middle categorization of the World Bank. A linear categorization scheme

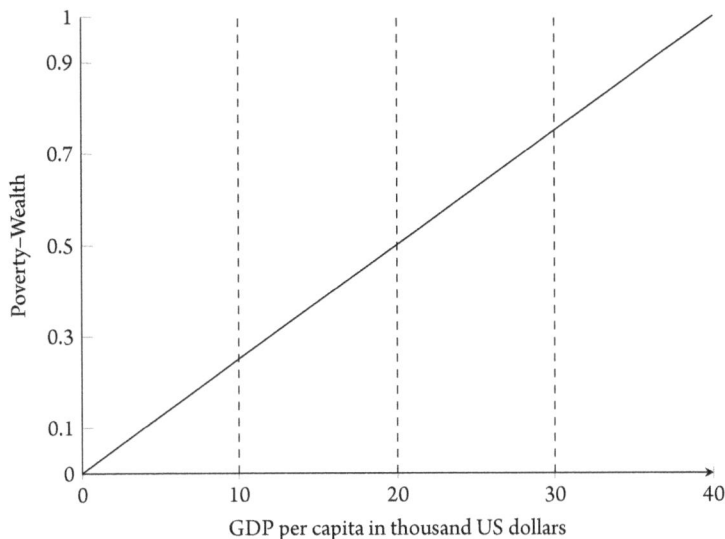

FIGURE 4.5. Poverty and wealth semantic transformations: default categorization and linear transformation using World Bank categories and GDP per capita.

would make the four categories the same size and divide the range of wealth into four equal parts, as indicated by the dashed vertical lines. This is definitely not the way the World Bank does things.

## The Bipolarity–Incompleteness Guideline and the Ragin Adjective Rule

Many World Bank consumption surveys are motivated in large part to analyze poverty. One might be descriptively interested in consumption in the sense of what people are spending their money on. If this is the case then the concept is really consumption. However, once one is interested in concepts like poverty or wealth, or one begins to use such concepts in causal hypotheses, then consumption is fundamentally an incomplete concept. Hence bipolarity in this example means that consumption ranges from almost none to huge dollar amounts. It is incomplete as a measure of poverty, one end of the continuum of consumption.

Because these concepts like consumption, education, GDP per capita do not distinguish between the poles, I call them bipolar concepts or indicators. What makes it incomplete is that they do not conceptualize one pole or the other. To make consumption work with the concept of poverty one needs to include other criteria. In the poverty literature this is the concept of a poverty line. The concept of a poverty line completes consumption by focusing in particular on low levels of consumption.

Typical conceptual asymmetry is the WHO definition of health versus illness: "Health is a state of complete physical, mental and social well-being and not merely the absence of disease or infirmity" (Preamble to the Constitution of WHO as adopted by the International Health Conference, 1946). This kind of claim almost always appears in concept pairs:

Bipolarity–Incompleteness Guideline: Does the concept of interest focus on one pole but the data, indicator, index run from one pole to its opposite? If so, what is the conceptual and mathematical operation on the incomplete concept-indicator (e.g., consumption) to arrive at the concept of interest (e.g., poverty)?

This means that when one is taking the incomplete concept, completing it for one pole involves operations that will be different from completing it for the other pole. The way you construct a wealth line will be different from constructing a poverty line for the same underlying consumption data.

The Bipolarity–Incompleteness Guideline then focuses on these bipolar, but generally incomplete concepts. Typically there are two operations, one involving the basic continuum between the two poles, and the second modifying that in various ways to arrive at the final concept of interest.

This guideline is central because of the fundamentally asymmetric nature of most bipolar concepts. This volume argues throughout that these traditional opposites such as war–peace involve conceptual asymmetry: one is not the mirror image or inverse of the other.

Our conceptualization and measurement of war (i.e., highly militarized and hostile relationships) involve different defining features from the concept of interstate peace (Goertz et al. 2016).

Ragin and Fiss (2017) provide a nice series of examples illustrating this crucial point. They use a variety of incomplete variables to create the concepts of theoretical and empirical interest. Here are some examples with the incomplete variable followed by the concept of theoretical and empirical interest (raw data indicator: concept of theoretical interest):

- AfQT ("intelligence") test scores: low, high
- years of education: educated, highly educated
- income: poor, wealthy

For instance, they state that "the set of respondents with low-income-parents is *not* the exact negation of the set of respondents with high-income-parents, nor is the set of respondents with low-AfQT-scores the exact negation of the set of respondents with high-AfQT-scores" (p. 64). When they talk about not the exact negation they mean high and low are asymmetric.

Causation is critical here because one needs a methodology for concepts that fits causal hypotheses. There are many hypotheses about the causes and effects of poverty. The concept and measure must reflect this causal interest: that is why consumption is fundamentally incomplete if the concept of interest is poverty. For Ragin and Fiss, not-in-poverty is different from wealthy.

These considerations lead to the Ragin Adjective Rule:

Ragin Adjective Rule: In general nouns should be converted to adjectives as part of conceptualization and measurement. For example, "years of education" becomes "educated person" or "transparency" (e.g., the Transparency International global index) becomes "transparent government."

If the noun or concept does not lend itself to becoming an adjective, that suggests a potentially problematic situation. A good example in the context of this book is consumption as a part of the concept of poverty. Consumption does not lend itself to being an adjective; one is forced to modify it by requiring poverty to be low levels of consumption. The second scenario is when the incomplete concept does not suggest which end of the spectrum or continuum is of research and causal interest. Here the factor "years of education" does not tell us whether we are interested in educated as the key causal variable. Hence we need to convert years of education into the concept of educated, as illustrated in figure 4.1.

The role of adjectives is that they demand empirical anchors and thus the input of substantive knowledge. By contrast, the conventional variable (abstract noun) is completely untethered. All that matters is that it offers variation.

## Default Fuzzy-Logic Semantic Transformation

As one can see from figures 4.2 and 4.5, the two default perspectives on semantic transformations are the linear and dichotomous transformations. From the fuzzy logic as well as semantic perspective these often appear problematic. This section reviews the issues regarding mapping semantics as well as the standard defaults when taking a fuzzy-logic view on transformations. These defaults, like all defaults, need to be questioned and evaluated, but the default does provide a good place to start.

The mapping for the concept of wealthy country in figure 4.4 illustrates the default semantic transformation using the fuzzy-logic framework, as well as figure 4.1 for educated. This S-curve, logit- or probit-like, is what fuzzy-logic software will do by default (see Ragin 2008 for an extended discussion and Dusa 2018 for R software applications).

In general, a key decision is where to establish the 0.50 membership level. The 0.50 membership value is a "crossover" point: it is where cases move from more in to more out of the concept. It is the half-empty and half-full point. It is also the zone where small changes in the data can mean large conceptual differences (see below). In the case of figure 4.4 I have used the middle of the upper-middle-income group, i.e., $8,096. The 0.50 point becomes important when one generates smooth, logistic, S-curves because it is a key inflection point.

Once one begins to think of things via the fuzzy-logic perspective then using the middle of the upper-middle-income group as the 0.50 transition point makes less and less sense. As one can see from the figure, and discussed above, the middle is often not the semantic middle point. Given the nature of the skewed GDP per capita data it might make much more sense to move the 0.50 transition point upward, closer to the 1.0 point for wealthy countries.

The 0.50 membership value should not be automatically determined by the distribution of the data. In general, one would almost never use the mean of the data as the 0.50 level in fuzzy-logic analysis. For instance, one would almost certainly not use half the seats occupied as the 0.50 semantic value for the concept of full planes. There are various ways that one might do this, a number of which are discussed in the next chapter. Again, the key point is that mindlessly choosing the middle of the data scale or the statistical mean or median of the actual values is not necessarily a good idea, and in fact usually is not. These can inform the choice, but they should not completely and automatically determine it.

For the concept of educated, clearly something around a completed secondary education is the transition point and the 0.50 level. One can see this quite clearly in figure 4.1 where the $Y$-axis values of 0.40 and 0.60 are right around the end of secondary school.[6]

Two other key choices are the inflection points at the top and bottom of the S-curve. These are critical points where the changes in $X$ toward 0.0 or toward 1.0 have little semantic meaning. These might be called the points of "relatively flat semantic returns" in analogy with the log. Conversely, in the middle zone, small changes in $X$ have large meaning changes. This makes the choice of 0.50 critical, because it in part determines this zone of "steep semantic returns."

Putting figure 4.4 in the context of figure 4.2, one sees that the linear semantic transformation is the case where the two flat ends shrink

6. For technical reasons downstream in QCA, one tries to avoid coding cases at 0.50.

to zero; the middle slopping part is now the whole transformation. The dichotomous transformation is the other extreme, where the slope explodes to infinity and occupies a single point on the $X$-axis; now the top and bottom flat parts occupy almost the whole spectrum.

All fuzzy-logic textbooks extensively discuss various common transformations and we will see many of them in this chapter or later chapters. The sections below discuss some core features of common semantic transformation functions.

## The Principle of Unimportant Variation

As seen in figure 4.4 there are alternatives to the linear default transformation. Almost all of these nonlinear transformations—including dichotomization—have regions where changes in $X$ mean no change in $Y$. As an almost inevitable consequence of this, there are regions of $X$ where small changes have a big impact on $Y$. This section and the next explore these two core points about nonlinear semantic transformations.

I can now state a fundamental principle of many semantic transformations:

Principle of Unimportant Variation: There are regions in the data–indicator that have the same or virtually the same semantic meaning.

For example, as the number of seats occupied in the plane increases from 95 percent to 100 percent this does not change the characterization of the plane as full at all: it is still 1.0 full. Dichotomous versions of data–indicators illustrate the extreme version of this. In figure 4.2, all country years from $-10$ to 6 are 0.0 democracies, while those from 7 to 10 are 1.0 democracies.

One common methodology of estimating poverty in a society involves determining (1) a poverty line and then (2) the degree of poverty of those below the poverty line (e.g., see Ravallion 2016 for a nice survey). Taking total household consumption as the basic data–indicator then the households in poverty are those below the line. The degree of poverty of those in poverty is the ratio of the individual's income to the poverty line.

As the use of a poverty line illustrates, for many concepts, indicators, and global indices there are thresholds above which increased values have little or no impact on the final evaluation. This is seen in figure 4.4 by the fact that once above the poverty line, the country or individual has value 0.0 on the poverty concept.

In general, particularly in the global index industry, the use of a threshold almost automatically means that the Principle of Unimportant Variation is being applied.

## Large Change Zone

The default fuzzy-logic transformation has a middle—typically gray—zone where small changes in $X$ have large changes in semantic meaning. A key design decision is how flat or steep the slope should be in this region. Starting from a steep slope, as one flattens the slope the transformation becomes closer to the linear one. The other extreme is dichotomization, where the semantics change with a huge jump at one point.

Using the wealth–GDP per capita example in figure 4.4, the key point is quite intuitive: a difference of $4,000–$5,000 at the top does not matter much at all, but that same difference in the middle can be hugely important. Just as there are ranges where differences in GDP per capita do not matter for membership in the set of wealthy countries, there are other ranges where these differences are magnified. The magnified differences occur for membership values less than 1.0 and more than 0.0. Here, small differences in GDP per capita are translated into big differences in membership in the set of wealthy countries.

In figure 4.4 the exact position of the poverty line does not matter too much, though this of course depends on how many observations lie in the region where lines are being drawn. All scholars who actually estimate poverty lines (e.g., Alkire et al. 2015) test the robustness of their estimated lines. Ideally, varying the chosen point does not affect much the number of people or the estimated total amount of poverty.

This preference for robustness of the poverty line means that one prefers transformations that are relatively flat in the region of the poverty line. In figure 4.4 the transformation line is pretty flat around the poverty line and hence would be pretty robust. One can flatten it further by moving the poverty line up, i.e., to the right on the $X$-axis, which decreases the slope of the linear segment below the poverty line. In terms of semantic transformations, "robustness" means a preference for flat curves around the poverty line.

The extent of these differences depends on two basic factors. The first is the slope of the line where the poverty line is drawn and the second is empirically the number of people located in that region. With heavily skewed data—which is what most poverty and GDP per capita show—as one moves to lower the line, the bigger the impact of the poverty line on robustness.

## Normative Issues

The global index industry is full of quite clear normative evaluations. When establishing a "blacklist" one is clearly making a normative claim. These reports are full of language about "offenders" and the like. A core use of these indices is to change policy and shame governments (see the Kelley and Simmons–edited *International Organization* special issue 2019, as well as Kelley 2017; Kelley and Simmons 2015). Thus the choice of threshold is highly charged and normative.

While chapter 6 deals extensively with aggregation and weighting, semantic transformations can often imply a kind of weight in terms of the membership in the concept. For example, one might have a "preference for the poor." Rawls's philosophy clearly expresses a priority given to those worst off in society.

One way to give this preference for the poor and least well off of society is via semantic transformations that give increasing importance to those people. Probably implicit in these normative positions is the

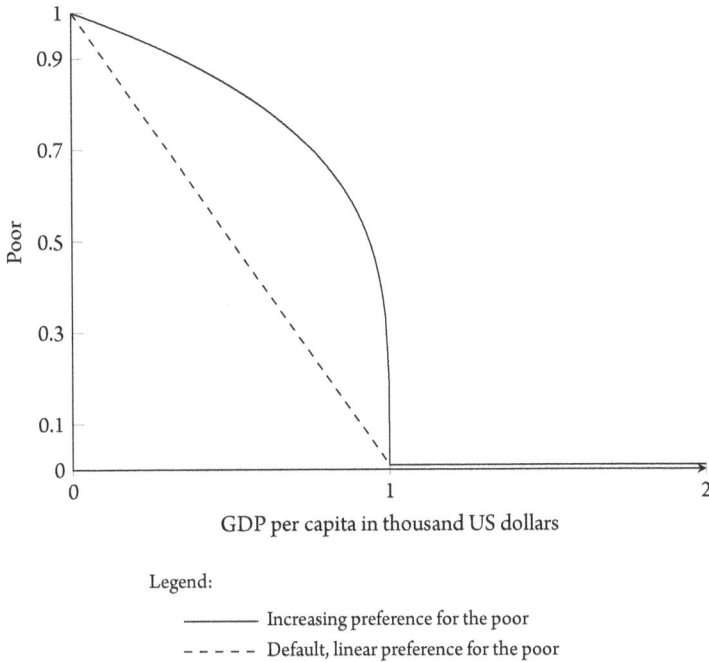

Legend:

————— Increasing preference for the poor

– – – – Default, linear preference for the poor

FIGURE 4.6. Normative issues: privileging the very poor.

contrast with the equal treatment of utilitarian philosophies. The linear semantic transformation often represents that position.

In normative terms the poverty line has the disadvantage of treating those just above the poverty line the same as the very well off. That too is a normative position that needs defense. The Principle of Unimportant Variation often has a normative claim that those in that zone do not deserve any different treatment. For example, all those with 1.0 membership in the set of poor people get the same treatment. It also means that those just above the poverty line get the same treatment as the superwealthy.

Most of the work on poverty (e.g., World Bank) is really about the degree of poverty of poor countries or people, where the poverty line defines poor country or people. Figure 4.6 illustrates the main methods for thinking about this. They all agree that the first step is to construct a poverty line. The "head count" approach to poverty is a dichotomous one: one is either poor or not-poor, so those greater than the poverty line receive value 0.0, while those less than the poverty line receive value 1.0. Total poverty is the sum of the poverty scores across the population.

The solid line conceptualizes poverty as the ratio of the individual to the poverty line: this is a linear transformation. As we have seen, linear is the standard default; poverty is just another illustration of that.

One of the advantages of the semantic transformation methodology is that it allows one to conveniently compare traditions and schools of thought. The linear-flat transformation (the dashed line in figure 4.6) is very common in the literature on poverty. One could do the same thing with democracy: a linear transformation to Polity level 7, then flat to 10. One could do the same thing with latent variables (e.g., the V-Dem measure of democracy, https://www.v-dem.net/en/about/). However, in the democracy tradition no one does that, and if they did there would be loud complaints, whereas in the poverty literature the linear transformation to the threshold is by far the most common practice (see chapter 6 for more on threshold functions).

There is no one inherently right, correct, or proper transformation. However, in different traditions and cultures some defaults are so hardwired as to be virtually invisible. The point of the semantic transformation approach is to make visible—and hence up for discussion—these defaults.

Within the poverty line approach one could use a different semantic transformation to convert the ratio (consumption/poverty line) to give more rapidly increasing higher values to the poorer. Perhaps the most common way to do this is by including an exponent $\alpha$ in the ratio, i.e., $(1 - \text{consumption/poverty line})^{\alpha}$ for all individuals less than the poverty line. Figure 4.6 gives an example of this where the line represents a "strong" ($\alpha = 0.25$) preference for the poorer. The preference for the poorer can be seen by the fact that the curved line lies above the default dashed line. Using the curve means that total poverty will be greater than that calculated by the linear value, and greater the larger the number of very poor in the country.

If one is interested in the total amount of poverty in a country, the relative preference given to the very poor can, not surprisingly, radically change the total amount within a country and the relative rankings of countries. Not only does one *have* to make a normative choice about how to give preference to the poor, but it will then be reflected in descriptions of the amount of poverty in a given country, region, or world.

The various semantic transformation lines in the poverty zone reflect different normative, philosophical, and moral perspectives on poverty. Utilitarianism is naturally associated with linear transformations, while Rawls's and other moral arguments give additional weight to the very poor.

There is no "nonnormative, objective, neutral" perspective. One must choose a transformation and defend it.

## Semantic Transformations and Intensity-Modifying Adjectives

As stressed by the Multiple Word Guideline, concepts often involve using modifying adjectives such as "extremely," "very," or "somewhat." For example, we have a root concept, say wealth, modified by an adjective to create the concept very wealthy. Fuzzy logic provides a nice semantic approach that works easily with continuous concepts.

The standard approach to creating a category of "very poor" countries takes the range below a certain level, e.g., say $500 GDP per capita, to define the set of very poor countries or in the case of individuals the "destitute." So in addition to the four categories discussed above, one has added a fifth.

Instead of creating a new category—which is pretty much the default procedure—this chapter argues that instead one should think about modifications of the basic, root concept. This is what is happening semantically when one uses adjectives like very, somewhat, or extremely.

The key feature that goes unnoticed is that *the set of very wealthy countries is a subset of the set of wealthy countries.* Hence semantic practice with intensity-modifying adjectives such as very, somewhat is the following:

> Intensifying or moderating adjectives invoke sub- or supersetting operations respectively.

The basic rule for intensifying adjectives like very, extreme, and exceptionally is that the membership scores are less than that of the root concept. This means, for example, that the concept of very educated is a subset of educated. For moderating adjectives it is the opposite: they are greater than or equal to the root concept.

With this basic semantic practice in mind one has the principles to deal with continuous membership functions. Using the case of very wealthy, the membership values must be equal to or less than those for wealthy countries. In figure 4.7 the dashed line gives a semantic transformation for very wealthy. For purposes of illustration this is defined as zero for the upper middle and lower. Full membership starts in the World Bank's wealthy (i.e., high income) range of $20,000 per capita. Graphically, "very" means that the very wealthy curve lies below or on the wealthy curve.

In short, the fuzzy-logic semantic approach to adjectives like "very" is to take the semantic transformation of the main concept, e.g., wealthy, and modify it to carry the meaning of "very." Ireland might be a 1.0 member of the set of wealthy countries, but only a 0.75 member of the set of very wealthy countries. Mathematically this means that the score of a given country, such as Ireland, for very wealthy is less than (or equal to) its value for the concept of wealthy, e.g., $0.75 < 1.0$. So in figure 4.7 the semantic transformation places the curve for very wealthy below that of wealthy.

With adjectives, like "somewhat," that weaken the intensity of the root concept, a superset of the root concept is formed. This means that their membership scores are always greater than or equal to the root concept values. In figure 4.7 this is the dotted line, which lies above or on the wealthy line.

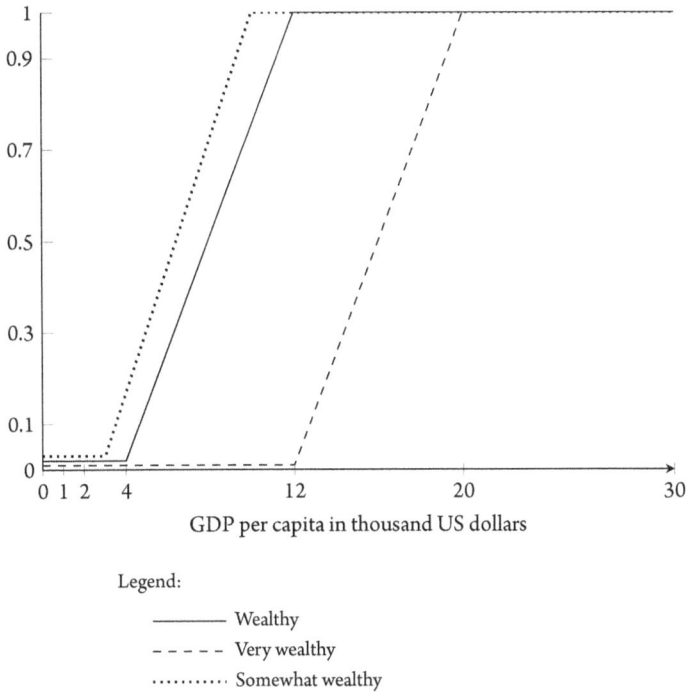

FIGURE 4.7. The semantics of intensity-modifying adjectives: somewhat wealthy
and very wealthy countries.

Fuzzy logic gives a way to deal with a popular class of adjectives when
applied to root concepts. Adjectives "very," "extremely," "somewhat"
and the like imply a transformation that is typically above or below that
of the root concept. The key methodological point is that intensity-
modifying adjectives invoke supersetting or subsetting operations.

## Breaking the Underlying Continuum into Categories, Semantic Neighbors as Overlapping Concepts

In addition to conceptual opposites, one often sees an underlying continuum broken into three or more pieces. Those who have developed
various global indices find it quite useful to move from interval or
ratio to ordinal categories (see chapter 5 for more on this). Instead

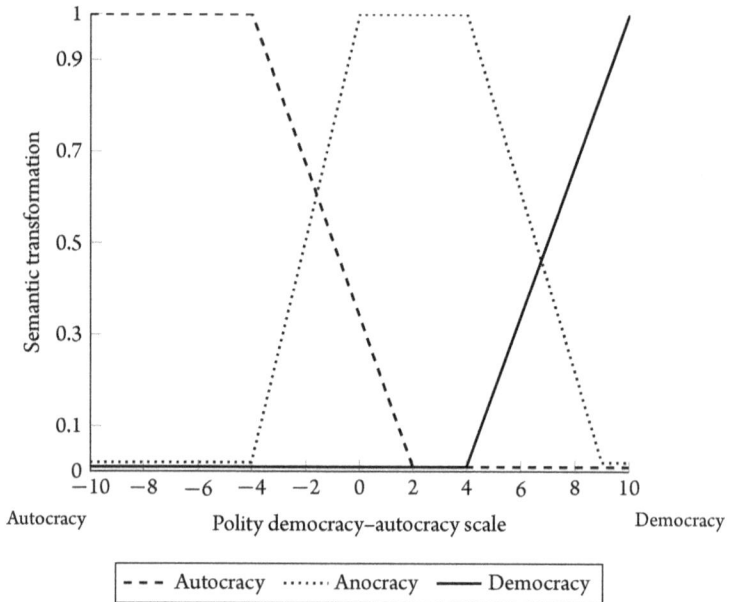

FIGURE 4.8. Overlapping categories and semantic neighbors: autocracy, anocracy, and democracy.

of dichotomizing, e.g., figure 4.2, one creates three or more adjacent categories as in figure 4.5.

Fuzzy logic embraces the philosophy that there should be no sharp boundaries between adjacent semantic categories or concepts. One way to see this in the context of conceptual asymmetry and the popularity of categorization of an underlying scale is to go back to democracy. As discussed at length in chapter 7, many scholars, particularly in recent decades, have been very interested in the middle zone between autocracy and democracy. Over the last 50+ years the world has gone from very few democracies to now well over the majority that are at least partly democratic. This, plus the move in the less democratic direction in many Western democracies due to the rise of the extreme right, means that the middle zone between democracy and autocracy is important.

Figure 4.8 illustrates that normally there should be overlapping boundaries between semantically neighbor concepts on the continuum. When people divide up a conceptual continuum into adjacent categories, almost by definition there is going to be conceptual overlap between neighboring categories. More generally, as discussed in chapter 8 on typologies, there is conceptual overlap between members of the typology, e.g., of autocratic regimes. There are no nice and neat boundaries between these types because they are neighboring categories. Any attempt to draw clear boundaries is going to be conceptually, as well as empirically, problematic. Having overlapping membership functions describes the empirical reality of overlapping boundaries.

The core guideline for this situation lies in refusing to make either-or decisions regarding the boundary cases, allowing that they have partial membership in adjacent categories:

Semantically close concepts should have overlapping membership functions.

It is quite possible for example that, following the Defining Attributes Guideline, semantically adjacent concepts have some defining attributes in common, hence ontologically they overlap. For example, competitive–authoritarian regimes have some democratic features, hence they should overlap to some degree with democracies.

Because these categories are semantically neighbor concepts there is a gray zone between them. This means that the semantic transformation of each overlaps because there is no neat dividing line between them, as illustrated by the epigraph to this chapter by Lotfi Zadeh, the inventor of fuzzy logic.

## Categorization as Nonlinear Semantic Transformations

One of the core claims of this chapter is that while the quantitative methodology of concepts and measurement is often assumed to be linear, semantic practice is frequently nonlinear. The discussion here is continued in more detail in chapter 5 on scaling.

If categorization followed the default linear approach then the "obvious" thing would be to divide the indicator into three to five evenly spaced categories. If the World Bank followed the linear rule it would divide the GNI per capita range into four equal categories. If it did so then the semantic transformation would be linear. When scholars, states, IGOs, NGOs create two or more categories, they often do so in nonlinear ways. Figure 4.5 illustrates this by putting dashed vertical lines that equally space the GDP per capita continuum and would be the default categorization of poverty–wealth into four categories.

In the case of democracy and using the Polity indicator, because scholars prefer three categories they often divide the spectrum into $-10$ to $-5$, $-5$ to $5$, and $5$ to $10$. As far as I can tell this has never been justified and seems clearly a matter of symmetry, based on no real substantive or semantic considerations.

The categorization of the Polity democracy measure into three parts, symmetric around the middle, is not alone. In chapter 1, I used the OECD concept of quality of life aka "How's life?" as an example of the basic framework. When giving descriptive analyses they resort to a default breaking of the continuum into three parts, based on the percentiles of the data in the OECD population:

> Quality of life is measured through 15 indicators spanning 8 dimensions: work–life balance, health status, education and skills, social connections, civic engagement and governance, environmental quality, personal safety and subjective well-being. For each indicator, countries are scored according to their comparative performance ($0 =$ bottom third of the OECD, $5 =$ middle third of the OECD, $10 =$ top third of the OECD). (OECD 2017, 23)

This is an interesting example because unlike the equal division of the underlying scale as illustrated by Polity, here it is the equal distribution of the actual data in terms of percentiles.

Categorization is a common part of bureaucratic life and has important implications for decisions. In the debate about the *bell curve*, people use the United States armed services test scores as the measure of intelligence. It would be possible to use just the raw scores or percentiles, but in fact Ragin and Fiss (2017) follow the US military and use the military's categories, where the concept is "high AfQT scores," which is treated as some measure of intelligence or ability:

> To construct our two fuzzy-set measures based on the AfQT [military test scores], degree of membership in the set of respondents with high AfQT scores and degree of membership in the set of respondents with low AfQT scores, we rely on categories used by the Department of Defense to place enlistees. The military divides the AfQT scale into 5 categories based on percentiles. These 5 categories have substantive importance in that they determine eligibility for as well as assignment into different qualification groups. Persons in categories I (93rd to 99th percentile) and II (65th to 92nd percentile) are considered to be above average in trainability; those in category III (31st to 64th percentile) are considered about average; those in category IV (10th to 30th percentile) are designated as below average in trainability; and those in category V (1st to 9th percentile) are designated as markedly below average.... The threshold for full membership (.95) in the set of respondents with high AfQT scores was placed at the 93rd percentile, in line with the military's designation of the lower boundary of their highest category; the crossover point (.5) was set at the 80th percentile; and the threshold for full nonmembership (.05) in the set of respondents with high AfQT scores was placed at the 65th percentile, the bottom of the military's second-highest AfQT category. (Ragin and Fiss 2017, 73)

While I do not include the semantic mapping figure it is clear from this description that the semantic transformation for "high test score" is very asymmetric and nonlinear to the underlying percentiles. For example, 0.0 membership starts already at about the 60th percentile and 1.0 membership starts at the 93rd percentile, while the "middle" is the 80th percentile.

In general, the linear semantic transformation underlies the continuum when it is equally categorized. A hypothesis for future research is how widespread the linear categorization is. My hypothesis is that if one looked systematically at the Kelley–Simmons or Broome et al. data sets of GPIs, linear categorizations would be relatively rare.

The key point here, illustrated by the World Bank example, is that when one is trying to understand and explore these categorization schemes, it is critical to draw the figure looking at the underlying indicator on the $X$-axis with the categorizations and their corresponding values on the $Y$-axis.

While this is rarely discussed, the semantics of the labels is quite important and signals some underlying interests and concerns. For its four categories, the World Bank uses the labels high, higher middle, lower middle, and low. The United Nations has a related scale of human development, HDI, with labels very high, high, medium, and low (http://hdr.undp.org).[7] Notice that the top categories are very high and high, which suggests a different semantic transformation from the World Bank's semantics which puts two categories in the middle of the scale.

The semantics are the criteria are for drawing the boundary lines between categories. That determines what real-life empirical cases fall into the different categories. These categories often have a life of their own and inform major policy decisions. The World Bank categories are not infrequently used to decide which countries are eligible for development aid. So these categorization decisions are fraught with potentially important policy consequences in terms of decisions made by national governments and international organizations.

All this reinforces the point made at the beginning of the chapter with "full" airplanes. There is a nonlinear relationship between the number of seats occupied and the use of terms like full and empty. If one starts from the assumption that semantics are nonlinear in general,

---

7. These four categories are based on quartiles, and thus are a linear transformation based on the empirical distribution of the data. This is something that this volume generally does not recommend, i.e., conceptualization completely based on the empirical distribution of the data.

then when one sees an equal categorization the conclusion is that the scholar, NGO, or IGO has not really thought much at all about the empirical and semantic continuum. Equal categories reflect a lack of serious thought about conceptualization and the connection between data, categories, and concepts.

## Logging as a Semantic Transformation

Power [e.g., log] transformations can make a skewed distribution more symmetric. But why should we bother?

(1) Highly skewed distributions are difficult to examine because most of the observations are confined to a small part of the range of data.

(2) Apparently outlying values in the direction of the skew are brought in toward the main body of the data when the distribution is made more symmetric.

(3) Some of the common statistical methods summarize distributions using means. The mean of a skewed distribution is, however, not a good summary of its center.

JOHN FOX

The epigraph to this section comes from a popular statistics textbook. It illustrates how one might deal with "problematic" empirical data in standard statistical analyses. It illustrates a rationale that has nothing to do with increasing the meaning of an indicator, measure, or numeric data.

Logging a variable (i.e., using the natural log of the variable) is very common and often recommended in statistical research. To take a classic example, the decision to log GDP per capita is rarely con-troversial. In fact, not-logging for GDP per capita probably produces more objections. Although not all scholars carry out this transforma-tion, one can find countless examples of research of all kinds where they do, and for many variables in cross-national research it is the norm. In a cross-national study, easily 50 percent of the continuous variables could be logged. Does logging increase or decrease semantic validity?

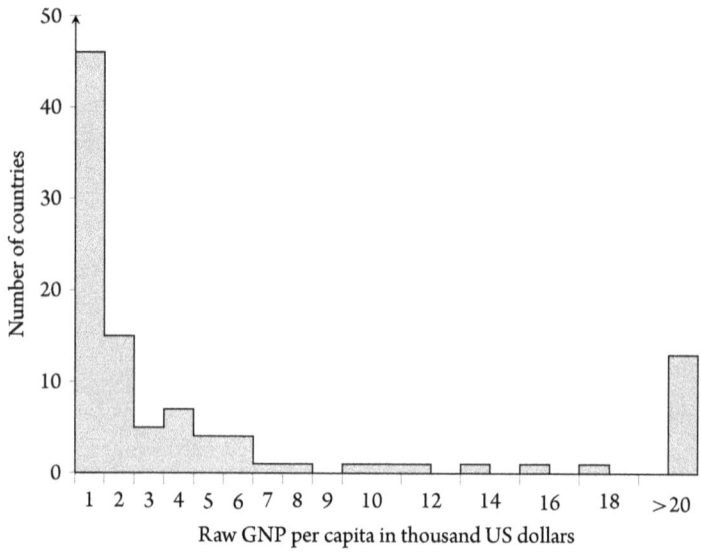

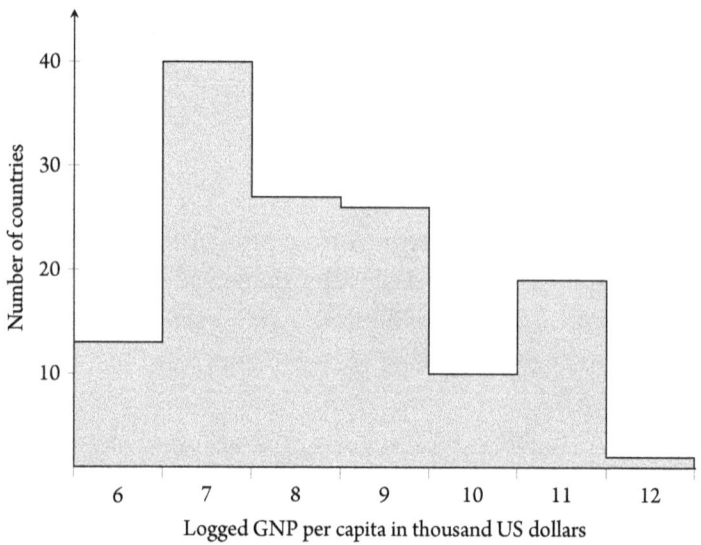

FIGURE 4.9. Distribution of countries by levels of raw and logged GNP per capita.

The most common rationale for logging, however, has nothing to do with semantics. If one were to ask why a scholar is logging data in a statistical analysis, almost certainly the answer would be because the data are skewed, as seen in the top panel of figure 4.9. The big majority of cases are toward the low end and the long tail is typical of skewed data. This kind of skewed data is very common in the social sciences.

What logging does is make skewed data look more normal, bell shaped. This makes it more suitable for many statistical analyses. The lower panel of figure 4.9 makes clear the radical changes that are produced in the distribution of cases when the logged value is used. The data now approach a normal distribution. This distribution was created by making large distinctions among the many countries that have very low levels of GDP per capita. Thus, in the lower part of figure 4.9, countries with less than $2,500 GDP per capita make up much more of the variation on the left-hand side of the histogram.

Occasionally, one will find scholars debating whether improved fit justifies a particular kind of variable transformation. For example, Kurtz and Schrank (2007) argue that governance is not related to economic growth. The World Bank economists in their response say, "In the next panel we show the effect of two minor departures from the original Kurtz and Schrank specification. Instead of entering per capita GDP in levels as they do, we enter it in log-levels. This is a very standard practice in cross-country empirics and statistically is more appropriate since the relationship between the dependent variable and log per capita GDP is much closer to being linear, and we are using a linear regression model" (Kaufman et al. 2007, 59). This means that semantic transformations have important causal inference implications in addition to semantic ones.

In general, the underlying motivation for logging skewed data is in fact a better fit in (linear) statistical analyses. Now, "curve-fitting" is widely considered bad practice, particularly in economics. If I were to say that I was doing an arcsine transformation because I got more significant results, then people would complain. This sort of rationale falls under the rubric of specification searches (e.g., Leamer 1978), which have been extensively debated by statisticians over the decades.

One could imagine doing all sorts of variable transformations and then picking the one that gives the strongest results. However, given the conventional nature of logging, its curve-fitting rationale is acceptable practice.

There are good reasons to log or perform related transformations. By far the most common is that the theorist is arguing diminishing returns. The claim is that a 1, 000 USD increase for a wealthy person or country means a lot less to them than a 1, 000 USD increase for a poor person. This produces the flattening curve in the upper regions of GDP per capita. This is another example where normative concerns often play a role.

Logging is not inherently an invalid transformation. As with all variable transformations, one must give and defend the rationale for the transformation. Logging is typically done for curve-fitting or skewed-data reasons: these are statistical rationales not semantic ones. However, logging for statistical reasons still has a semantic effect: it changes the meaning of wealth, poverty, etc.

## Conclusion

Variable transformations have been treated here in terms of whether they increase or decrease semantic validity. Depending on the perspective, there are various default transformations, e.g., linear or dichotomization. These are in fact often not seen as transformations at all.

However, with fuzzy-logic methodology in hand one can begin to explore various defaults and common practices such as logging. The advantage of forcing everything into the [0, 1] range is that one *must* confront this question. The standard linear transformation is certainly one option, but one that often clashes with the semantics of the concept. What is typically seen as a small technical question—common scale—becomes an important theoretical, descriptive, normative, and causal issue.

One cannot talk about semantic transformations, measurement, and concepts without thinking and considering the causal use for them.

Not surprisingly, semantic transformations such as logging have an impact on statistical analyses. In fact, that is the fundamental rationale. The whole purpose of calibration and semantic transformations is to produce variables that match the concepts which themselves are embedded in causal hypotheses and models. Transformations need to be faithful to the causal environment within which they are to function.

The debate between Ragin, and Lucas and Szatrowski (2014) illustrates nicely what is at stake. The empirical example is the explosion of the space shuttle Challenger. This works well because there is consensus on why the space shuttle exploded. We can contrast or compare various statistical or set-theoretic methods of data analysis against the "true value." The key issue is the concept of "temperature" versus "low temperatures" in the context of the O-rings which were the cause of the explosion.

The standard, statistical, linear default would be to include temperature *tout court*; with fuzzy-logic calibration it is all about "low temperatures" in the context of O-rings. Core to Ragin's argument is that one needs to semantically transform temperature into the relevant context of what constitutes low temperatures for the space shuttle. I encourage the reader to read the whole debate but the core feature for our purposes is the following:

> Sets and set labels almost always involve adjectives in some way. For example, it is possible to assess degree of membership in heavy; it is not possible to assess degree of membership in weight. This aspect of sets is fundamental to set-theoretic analysis. L&S [Lucas and Szatrowski] violate this principle by using mechanistic calibrations based on ranges. This issue is especially important for the calibration of temperature because the overarching engineering concern was for temperatures that were low, a unipolar concept. Thus, L&S should have calibrated degree of membership in low temperature, based at least in part on case knowledge. Instead, they tried to calibrate degree of membership in temperature, which is nonsensical. (Ragin 2014, 90–91)

In his analysis Ragin finds that the appropriately transformed "low temperatures" generates the correct results while the generic, linear "temperature" does not do the job. That, in many ways, summarizes a core theme of this chapter: one needs to match the semantic transformation with the substantive content of the theory or hypothesis under examination.

Basic-level concepts and indicators are often broken into multiple categories. Often a two-category breakdown becomes a concept pair like poverty–wealth. It can easily be extended to three categories as illustrated by democracy, or four categories as illustrated by the World Bank. No matter how many categories, the same basic principles apply.

This chapter treated categorizations that had an underlying continuous scale, data, or indicator. These categorization schemes by definition create ordinal variables. The advantage here is that we can connect these ordinal categories to some underlying continuous indicator. The next chapter deals with the common case where we have ordinal categories but no underlying continuous data. The methodological, conceptual, and calibration problem is how to convert them via semantic mappings into the [0, 1] common scale.

There is no inherent reason why these semantic transformations cannot be used in statistical analysis. Within the statistical framework, they are just variables that range from 0 to 1. The extent to which, and how, these transformations influence causal analyses remains to be investigated.

It is important to realize that, as always, terminology is important. While often one is explicit about the "very," sometimes it is implicit. When one reads about "positive peace" versus "negative peace" this could be translated as positive peace being "very peaceful." Similarly, the use of "quality of" signals an intensification of the root concept; "high-quality democracy" means "very democratic." This use of adjectives with root concepts is built into our language.

The fractal character of the basic framework means that the semantic issues are pervasive. One can take existing data for the basic-level concepts and apply the procedures discussed in this chapter. One can go to the bottom at the data–indicator level and for each of the indicators of a secondary-level dimension the same issues arise. As such, the semantic mappings are a pervasive issue in linking numeric indicators and data to concepts.

As discussed in the next chapter, these have important implications because one must have a common scale for aggregating different dimensions. So, as one works one's way up from the bottom to the top in terms of measurement, one must make a variety of semantic mapping and transformation decisions to get from the raw data–indicators at the bottom to the more abstract concepts at the top.

Not to decide, and to use a linear mapping, is to decide. To dichotomize is also to make a semantic transformation. The issues outlined and discussed in this chapter cannot be avoided. A major goal of this chapter has been to open up these decisions to discussion and provide a methodology for comparing and contrasting alternative decisions.

The central question of this chapter is how to connect semantics with numeric and quantitative measures. Fuzzy-logic semantic transformations provide a framework for getting numeric measures from data–indicators, which can then be used in descriptive or causal analyses. Summarizing this chapter the core guideline is clear:

Semantic Mapping Guideline: Construct the semantic mapping between the data–indicator scale on the $X$-axis and the semantic content on the $Y$-axis.

# 5

# Scaling

Being so disinterested in our variables that we do not care about their units can hardly be desirable.

J. W. TUKEY

## Introduction

Given the fractal nature of the basic framework, scaling decisions are unavoidable. This is clearly related to the semantic transformations and mappings discussed in the previous chapter. This is also related to aggregation decisions to be analyzed in the next chapter. One must have a common scale for aggregating across indicators or secondary-level dimensions. In a more philosophical vein, people talk about various factors being incommensurable, but in practice one must make them commensurable otherwise research cannot proceed. So the question is not whether one should do it or not, but rather what is the best way to do it.

Semantic transformations connect to the canonical literature on scale types discussed in this chapter. The motivation here is the need for a common scale that allows a variety of mathematical operations to be performed on them as part of the aggregation process. Scaling and standardization are either not taught or taught in a completely conventional fashion. In my years of reading quantitative research, the issues raised in this chapter, while in some sense quite simple, are often ignored in practice. In political science at least they are barely taught at all, and certainly not seen as something that one must pay attention to in applied research.

In short, scaling is at the core of multidimensional and multilevel concepts. If one wants any kind of numeric measure or indicator, the challenge of scaling must be directly addressed.

Since most research design textbooks and almost all statistical work focus on measurement, this chapter connects the approach of this book with these traditional concerns. The best way to start is via a discussion of the standard typology of "scale types." Traditionally, there are four types: (1) nominal, (2) ordinal, (3) interval, and (4) ratio. As a rule, as one moves "up" the scale the type is more informative and valuable.

Related to this are various transformations of numeric measures. Chapter 4 introduced the concept of a semantic transformation: *any* mathematical transformation of the basic indicator involves meaning shifts. The traditional topic of types of scales also raises the issue of what are permissible transformations of the original scale, e.g., logging, addition, multiplication.

To analyze scaling and standardization issues, this chapter uses the conceptual framework and the fuzzy-logic approach to measurement, scaling, and semantic transformations developed in the previous chapter.

## Varieties of Scales

### Nominal "Scales"

As always, terminology is important. The classic discussion uses the language of "scale types" which goes back to the classic Stevens articles (1946; 1968). A key question is the extent to which nominal indicators constitute a scale. A typical coding of 0 and 1 (e.g., absence–presence) suggests that there is an underlying continuum between 0 and 1. Misleading in this coding is the implicit suggestion that 1 is higher on the underlying conceptual continuum. The first guideline requires one to be clear on this point:

Nominal Scale Guideline: Verify that 0 and 1 are in fact not ordinal and that there is no underlying continuum between them.

*The absolutely essential point is that "a" nominal variable is really two (or more) concepts.* If there is no underlying continuum then 0 and 1 are different concepts: there is no scale between them. Authors can disagree on this point: some treat 0 as "qualitatively different," while others imply a underlying continuum.

The Multidimensional Poverty Index illustrates how this works in a multilevel and multidimensional setting. At the core, bottom level of the concept are various data about dimensions such as health, education, or living standards. These basic data are dichotomous and aggregated usually via the maximum to produce 0 or 1 values for each of the 10 core indicators. Are these dichotomous indicators nominal, ordinal, or interval? The basic-level numeric value—the poverty measure—is the weighted sum of these 10 indicators. So the 0 or 1 for each indicator is an interval-level factor which is then weighted to produce the final sum. So what might appear to be a nominal indicator is an ordered [0, 1] variable which when weighted becomes an interval-level value for the degree of poverty of a given individual or household.

The distinction between nominal and ordinal is critical in the methodology of typologies (see chapter 8). Here too it is sometimes not clear whether the typology involves ordered categories or not. Typically, a typology is seen by default as involving nominal types. Thus, the discussion of typologies is an extension of the brief discussion here.

This makes nominal "scales" fundamentally different from the other types. The key question is whether there is an underlying continuum; for all the other scale types there is an underlying conceptual continuum. For nominal variables there are implicitly two underlying continua, one for each concept. To call a nominal scale a scale—hence the scare quotes in the title of this subsection—is fundamentally misleading.

## Ordinal Scales

Perhaps the most problematic and difficult to deal with are ordinal scales. We just saw that dichotomous values are often in fact ordinal. It is extremely common to see scales with three to seven different ordered levels. Quite uncommon are scales with ten or more ordinal levels. One tendency, particularly with ordinal scales with seven or more levels, is just to treat them as interval.

With complex concepts one must have a common scale, so we need a way to create an interval or ratio scale from these ordinal levels. The semantic transformations and mappings of the previous chapter provide one way to think about how to do this. As always on the $Y$-axis we have the $[0, 1]$ scale, which is the common scale for all components of the basic framework. On the $X$-axis I have placed the various ordinal levels, equally spaced, which suggests an interval-level interpretation of them.

If one does a linear semantic transformation then of course the ordinal variables are in fact treated as equally spaced interval values. But as we saw in the previous chapter, that often does not make semantic sense. One can apply the same logic to ordinal variables that we applied to interval or ratio variables in the previous chapter. We need to ask how the various levels of the ordinal variable map onto various points of the $Y$-axis, which then gives us the semantic transformation and at the same time provides ratio-level variables that can be used for other purposes.

As a concrete example I use the Political Terror Scale (PTS) which has five levels of human-rights violations from basically none to widespread killing, torture, and imprisonment of extensive parts of the population. Here is a brief description of the scale levels:

LEVEL 1: Countries ... under a secure rule of law, people are not imprisoned for their views, and torture is rare or exceptional.... Political murders are extremely rare....

LEVEL 2: There is a limited amount of imprisonment for nonviolent political activity. However, a few persons are affected; torture and beating are exceptional.... Political murder is rare....

LEVEL 3: There is extensive political imprisonment.... Execution or other political murders and brutality may be common. Unlimited detention, with or without trial, for political views is accepted....

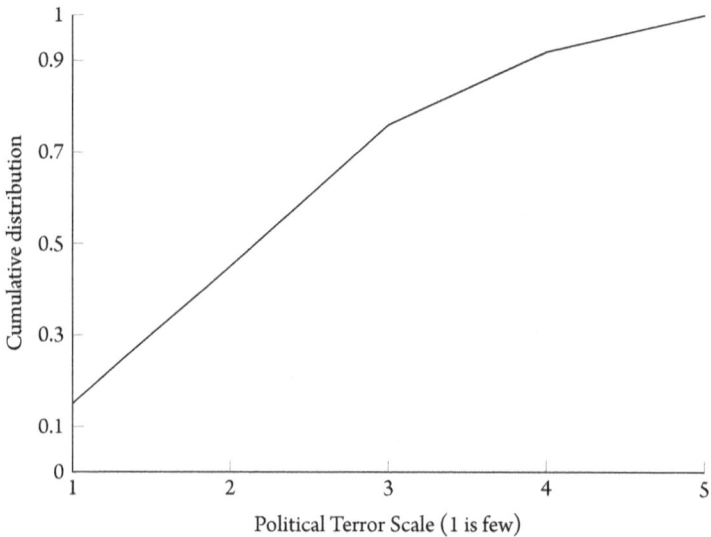

FIGURE 5.1. Political Terror Scale: empirical cumulative distribution, 1976–2017.

LEVEL 4:  The practices of Level 3 are expanded to larger numbers. Murders, disappearances, and torture are part of life.... In spite of its generality, on this level terror affects primarily those who interest themselves in politics or ideas.

LEVEL 5:  The terrors of Level 4 have been extended to the whole population.... The leaders of these societies place no limits on the means or thoroughness with which they pursue personal or ideological goals. (Wood and Gibney 2010, 373)

One of the things that one can do in making these transformations, as a guide, is to look at the actual distribution of the cases; see figure 5.1. In fact, in the fuzzy-logic literature on poverty (e.g., Cerioli and Zani 1990; see Alkire et al. 2015 for a critical overview) this is the main approach: one uses the cumulative distribution function as a way to calibrate and transform the underlying data into the [0, 1] interval. While this should not be done in an automatic fashion, it does provide a way to think about the levels. One of the things that comes out when looking at the histogram of the PTS data, as with much social science data, is that they are skewed: there are relatively few cases at the highest level of

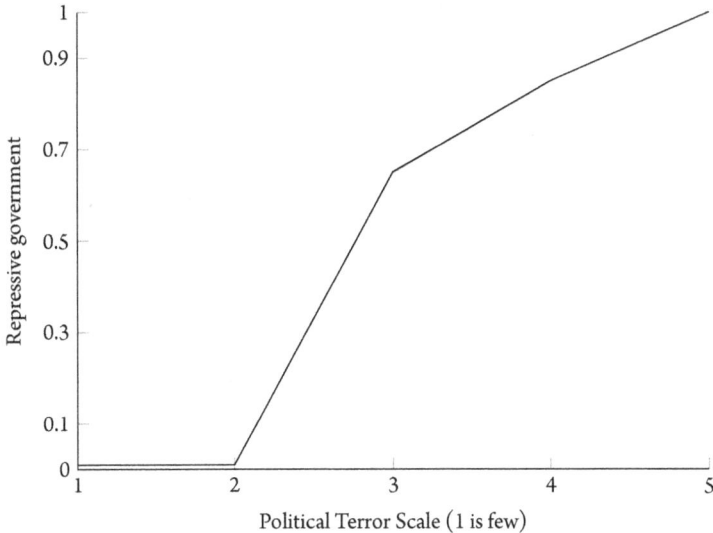

FIGURE 5.2. Political Terror Scale, "repressive government": semantic transformation of an ordinal scale.

human-rights violations, less than half those with the best scores. One can see this because the top three levels have only about 25 percent of the cases. The data are clearly skewed to the right toward the side of fewer human-rights violations.

Figure 5.2 illustrates one transformation of the PTS scale onto the [0, 1] standardized scale. As with educated versus education, the concept of interest here is "repressive government," not repression. Notice that the high end, levels 4 and 5, receives quite high codings of 0.8 and 1.0. The 1 and 2 levels have 0.0 membership in repressive government. The curve, not surprisingly, has roughly a skewed-S shape. It is also worth stressing that we are interested in the concept of repressive government. This means that levels 1 and 2 have very low levels of membership in the concept. This is exactly analogous to what the last chapter did in contrasting the concept of poverty with wealth.

The natural thing would be to use level 3 as the 0.50 crossover point because it is the middle of 1–5. It is again important to look at the meaning of that level in the coding rules, as well as specific cases that get that particular coding. If one does so, it seems pretty clear that 0.50 is too low for the concept of repressive government. Level 3 is defined as "extensive political imprisonment" and "execution or other political murders and brutality may be common." So I have put level 3 at 0.65.

To repeat the point about conceptual asymmetry, if I'm interested in trying to explain why some governments respect human rights then I would draw a semantic mapping different from the one in figure 5.2.

Hence the methodology of semantic transformations can be used to convert ordinal concepts into ratio ones. The key features of this are exploring the meanings of the different levels.

It is worth contrasting figure 5.2 with what the previous chapter did with the ordinal World Bank groupings of poverty–wealth. The core difference is that the ordinal categorization of the World Bank has an underlying ratio variable of GDP per capita. Because of this underlying data, we can see that the distance covered by groups is definitely not equal. For the PTS we do not have such underlying ratio data. As a result we have to use other means to try to do the mapping. However, the basic semantics, logic, and methodology are not really that different.

This example leads to some general considerations:

Guideline: Explicitly decide which level of the ordinal scale is the conceptual middle point.

This then leads to some suggestions about the number of levels one should have in an ordinal indicator. Critical for concept development is the 0.50 point, the half-empty or half-full point. With an odd number of levels there will be a clear crossover point, e.g., 3 in a 1–5 scale.[1] For example, the Aid Transparency Index[2] has five categories: (1) very poor, (2) poor, (3) fair, (4) good, and (5) very good.

If one includes such a middle point one might ask about a three- versus five- versus seven-point ordinal scale. From a fuzzy-logic and practical point of view, there are good reasons to stick with five as the

1. For QCA users, things are complicated by the fact that in standard QCA practice 0.50 cases are excluded from the analysis. Hence, it might be good to have an even number of levels, such as 1–6 where 3 and 4 are just on either side of the 0.50 middle, of 3.5.

2. https://www.publishwhatyoufund.org

default number of levels. Recall from chapter 4 that the default fuzzy-logic semantic transformation is an S-curve. With three levels one can draw a curve, but to do an S-curve one needs the inflection points on either side of the middle to draw the curve.

While it is hard to generalize, when the researcher uses five or more levels I often feel that the distance between 4 and 5 (or 1 and 2) is smaller semantically than the distance between 3 and 4 or 3 and 2. This is illustrated in the Political Terror Scale where the bottom two levels are considered as not repressive at all and where the top two levels are also more closely grouped together. I think this is in reality quite often the case: the levels are in fact not equal and there is a grouping close together particularly at the extremes. Of course, this will vary from concept to concept but it is always worth asking about.

One can already see where this discussion is going:

Ordinal Scale Guideline: Consider transforming the ordinal scale into a fuzzy-logic one.

Among other things, on the statistical and mathematical side one now has a ratio variable and consequently the number of statistical options goes up dramatically (e.g., exploring function forms).

If one is going to use or create an ordinal scale it is worth considering (1) the number of levels, (2) what the conceptual middle 0.50 level is, and (3) whether some categories are semantically closer together than others.

Recall that in the basic framework, or for any even slightly complex concept, one is going to need a common scale. It is not something that one can avoid so it is best to be rigorous and explicit. The basic semantic transformation methodology provides one way to do this in an explicit, coherent, and open fashion.

### Interval Scales

By definition, an interval scale means that there are equal distances between levels. The scale itself is movable—i.e., subject to linear transformations—and arbitrary as long the distances between levels are equal. So, for example, one can increase the distance between levels from 1 to 2.

In practice, probably the most common scale is the interval scale. As noted in the previous subsection, once one gets to the range of seven or more ordinal levels it becomes quite cumbersome to do statistical analyses. Therefore, the implicit move is to consider an ordinal scale with, say, ten levels as in fact interval. Of course, how justifiable this is depends on the concept.

Latent variable statistical measurement produces interval measurement of concepts. The unmeasured variable is usually standardized by fixing the standard deviation as 1.0 and the mean as 0.0.

In terms of concept semantics there is an implied linear relationship between the interval scale and the concept. The fuzzy-logic approach suggests that this assumption can be challenged and that it is quite possible to perform semantic transformations on the underlying data or indicator. A standard example in chapter 4 was modifying the Polity democracy indicator to fit better my concept of democracy. This is possible for any interval or ratio indicator or data. There is no reason why it cannot be applied to the V-Dem measure of democracy or any other interval-level indicator.

A key problem with interval indicators and data is the confusion between interval and ratio.

## Ratio Scales

The most common definition of a ratio scale is that it has a true zero. This means that it is not moveable like interval scales: the zero is a key feature of the concept and has real meaning. From our bank accounts we know that positive amounts are different from negative amounts, and zero means no money. In a very famous early book, Bueno de Mesquita (1981) hypothesized that a positive expected utility was a necessary condition for war initiation. This means that the zero was not an arbitrary point.

The second, less popular definition focuses on the name itself, ratio. With ratio indicators one can say that one observation is "twice as big" as another. Interval scales do not allow this. For example, using the

Polity scale of democracy one cannot say that a country with a 10 is 5 times more democratic than one that scores 2. However, it makes sense to say that someone is twice as rich as another person.

The problem, see below for more, is that it is not clear whether the zero is a real zero or not. It might be that the theory or hypothesis requires a zero like Bueno de Mesquita's hypothesis about war initiation. The main factor that generates confusion between interval and ratio scales is that, in general, statistics only needs interval scale variables. Since it does not usually matter for the statistical method, it is not really a source of concern or interest.

Fuzzy-logic concepts are ratio because the zero is a real zero; it is 0.0 membership in the concept. Zero means the complete absence of the property.

Semantic transformations are a means of converting ordinal or interval indicators into ratio ones. Whether this makes sense or not depends on the semantics of the concept. In the previous chapter we saw that dichotomization of variables with an underlying scale is just a certain kind of semantic transformation operation.

### Fuzzy-Logic Scales

So how do these scale types match up, or not, with membership functions in fuzzy-logic analysis? A good place to start is with the zero point. Interval scales differ from ratio scales in that the latter have a true zero while the former do not.

The 0.0 membership value in fuzzy-logic analysis does not play the same role. In fuzzy-logic analysis, the 0.0 value indicates the complete lack of *membership in a set*. For example, a country with a GDP per capita of $500 would doubtless receive a 0.0 membership value in the concept "wealthy country." In this sense, the 0.0 value in fuzzy-logic analysis is closer to the idea of the minimum point on a continuous scale.

A similar point can be made for the 1.0 membership value in a fuzzy-logic scale. The 1.0 value indicates full membership in a set. It plays a role somewhat similar to the maximum point on a continuous scale. In the classic scaling schemes, there is no notion of a true maximum (or minimum). For example, what would it mean to say that an individual has a maximum level of wealth? The individual could always have one dollar more.

In classic measurement theory, dichotomous variables are seen as occupying the bottom of the hierarchy of scales. If one has continuous data, it is almost always considered a bad move to dichotomize, since this involves throwing away information. Fuzzy-set analysis offers a quite different view of dichotomization.

Figure 4.2 in the previous chapter shows the common dichotomization scheme that scholars apply to the Polity data, where 7 is the cutoff point for democracy on the scale $-10$ to $10$. From a statistical standpoint, one loses a tremendous amount of information by dichotomizing the Polity data: we go from a 21-point scale to a 2-point scale. By contrast, from a fuzzy-logic point of view, dichotomization is just another semantic transformation function. The fuzzy-logic objection to dichotomization of this sort is not the loss of information. Rather, the objection is that the slope of the curve, i.e., the vertical line at 7, is far too steep (the derivative is infinite). Here is a case where the cutoff point really matters: the slightest change in data could lead to a complete shift in semantic meaning for some observations: as the Zadeh epigraph at the beginning of the previous chapter stresses, one needs a more gradual change when moving semantically along the $X$-axis, not such an abrupt one.

In summary, a key conceptual issue is whether there is a conceptual continuum underlying whatever measurement scale is being used. The fuzzy-logic semantic transformation presents a unifying perspective. Whether there are 2 levels (dichotomous-ordered), 5 levels (ordinal), 20 levels (treated as interval), or an infinite number of levels (interval or ratio) on the $X$-axis, the conceptual and semantic question is the relationship of those levels to the underlying concept on the $Y$-axis.

## Implicit Conversion to Interval or Ratio Scales

The previous section briefly surveyed the basic scale types and some core issues in thinking about them. This section treats briefly the fact that one combines indicators and dimensions. Chapter 6 on aggregation assumes features of secondary-level dimensions or indicators that may in fact be problematic when they are combined via various, simple, mathematical operations.

One of the most common index-, concept-, or scale-building procedures involves having a number of dichotomous indicators of some concept and then summing them to get an overall level of concept X. Typically, these dichotomous indicators will be coded 0–1 before they are added, e.g., the Multidimensional Poverty Index. Thus the following point is key:

> Adding dichotomous, e.g., 0–1, indicators converts those indicators into the interval scale.

Adding not only makes the 0–1 indicators ordinal, but makes them interval. This arises because addition is not a permissible mathematical operation on nominal or ordinal variables.

The classics of measurement of the 1960s in psychology (e.g., Suppes and Zinnes 1963) discussed at some length these issues of permissible mathematical operations depending on scale type. However, (1) these discussions did not seem to make it into more distant disciplines like political science and economics, and (2) have probably been dropped over the decades in psychology methods classes.

This automatic conversion is so common that it is almost never noticed. For example, to get an estimated value for observations in latent variable models, one uses the factor scores in a weighted sum of the indicators. No matter what the original scale type of those indicators, they are automatically converted by the weighted sum into interval-level indicators.

The same sort of thing occurs when one calculates ratios. For example, international conflict scholars often want to know the relative military capabilities or power of various states. They calculate the ratio of the military capabilities (e.g., the widely used CINC military capability variable from the Correlates of War project). No surprise, when one calculates a ratio the power variables are automatically converted into a ratio scale. This may not be invalid: 0.0 on power might be a real zero.

Whether adding–subtracting for interval variables or multiplying–dividing for ratio variables is valid depends on the underlying concept and its relationship to the indicators and scale. One advantage of the fuzzy-logic approach is that everything is converted into real numbers. Hence, there are no issues about what mathematical operations are permissible or not.

Some might object to the fuzzy-logic transformation of ordinal to ratio, described above as being "arbitrary." However, I would suggest that converting a bunch of ordinal dummy variables into an interval index via addition is more problematic and arbitrary.

The basic guideline is to think about what it means when combining indicators:

> Scale Combination Guideline: Any time that indicators, measures, or indices are combined via some mathematical operation, e.g., addition or multiplication, decide whether the scale conversions are justified.

## Beware of Zero

All of these scales from nominal to ratio may contain a 0: the scale could be [0, 1], [0, 5], [−10, 10]. This can lead to problems if one is not careful. This leads to one immediate guideline:

> Zero Point Guideline: Do not use zero unless it is a ratio scale.

The biggest problem probably is distinguishing between interval and ratio. Usage varies along with interpretation. For example, the original Polity concept of democracy probably had a real zero at 0 since −10 to 0 was autocracy, while 0–10 was democracy. This then implicitly shifted with dichotomization rules whereby democracy was greater than (or sometimes equal to) 6.

Bueno de Mesquita's hypothesis about a positive expected utility required a ratio measure of preference (called tau-beta), and it varied from −1 to 1, with 0 as the implicit middle point.[3] The popular S

---

3. In fact there was some controversy over the exact means of calculating the zero point, which I discovered when using it as a ratio variable and receiving critiques from Bueno de Mesquita about my choice of zero.

measure (Signorino and Ritter 1999) is an interval measure. However, they make it seem like a ratio by rescaling it to $[-1, 1]$.

Once you begin to have interaction terms it means that you are multiplying two variables. With ratio variables this is no issue. However, because interval variables can move around they can be both positive, both negative, or some part positive and some part negative. Individually this makes no difference, but once one multiplies it obviously does.

Then one can throw zero into the interaction mix and obviously that is going to matter. So if the variable contains 0 then in the interaction one will be multiplying by 0 sometimes. This might seem so obvious as to be insulting. However, in practice it is not always on people's radar.

Braumoeller (2004) and Brambor et al. (2006) raised awareness in political science to the fact that there are many easy-to-fall-into pitfalls in the use of interaction terms. One important implication of the presence or absence of a zero point is exactly the role that ratio variables play in interaction terms.

One issue in interaction term analysis lies in the interpretation of the individual terms of the interaction term, e.g., $\beta_1 X_1$ and $\beta_2 X_2$. Typically, the interpretation is that $\beta_1$ is the impact of $X_1$ when $X_2 = 0$. This then assumes obviously that $X_2 = 0$ really means something. If $X_2$ is an interval variable then $X_2 = 0$ is completely arbitrary (see Friedrich 1982 and Allison 1977).

Another issue with zero is that sometimes it means "in the middle" and sometimes it means "completely absent." In fuzzy-logic usage, 0.0 means completely not a member of the concept, while 0.50 is in the middle. In the examples where the scale is in the $[-1, 1]$ range, 0 is in the middle and $-1$ means (often implicitly) completely absent.

Latent variables have no scale as interval variables, so they may or may not include zero and because they are interval they can be moved around. Standard practice is to have zero as the middle, i.e., mean, point.

Similarly, standardization of variables with mean 0 is common. For example, Beck et al. (2000) do this for all the variables in their neural net analysis. These standardized variables are then used in a large variety of interaction terms.

In summary, one needs to ask about the existence or not of zero points. Does the theory need them? Does the use of the variable in interaction terms and the like imply that there is a true zero point?

This subsection started with a guideline to avoid zero unless it is really a zero. This brief discussion illustrates some of the pitfalls of using zero in nonratio indicators. My concept exercises contain a fair number of examples where the zero has been problematic. The existence of these exercises motivated the writing of this subsection.

## Standardization

Standardization is a critical operation in the construction of complex concepts and their measurement. In order to aggregate across dimensions at any level requires some common scale. This section reviews the common and not-so-common ways to deal with this fundamental issue of conceptualization and measurement. Before one can aggregate—the topic of the next chapter—all indicators must be converted to a common scale. For example, all the various global indicators have to solve this problem.

The basic idea behind all these standardization techniques involves having some sense of what is high or low for a given indicator or dimension. All of the methods discussed below implement this in different ways, but the common scale puts "high" on dimension 1 together with "high" on dimension 2 as the same on the common scale, typically [0, 1] or [1, 100]. The substance of the dimensions can vary widely, but what one needs for standardization is some underlying continuum of low to high. This can be as simple as the ordinal 0–1 scale, as long as there is a clear sense that 0 means none or low, and 1 means high on the continuum.

It is worth noting in passing that standardization assumes that the dimensions are commensurable. While one can debate, often philosophically, the commensurability of various dimensions (e.g., Chang 1998), for the purposes of this book, as well as in practice, commensurability is assumed as part of the standardization process.

Not surprisingly, economists often standardize by trying to convert everything into constant—across time and space—dollars. This is a complex and tricky operation that requires calculating purchasing power equivalencies in different countries, which can then be complicated if the data are to cover extended time periods.

"Different" goods are converted into their dollar values, which gives a ratio scale. Now all kinds of mathematical operations, e.g., aggregation, can be performed on these standardized dollar indicators.

As we have seen, problems arise when it is hard to give dollar values to specific dimensions. For example, how much is liberty and lack of repression worth in dollars?

More generally, production and utility functions aggregate different dimensions, e.g., classically, labor and capital in production functions. Sometimes "utils" are the common scale in utility functions. Production–utility functions play a key role in aggregation, the topic of the next chapter.

## Statistical Standardization

A popular transformation is to standardize a variable. To recall, the formula when standardizing variables is $(x_i - \bar{x})/s$, where $\bar{x}$ is the mean and $s$ is the standard deviation. For example, the raw data of the Polity scale of democracy codes cases from $-10$ to $10$ (Jaggers and Gurr 1995). Standardization converts these numbers into a new scale of standard deviations from the mean. The most common rationale for statistical standardization lies in getting the same scale for all the variables in an analysis.

Standardization is quite common in psychology and sociology, rare in political science, and probably rare in economics. Statistical standardization can be common in some disciplines like psychology but be a contested area for some statistical techniques like cluster analysis (Milligan and Cooper 1988). For example, in an oft-cited work, Kim and Ferree (1981, 187) in their first sentence talk about "the long-standing debate in the social sciences over the desirability of using standardized coefficients in regression." What is not in doubt is that the rationale behind statistical standardization is to have the same scale for, typically, all the independent variables, which then allows for comparisons of the relative impact of different $X$ variables.

The results of standardization obviously depend on the underlying data, not on anything related to the definition of the concept being measured. A core guideline is to be wary of making conceptualization decisions based on the empirical distribution of cases (see chapter 9). The same, not surprisingly, is true of semantic transformations. This is not to say that one should be completely immune to empirical distributions. However, any transformation that depends heavily or exclusively on the distribution of the data is problematic. Statistical standardization certainly relies on the distribution of the data and hence on a particular data set.

The statistical mean and standard deviation usually change as the underlying data change. In fact, with standardization the score for any one case can easily change if the scores for the other observations are altered. A case might not experience any real-world change, yet its coding shifts because values for other cases are changing. From a semantic as well as descriptive perspective this seems odd: Why should the score for a case depend on how other cases happen to be coded, or on changes in their values? Of course, if the concept is relative and relational to begin with, e.g., inequality or positional goods, then how other cases are coded does and should matter.

To make this more concrete, consider the Polity data set on level of democracy. A qualitative researcher might develop the rule that "full democracy" characterizes those cases beyond some threshold, such as all cases with values from 7 to 10. Under this rule, any proportion of the cases, including all or none of them, could be full democracies, depending on whether they meet the threshold. If the data are presented as standardized values, however, one must use a different rule, such as full democracy characterizes those cases that are at least 2 standard deviations above the mean. This rule ensures that only a small proportion of the cases will be coded as full democracies.

A given case can slip in and out of the category of full democracy depending on how the other cases are coded. From a semantic perspective, this is problematic. Whether a case is a full democracy or not depends on the definition of that concept and the features of the case, not on the distribution of levels of democracy within the population as a whole.

The use of standardized values can also have other consequences for research. For example, consider the advice that one should standardize variables in order to select case studies based on their "extreme" values (Seawright and Gerring 2008). There are good reasons why one would want to look at extreme cases. Given this, standardizing values is an obvious choice because we have some idea about what extreme means in terms of standard deviations: an observation that is at least 2–3 standard deviations from the mean is extreme.

From a semantic perspective, the approach is troubling. The standardization approach defines extreme values in terms of their relationship to the sample mean, which is treated as the "middle point." But from a semantic point of view, the sample mean may, or may not, represent the middle point of a concept. The middle point corresponds to the *conceptual* middle value. For instance, with the Polity scale, which ranges from −10 to 10, the conceptual middle point might be 0.[4] By contrast, the sample mean for Polity is about +3.

With the Polity data, one consequence of standardization is that the most extreme cases are always autocratic regimes. Because the sample mean is about +3, the autocratic cases of −10 always have larger absolute standardized values than do the complete democracy cases with a value of +10. From a semantic perspective, however, standardization is counterproductive and problematic: the extreme values are "obviously" the −10 and the +10 cases.

Semantic transformations usually have an impact on causal and statistical analyses. For example, in the (in)famous *Bell curve* debate, standardization significantly changes the statistical and substantive analyses (see Fischer et al. 1996). What is significant in the original book

---

4. Given that the Polity measure of regime type is democracy minus autocracy, where both democracy and autocracy range from 0 to 10, there is much in the Polity procedure that would imply that 0 is the conceptual middle point.

as standardized changes significantly when nonstandardized variables are used.

In summary, statistical standardization is usually motivated by getting a common scale, not by increasing the semantic validity of the resulting variable. In addition, it relies heavily on the empirical distribution of data. Both these features lead to a recommendation that one should not statistically standardize variables.

## Standardization via the Minimum and Maximum

Another approach, extremely popular in the global indices literature, rescales by using some version of the minimum of the data to determine "low" and some variant of the maximum of the data to determine "high." The minimum and maximum are used to rescale everything, typically into [0, 1]. The use of the min-max procedure, or variants on it, has become the default in the global indicators industry.

As with statistical standardization, this obviously depends on the data. As such, it has all the problems of data-driven standardization procedures.

A core issue with this approach is that there might be "outliers," which can significantly extend the scale in one or both directions. The scare quotes on "outlier" suggest a problem: one person's outlier might be another person's "good case" or "ideal type."

Sachs et al. (2019) illustrate a possible—and perhaps common— simple response to this outlier problem. Basically, one removes the outliers from the empirical data. The definition of an outlier could be, for example, the top percentiles 97–100 and the bottom percentiles 0–3:

> To determine the worst value for each indicator, we first remove the worst 2.5% of observations in order to ensure that our scoring is not overly influenced by outliers. We then identify the next-worst value on each indicator and apply this value to the bottom 2.5 percentile of the distribution.... Here we use the average of the top 5 values in the sample of countries for that indicator. All

countries that exceed the average of the best values are assigned the best value. (Sachs et al. 2019, 13–14)

The OECD (2008) similarly recommends removing the effect of extreme values, which can skew (to use their problematic term) the results of a composite index. It recommends truncating the data by removing the top and bottom 2.5 percentiles from the distribution.

The UNDP recognizes the problems with setting absolute minima and maxima, particularly based on empirical data over time:

> The main problem with shifting the goal posts annually is that it precludes meaningful comparisons over time: a country's HDI could change from year to year for reasons that have nothing to do with its performance. So, this year, we fix "normative" values for life expectancy, adult literacy, mean years of schooling and income. These minimums and maximums are not the observed values in the best or worst-performing countries today but the most extreme values observed or expected over a long period (say, 60 years). The minimums are those observed historically, going back about 30 years. The maximums are the limits of what can be envisioned in the next 30 years. Demographic and medical information suggests that the maximum average life expectancy for the foreseeable future is 85 years. Similarly, recent economic growth rates indicate that the maximum income that the richest countries are likely to achieve by 2020 is $40,000 (in 1990 PPP dollars). (UNDP 1994, 92)

Interestingly enough, this outlier fix produces basically the S-curve default of fuzzy logic. The popular min-max standardization with "outlier correction" (i.e., cutting off the top and bottom 2–5 percent) produces the fuzzy-logic default S-curve transformation; however, the route to that transformation is radically different: it is not semantics but data outlier problems.

There are fancier and more sophisticated ways to use the maximum. In economics there is the core concept of production frontiers. These are essentially the maximum that one can produce given a certain

context of technology, corporate organization, etc. There are statistical techniques for estimating these frontiers or, in other contexts,
data envelopes (see Dul 2016 or Goertz et al. 2013 for other statistical ways of thinking about these frontiers) that then can be used to
standardize data:

> Building on the long-standing framework of "production possi-
> bility frontiers" used in economics, we construct Achievement
> Possibilities Frontiers by plotting the value of a given socioeco-
> nomic indicator against available resources for all countries and
> then identifying the outer boundary of the plot. Just as a produc-
> tion possibility frontier shows the maximum output of a good
> possible for any given resource input, the APF reveals how well
> a country can perform—the level of social and economic rights
> it can provide—at any given level of resources. (Fukuda-Parr et
> al. 2015, 42; see figure 3.1, "Prototype achievement possibilities
> frontier").

As this brief survey has suggested, there are a variety of ways to use
the empirical distribution of data to do standardization and which are
also semantic transformations. The key guidelines here are not only
to examine carefully how the empirical data are being used, but also
the extent to which some external goalposts are being used that do
not rely at all on the empirical distribution of data. Not surprisingly,
in the global indicator industry one can find varying mixes of external,
often normative, means for determining the semantic transformation
along with the empirical distribution of data. The position here is that
the empirical distribution of data can help inform but it is semantics,
normative concerns, and the like that should determine the semantic
transformations.

## Hybrid and "Natural" Standardizations

It is very common to use the empirical minimum and maximum, perhaps with some cutting at the ends for standardization. Particularly in
the global performance index industry, there are often combinations of

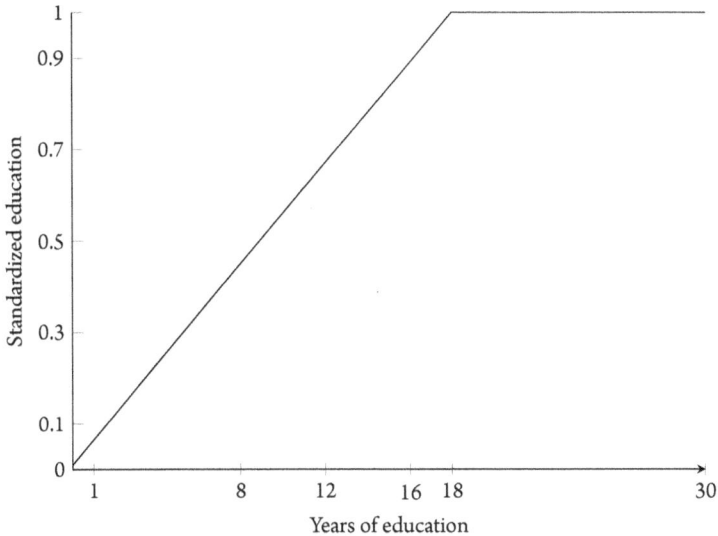

FIGURE 5.3. Standardizing education according to the UNDP.
*Source:* Based on UNDP (2018a).

"natural zeros" along with some threshold for the maximum. These are so common that they are worth special mention.

Figure 5.3 illustrates the UNDP's semantic transformation of years of education into a standard [0, 1] scale. Here there is a real natural zero for years of education, because there are people with 0 years of education. There is, on the other hand, no obvious maximum for years of education. As with many skewed social science data, the tail can be quite long as people can spend many years in education. The UNDP following social conventions about meaning fix the maximum at roughly a master's degree. This then produces a linear standardization from 0 to the threshold of 18 years. We have seen the same procedure with measures of poverty where the natural zero is not easy to determine, e.g., "existence-life minimum."

Thus it occurs quite frequently that one end of the standardization scale can be quite fixed and clear, and this is often at the zero end. Sometimes the maximum is fixed by policy goals, as in the SDGs. In this case the maximum is fixed by the policy instead of social conventions, as is the case for education in figure 5.3. Frequently the maximum is unclear because of skewed data and long tails. Then, some strategy is needed to fix the threshold, which then produces the linear-threshold standardization semantic transformation.

## Percentiles, Categorization, and Standardization

We have seen that categorization schemes such as those in the global performance indicator industry often imply a nonlinear relationship between the underlying indicator and the categories. The Human Development Index (HDI) divides countries into four ordinal categories: (1) very high, (2) high, (3) medium, and (4) low. It is always interesting to see how the ordinal categories are labeled and the use or nonuse of adjectives. So, for example, for HDI we have very high, but not very low. Why not do high and very low instead? Contrast that with the World Bank's categories of high, higher middle, lower middle, and low.

One might ask how the UNDP got these explicit cutoff points. The UNDP uses percentiles for its categorization scheme (exact details do not seem easily available): "HDI classifications are based on HDI fixed cutoff points, which are derived from the quartiles of distributions of the component indicators. The cutoff points are HDI of less than 0.550 for low human development, 0.550–0.699 for medium human development, 0.700–0.799 for high human development and 0.800 or greater for very high human development" (UNDP 2018a).

Here is an example of what I would call "second-order linear thinking." If one wants five categories, then break raw data into *equal* percentiles corresponding to those five categories. This is essentially the same as using the cumulative distribution function to do calibration and standardization.

One simple and obvious system for standardization uses the empirical distribution of the data and takes the percentiles as the semantic transformation. This, in one form or another, is quite common and often recommended:

> The simplest normalization [standardization] method consists in ranking each indicator across countries. The main advantages of

this approach are its simplicity and the independence to outliers. Disadvantages are the loss of information on absolute levels and the impossibility to draw any conclusion about difference in performance. This method has been employed to build a composite on the development and application of information and communication technology across countries and also in the Medicare study on healthcare performance across US States. (Eurostat 2005, 46)

One can use percentiles in nonlinear semantic transformations. For example, here is one from Eurostat (2005, 49):

- Top 5 percent get a score of 100.
- 85–95 percentiles get 80 points.
- 65–85 percentiles get 60 points.
- 35–65 percentiles get 50 points.
- 15–35 percentiles get 40 points.
- 5–15 percentiles get 20 points.
- 0–5 percentiles get 0 points.

This is one that is nonlinear but symmetric around the middle of the 50th percentile. Again, there is no reason why the 50th percentile is the conceptual 0.50 point. If one follows the Ragin Adjective Rule then these kinds of symmetric categorization decisions are unlikely to occur.

Because the underlying data used by the UNDP are highly skewed, percentiles produce quite uneven categories. Even normal distribution data would produce unequal cutoffs based on equal percentiles. This is why second-order linear thinking using percentiles produces first-order, quite unequal categories.

A variation on percentiles is to use ordinal rankings. Ranking is a simple normalization technique based on the data. This method is not affected by outliers and allows the performance of countries to be followed over time in terms of relative positions (rankings). Some examples that use ranking include the Information and Communications Technology Index (Fagerberg 2001) and the Medicare Study on

Healthcare Performance across the United States (Jencks et al. 2003; see OECD 2008, 27).

There is an inherent tension in the linear standardization, which is based on the empirical range of the data, e.g., min-max, versus the almost inevitably nonlinear transformations based on second-order linear thinking in terms of percentiles and cumulative distribution functions. As far as I'm aware no one in this global index industry has really discussed the tensions between them.

From a semantic point of view these are all problematic because they relatively mindlessly use empirical distributions of data to form categories or do standardization. Hence the categories really are empirical data descriptions which may only be weakly related to what scholars, societies, organizations mean by the underlying concepts.

## Normative Issues

Standardization can easily have a normative dimension. This is related to the idea of thresholds in the literature on poverty. Moving the threshold up or down is making an assessment about the individual and probably whether they deserve some kind of public support. "Low values" should be determined by policy and normative goals and not just the distribution of the data. Those goals, for example policy targets, have clear normative underpinnings and dimensions. This is yet another reason why using the distribution of the data to standardize is implicitly a normative choice.

There might be situations where the high and low on a given indicator can be determined substantively for that dimension. Sachs et al. (2019) use the United Nations's development goals to standardize some of their indicators: "We also create a best score. In most cases the best score is the natural 'perfect' and technically feasible target [e.g., MDG] in line with the principle of 'leaving no one behind' (e.g. zero extreme poverty, zero undernourishment, 100 percent school completion)." Curiously they do not talk about a natural minimum which might also exist.

There is sometimes a relative social consensus as to what constitutes good performance or high levels of achievement, e.g., educated. One can consider using these in the standardization process. Using society standards for standardization or categorization almost always means or implies a normative judgment.

Semantic transformations thus are one way to use substantive content and meaning to influence the standardization procedure. The semantic transformation mapping provides a nice visual device for illustrating what that mapping looks like.

## Conclusion

A main point and purpose behind the semantic transformations discussed in the previous chapter was to map substantive meaning onto numeric values. Standardization occurs because now everything is on the [0, 1] scale. High on each dimension is mapped to high on the other dimensions. However, instead of high being evaluated in terms of empirical distributions, it is evaluated in substantive terms.

It is extremely common for researchers to sum nominal or ordinal indicators to form an index of a concept: *this is not strictly speaking valid.* One needs to make the argument that these nominal or ordinal variables are in fact interval. Similarly, scholars like to multiply or divide variables to form indices: *this is not valid unless the variables are ratio.*

The key issue for nominal variables is whether in fact they are nominal and not ordinal. If there exists an underlying conceptual continuum then one needs to explore how the numeric values in the scale—ordinal, interval, or ratio—relate to the underlying conceptual continuum. The fuzzy-logic approach to semantic transformations permits a framing of this problem that makes clear what is going on. As illustrated in the semantic transformation figures, one should explicitly map the scale to a basic conceptual continuum.

The previous chapter essentially assumed interval or ratio variables when discussing semantic transformations. Here the critical point is dealing with ordered dichotomous data as well as ordinal scales. In particular, ordinal scales are tricky: this is true in statistics as much as in conceptualization. The semantic mapping methodology provides one way to convert these ordinal scales into the [0, 1] common scale, which can be used for aggregation and other purposes.

In the multidimensional and multilevel concept setting one has no choice but to standardize. So the question is how to do this in a manner that is as faithful as possible to the underlying meanings of the categories and often their implied distance from each other.

In order to aggregate—the topic of the next chapter—one needs standardized ratio variables. Scaling and standardization decisions are thus critical in the construction of numeric measures of concepts. While these are typically seen as technical decisions and operations—and often noncontroversial—they have semantic consequences. Ideally, ontology, semantics, normative issues, and descriptive accuracy should motivate and determine scaling and standardization decisions.

# 6

# Concept Structure

AGGREGATION AND
SUBSTITUTABILITY

## Introduction

The basic framework, figure 6.1, provides a methodology for analyzing and creating multilevel and multidimensional concepts and their connection to measurement. It outlines the core structural decisions that must be made in getting to a final numeric measure of a concept.

In the literature—e.g., on composite indicators—many of these decisions fall under the rubric of aggregation. This chapter addresses many traditional issues dealing with aggregation. However, as always, terminology is important. These "aggregation" decisions in fact are decisions about the *structure* of the concept. I prefer the term concept structure to aggregation; however, if the reader prefers aggregation that often works as well.

Virtually all of the literature on "composite" indices assumes a multidimensional structure. This dimensional structure generates the problem discussed in the previous two chapters of getting a common scale for these dimensions. The multilevel nature of the basic framework is much less clear in the methodological literature on composite indices. If one were to diagram the many—if not virtually all—global indices they would have at least three levels, if not more.

The basic framework has a fractal character. While there are many question marks in the figure, the basic fractal character consists of

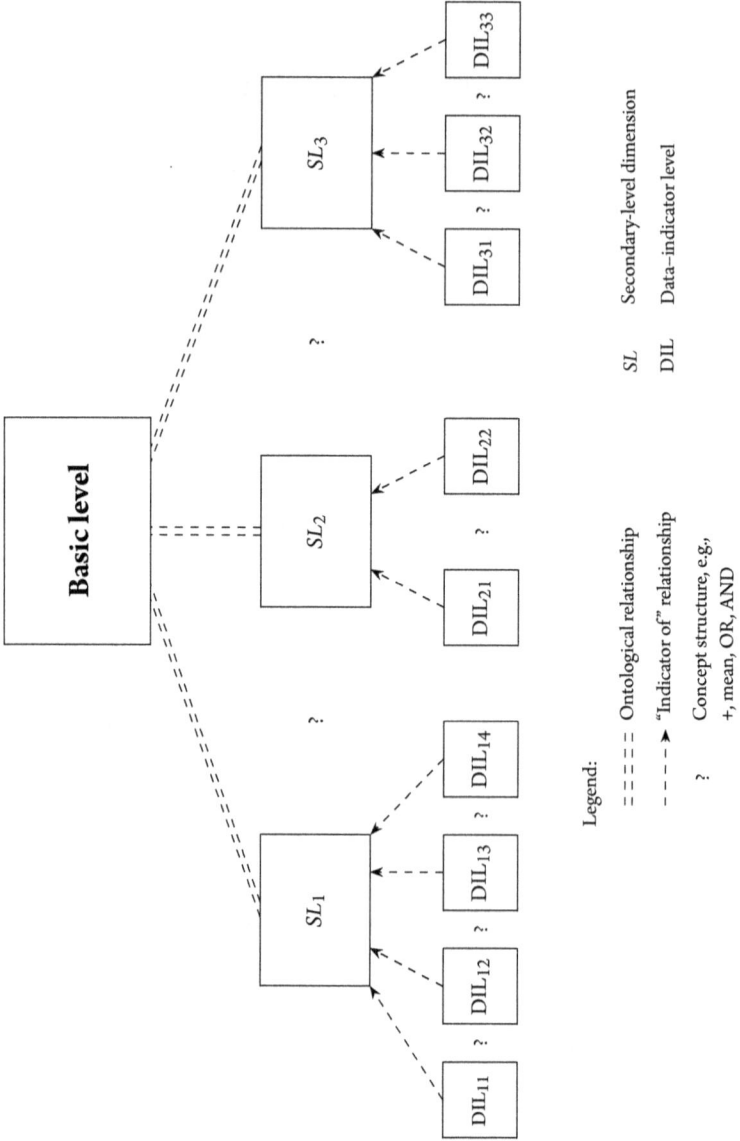

FIGURE 6.1. The basic three-level framework: concept structure and aggregation.

Legend:

= = = = Ontological relationship

- - -▶ "Indicator of" relationship

? Concept structure, e.g., +, mean, OR, AND

*SL* Secondary-level dimension

DIL Data–indicator level

just one question mark. Any time there are two or more boxes that lead upward to another box there are structural decisions. Thus the simplest is when one is linking just two indicators or dimensions. The basic structural decisions and features do not really change from two to some larger number. The number of dimensions really matters when one is in the weakest link or best shot classes of aggregation because of the nature of substitutability. But the basic fractal character of concept structure means that the basic issues apply when there are only two dimensions or indicators.

Concept structure typically means using the same function, e.g., addition or the logical AND, for all secondary-level dimensions or all indicators of a secondary-level dimension. However, there is nothing to prevent one from having some of the "?" at the secondary level in figure 6.1 be ANDs and some be ORs, or some be $+$'s and some $*$'s (addition or multiplication). The next chapter explores these "hybrid" concept structures. We will see that they seem particularly appropriate for gray zone concepts. For the purposes of this chapter, however, I follow the aggregation literature and assume that the aggregation operator is the same for all the factors being aggregated at a given level.

The basic framework makes the secondary level the ontological, definitional, constitutive level. For this reason the relationship between the secondary level and the basic level *always* uses the dashed equal signs to signal this ontological relationship. As discussed in chapter 1, key are the Completeness and the Redundancy Guidelines. In general this chapter assumes that the concept is complete.

Redundancy, however, is absolutely central to the whole chapter, because redundancy is all about substitutability. The Continuum Guideline suggests always thinking about the underlying continuum of a concept. The central underlying continuum of concept structure is substitutability. The key question is the extent to which high values on one dimension substitute for low values on the other. The substitutability continuum has three core regions. At the bottom are "weakest link" structures, where the default is the minimum, but there are weakest link measures that allow less substitutability than the minimum. At the opposite end of the spectrum lie the "best shot" structures, for which the maximum is the default. These allow for very high levels of substitutability. In the middle zone lies the "mean" aggregation *class*, which allows for some substitutability between dimensions. Of course, the average is the default mean aggregation procedure in this zone. This chapter introduces systematically these three classes of concept structures.

Core to the framework is that it is multilevel. These levels can play different roles in conceptualization and measurement. This is perhaps one of the main reasons that my approach differs from the general literature on composite indices. In this literature there is no distinction between the ontological secondary level and the data–indicator level. Any World Bank, Eurostat, or OECD publication on the methods of composite or multidimensional indicators has a section on aggregation, but almost never anything about different and multiple levels with different aggregation strategies.

Connecting the data–indicator level and the secondary level in figure 6.1 is the "indicator of" relationship. In general, the Completeness and Redundancy Guidelines do not apply here. In fact, it is often the opposite: indicators are ideally redundant, i.e., measures of the same thing. One does not want a "complete" set of indicators, but a reasonable number of good (e.g., highly correlated) indicators.

The mathematics must be in sync with the structure of the concept and how the different levels incorporate different logics of aggregation. This is why one must stress that the basic framework is multilevel as well as multidimensional.

This chapter provides an introduction to the core issues of aggregation, as well as some of the common methods of aggregation. The chapter does not require a lot of mathematical background. The goal is to provide the intuitions and logics behind aggregation decisions, which often appear quite technical. As with all concepts, these "technical" decisions have semantic, descriptive, causal, and normative dimensions that should drive the technical ones.

Chapter 9 discusses the impact of structural decisions on description in the sense of how many or few cases are coded to have nonzero membership in the concept. Structure essentially determines how strong or lenient the concept is in terms of including cases of the concept.

A "restrictive" definition of poverty defines fewer cases of poverty, a less restrictive definition allows more cases. Historically in philosophy and political science, this becomes the issue of intension–extension: How does the structure of a concept relate to its empirical coverage?

This chapter assumes that one has solved the problems of a common scale discussed in previous chapters and that everything lies in the [0, 1] interval. Hence we have ratio, real numbers, and no worries about permissible operations on dimensions or indicators.

In short, this chapter provides an introduction to the issues of concept structure and is intended to provide a set of tools for scholars and researchers to evaluate their own structural decisions and those that lie at the heart of all complex concepts and measures. The goal is to encourage researchers to decide first on the core structure of the concept, its substantive content, and the key nature of relationships in that structure. *Then* one can explore the structures and mathematical options that fit well with the concept structure and content.

## Weakest Link Concept Structures

The philosophy approach to conceptualization originates with Aristotle and continues today in mathematical logic textbooks. The basic notion is that a good definition or conceptualization gives the necessary conditions, i.e., secondary-level dimensions, that are necessary and jointly sufficient to be a member of the concept.

The "weakest link" class of concept structures uses the metaphor of the weakest link in the chain as the measure of how strong the chain is. It is related to the intersection in Boolean algebra (e.g., Alkire et al. 2015 refer to it as the intersection aggregation function). The minimum fits nicely with the weakest link metaphor: the strength of the chain is the minimum of the strengths of all the links. In addition to being the metaphor used in the literature on the production of public goods, it has been widely used in the liberal peace literature (Dixon 1994 first introduced this idea into the debate, which then became completely standard practice). In fuzzy logic the weakest link constitutes a *class* of aggregation procedures that has the minimum as its largest value. This is discussed below in some detail.

In some substantive areas the weakest link is the default concept structure and so when structure is not specified one can often assume that it is of the weakest link sort. That is certainly true in conceptual discussions in a philosophical vein. In political science, it appears in many a qualitative methods' syllabus via Sartori's classic article. For reasons that are a little unclear to me, the weakest link structure seems to be quite popular in constructing data sets. Typically, a potential observation must satisfy all the coding rules (the sufficiency condition) and if it fails on one coding rule it is excluded from the population (i.e., necessity). See Sambanis's (2004) survey of civil war concepts and data sets for examples.

Democracy is a core ongoing example in this volume. The conceptual literature—ignoring the empirical implementation—on democracy most often uses the weakest link structure to think about democracy. This is explicitly true for the Democracy–Dictatorship group (Cheibub et al. 2010), also true of the conceptual background of the Polity measure, and explicitly in the case of Dahl's influential discussions (e.g., 1956; 1998) of democracy. A large portion of political philosophy deals with democracy and it too, usually implicitly, applies the weakest link structure for democracy. The weakest link concept structure is thus extremely common in conceptual, ontological, and definitional analyses.

The previous edition of this book contained a whole chapter dealing with this particular problem, using the example of democracy. This chapter has been cut from this edition, not because it is no longer valid, but because of space considerations. With very few exceptions, democracy is conceptualized via the philosophy approach with its implied weakest link aggregation procedure. In practice, sums and means are frequently used to measure democracy. That chapter took the Polity measure of democracy, which is conceptualized in necessary and sufficient condition terms, and redid the measurement model so that it was consistent with the conceptual structure. A major part of the chapter was exploring and comparing systematic differences between a measurement model that is consistent with the concept and the inconsistent Polity measure. It showed that simultaneously they were pretty highly correlated but systematically different in important ways.

Wuttke and his colleagues (2020) provide a very nice recent example of this kind of analysis. They discuss the currently very important topic of populist attitudes and more generally the concept of populism. As with democracy they note that it is typically conceptualized as a multidimensional concept using necessary and sufficient conditions: "Most scholars now concur that populist attitudes denote a multidimensional construct, composed of two or more concept components" (p. 1) and that "populism scholars uphold that the distinct conceptual characteristic of populism at the mass level is the concept's status as an attitudinal syndrome, which is defined in terms of necessary and sufficient conditions, more specifically by the simultaneous presence of the concept's constituent components." However, in terms of empirical operationalization, "scholars obtain individual populism scores by computing weighted or unweighted averages across the concept dimensions. More specifically, scholars aggregate the concept attributes manually by computing mean values or using data-driven approaches such as factor analysis" (p. 2). They then explore the nontrivial empirical and statistical consequences of constructing a populism measure faithful to the semantic structure of the concept.

Given the top-down, semantic view of conceptualization and measurement defended here, the key guideline is obvious:

Structural Consistency Guideline: If the concept is defined or constituted via a necessary and sufficient condition logic then that needs to be applied in aggregation.

One could decide to use averaging aggregation and then go back and change the conceptualization and ontology. This is the cart driving the horse. Conceptualization should drive aggregation and measurement, not the other way around.

In the pure weakest link model there is no substitutability. Ordinarily, when scholars use the term "necessary condition" they are explicitly, or more often implicitly, thinking in terms of dichotomous concepts.

However, with fuzzy logic as well as public goods production functions we can have continuous variables. With continuous variables we can address two core questions of concept structure: (1) the relative weight of the dimensions and (2) substitutability between dimensions.

The advantage of fuzzy logic or public goods production functions is that often it is hard to wrap one's head around the idea that some necessary conditions are more important than others. After all, they are each *necessary*. So while weighted means are easy and obvious, weighting necessary conditions is definitely not.

The easiest way to think of weakest link aggregation is as being like multiplication—assuming as always that all dimensions and indicators lie in the [0, 1] interval. The V-Dem project illustrates the link between necessary condition logic and multiplication. They define a measure of democracy following this logic:

> What we call the Multiplicative Polyarchy Index (MPI) is following this necessary condition logic: MPI = (Elected Officials) * (Clean Elections) * (Associational Autonomy * Suffrage) * (Freedom of Expression and Alternative Source of Information) [where all factors lie in [0, 1]]. A low score on *any* of the component indices thus suppresses the value of the overall index. (Teorell et al. 2019, 81)

One can define general weakest link aggregation as a function of the $D_i$ where $f(D_i) = 0$ when any $D_i = 0$. The minimum satisfies this since the chain has no strength if one of the links is broken.

More generally, we can extend this idea to continuous variables where 0 and 1 are the two extremes. Then we want aggregation functions with the following properties, assuming continuous nondecreasing functions:

$$C = f(D_1, D_2, \ldots), \quad D_i \in [0, 1], \quad \text{where } C = \begin{cases} 0 & \text{when any } D_i = 0, \\ 1 & \text{when all } D_i = 1. \end{cases}$$
$$(6.1)$$

The "ideal point" would be something that scores the maximum, i.e., 1, on all dimensions, giving us the maximum value of C, which is 1.0.

TABLE 6.1. A simple weakest link function.

| $D_1$ | $D_2$ | $C$ |
|---|---|---|
| 1 | 1 | 1 |
| 1 | 0 | 0 |
| 0 | 1 | 0 |
| 0 | 0 | 0 |

Throughout this chapter I use $D$ to indicate secondary-level dimensions or indicators, while using $C$ for the aggregated level, i.e., $D$ refers to dimensions–indicators, while $C$ refers to concepts. I do this to eliminate any kind of causal implications of notation using $X$ or $Y$.

The obvious example of such a model, but not the only choice, uses a multiplicative form. Such a model satisfies the fundamental requirement for a multivariate weakest link utility function, that a poor score on one dimension makes the overall value low. Hence, a basic model is

$$C = D_1 * D_2 * D_3. \tag{6.2}$$

This emphasizes that multiplication often characterizes weakest link aggregation functions. If we take the $D_i$ as dichotomous variables we get table 6.1. This is of course exactly the V-Dem example above.[1]

Equation (6.2) implicitly weights each dimension equally. This is of course one option, but probably not semantically, empirically, or causally accurate. Some goals are more important than others. Thinking of aggregation in terms of utility functions, reelection may be more important than policy goals; winning the war may be more important than the rules of war. Some goals are just more important than others. However, one can easily give differential weights to each dimension by

---

1. The Gini Index can be seen as basically a weakest link concept: Gini $= 1 - (1/N^2 \mu) *$ $\sum_{i=1}^{N} \sum_{j=1}^{N} \min(y_i, y_j)$, where $\mu$ is the mean. This version means that inequality is a function of the worst off of the two, a weakest link idea. The same logic is used in democratic peace literature for comparing two nations. See Sen (1973) for a nice discussion of the various ways to formulate the Gini Index.

adding parameters as exponents, giving us

$$C = D_1^{\beta_1} * D_2^{\beta_2} * D_3^{\beta_3}. \tag{6.3}$$

Equation (6.3) expresses this through different values of $\beta_i$. Since all the $D_i$ lie in the interval $[0, 1]$, if $\beta_i > 1$ then this goal is more important, since it reduces the overall evaluation more than dimensions with $\beta = 1$: e.g., $0.25 = (0.5)^2 < (0.5)^1$. If $D_i$ is a less important factor, then $\beta < 1$: e.g., $0.71 = (0.5)^{0.5} > (0.5)^1$. In this case the impact of a low $D_i$ is mitigated; its impact on the whole is not so severe. If all the $\beta_i = 1$ then we have equal weights for all parameters and equation (6.3) reduces to equation (6.2).

The limiting case of $\beta_i = 0$ provides a test of the importance of a given dimension since $\beta_i = 0$ means that $D_i^{\beta_i} = D_i^0 = 1$, $D_i \neq 0$. This says that $D_i$ has no impact on the overall evaluation: regardless of the actual value of $D_i$ (except for 0, when it is undefined), its contribution to the overall value is always the maximum, 1.

The noncompensatory model presented in equation (6.3) *does not* decompose into simple bivariate effects, as would be the case in additive utility functions. The only clear-cut bivariate effect occurs when $D_i$ equals 0.

If one were an economist, one would naturally turn to the Cobb–Douglas production function. Equation (6.3) is quite familiar to economists: it is the classic Cobb–Douglas production function, which has a venerable history going back to the 1920s (Cobb and Douglas 1928). As its name indicates, it models the production of (industrial) goods as a mixture of inputs, where the $D_i$ are capital and labor:

$$C = \alpha D_1^{\beta} D_2^{1-\beta}, \quad \beta \geq 0, \quad \alpha > 0. \tag{6.4}$$

It is clear that this is the sort of model described above.[2]

2. In the special case of $(\beta_1 + \beta_2 + \beta_3) = 1$ the function is said to be linearly homogeneous. This is actually the most common expression of the Cobb–Douglas production function in economics. Used in such a form, Cobb–Douglas statistical models are tested with restricted least squares (Greene 1993, 211–16).

Weakest link models have two key characteristics. The first is that they are nonlinear. Both the multiplicative form and the parameters in the exponents make the model very nonlinear. Secondly, the model is interactive in nature. A change in one variable (say from near 1 to near 0) can have a dramatic impact on the whole.

Figure 6.2 illustrates graphically some weakest link functions, and many of the points of this section. Within fuzzy logic (see any fuzzy-logic mathematics textbook) the minimum is the largest value of the class of weakest link aggregation functions. This means that in figure 6.2 weakest link aggregation surfaces all lie below the minimum. An example of this would be the product surface in the figure that lies below the minimum.

Critical in the theory of weakest link functions (causal as well as con-ceptual) is that each necessary dimension acts as a *ceiling* on the value of the whole aggregation. The metaphor of a ceiling or related ideas, e.g., veto players (Tsebelis 2002) means that one is in the domain of weakest link functions. The key point is that *a low value on one dimension con-strains the whole function*. A glass ceiling constrains how high women can go in a profession. Weakest link aggregation connects directly to constraint theories. These constraints can be called "ceiling effects" (Goertz et al. 2013).[3]

The ceiling effects appear when you fix either $D_1$ or $D_2$ at some value. If you fix $D_1 = d_1$ then the "ceiling effect" is the maximum value of $C$ that one can attain when $d_2 = 1$; this is the maximum utility one can get for that fixed value of $d_1$. Notice that when $D_1$ is small the noncompen-satory effect can be dramatic: at the limit when $D_1 = 0$, no matter what $D_2$ is then $C = 0$. In contrast, if $D_1$ is large (i.e., near 1), a lot depends then on the value of $D_2$.

3. For those interested in an extended discussion and methodology for looking at the ceiling and constraining effects of necessary conditions, I recommend the NCA (necessary condition analysis) methodology developed by Jan Dul, http://www.erim. eur.nl/necessary-condition-analysis/. This methodology describes various ways of calculating the ceilings and then evaluating their restraining effect, including probabilistic tests for these estimated ceilings.

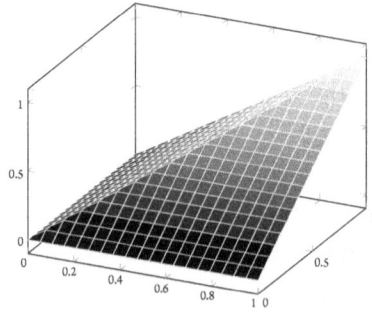

Minimum

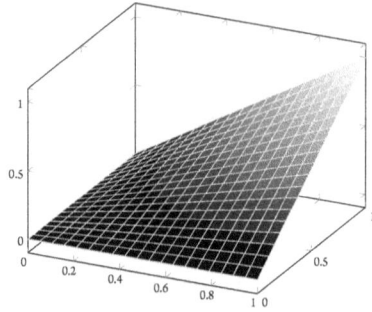

Product

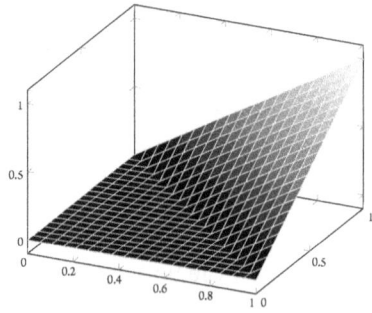

Threshold, $\max(0, D_1 + D_2 - 1)$

FIGURE 6.2. Weakest link concept
structures and aggregation functions.

These various examples show that the idea of weakest link and ceiling effects models make intuitive sense. Key are low values on central goals because they have a large impact on the overall utility function. This makes sense of the idea that because they are key goals we should, and are, hesitant to permit big compensatory effects. We *want*, if possible, something that scores relatively high on all our key ends. These weakest link functions put into mathematical form some deeply held intuitions.

Swiss decision-making about their nuclear bomb shelters provides a nice little illustration of how noncompensatory decision-making works in practice (Schärlig 1985).[4] Switzerland evaluated each feature of a nuclear shelter in a point system as follows: very good = 1, good = 2, usable = 5, and bad = 40. Defense officials' overall evaluation of shelters used the sum of ten criteria coded using this system. The decision rule was to use the sum of the ten criteria (so larger means worse) with the ordinal categorization scheme 10–11: very good, 12–20: good, 21–50: useable, and > 50: bad. As one can see, bad on any dimension basically means the shelter is virtually unusable. If one dimension is bad, i.e., 40, and the other nine are all very good, the total is 49. So if one dimension is bad the shelter is just barely "usable."

In the literature on decision-making, weakest link aggregation functions are known as noncompensatory decision-making models (e.g., Mintz 1993). If one examines bureaucratic and legal decision-making rules often there exist "requirements," "prerequisites," "sine qua non," "essential," or "veto" conditions that must be fulfilled. These all imply weakest link decision-making procedures (or as we will see in the next chapter, hybrid structures). Another class of weakest link procedures lies in constraints: a strong constraint must be satisfied; it is a necessary condition.

For each weakest link aggregation function we can ask the degree of substitutability across dimensions. With these highly nonlinear functions, substitutability varies not only with the size of the parameters but can change significantly as the values of $D_i$ change. Cobb–Douglas

---

4. I have lived in Switzerland on and off for a number of years and so I like this example.

illustrates this nicely: there is no substitutability when either factor is 0; the degree of substitutability increases as $D_i$ increases. For those interested in the details of this, any economics or calculus textbook provides a mathematical analysis. Weakest link language occurs naturally in the discussion of production functions, notably in the Cobb–Douglas context (e.g., Chambers's 1988 discussion of the "essentiality" of factors of production).

In short, there exists a class of weakest link aggregation functions, illustrated in figure 6.2, that can be used in concept structures. In practice they appear much more often at the secondary level than the data–indicator level. The philosophy approach emphasizes that conceptualization needs to be complete. Implicit is that each defining dimension is very important—otherwise it would not be there—which in practice means necessary. The philosophy approach also implements the nonredundancy, which tends to imply nonsubstitutability. This makes the weakest link a natural choice for secondary-level concept structures.

## Best Shot Concept Structures

Best shot aggregation in many ways is the opposite of the weakest link class structure for concepts. The weakest link is characterized by the minimum, multiplication, and intersection. The best shot is characterized by the maximum, sum, and union. The term "best shot" comes from the economics literature on the production of public goods (e.g., Sandler 1992).

A good example of a simple best shot rule for teachers would be that if a student gets an A on the final exam, they get an A for the whole course. In terms of substitutability, a good grade on the final substitutes for all the bad grades received during the semester.[5]

---

5. In my large Introduction to International Relations class I have used a variant on this whereby a bad grade in the first exam can be completely substituted for by high grades in the rest of the class. I tell them that they can skip the first exam and get a zero if they like and can still get an A.

Teorell et al. use this for part of their measure of democracy: "Since these are considered perfect substitutes (either a directly elected president or a president elected by a directly elected parliament suffices), the index value is arrived at by taking the maximum value of the two" (2019, 78). In short, in the substitutability continuum the weakest link implements no substitutability, while the best shot represents complete substitutability.

The generalized mean approaches the maximum from below so there is no bright line dividing the two. No surprise, there is a gray zone between the mean and the best shot as well as between the generalized mean and the weakest link. The key feature is that at the extreme, a high level on one dimension *completely* substitutes for low values on *all* other dimensions. It is symmetrically similar to the weakest link in that for the weakest link, a low value on one dimension trumps high values on all other dimensions.

According to the concept, literature, and tradition this might seem quite odd, indefensible, and the like, or quite common. For example, in the literature on public goods the best shot is a commonly discussed and used aggregation function.

Within fuzzy logic the best shot constitutes a class of aggregation functions bounded from below by the maximum. Figure 6.3 illustrates some best shot aggregation functions. Not surprisingly they mirror the weakest link ones. Since the maximum is the smallest best shot function, this means that all best shot functions lie above the maximum. This is analogous to weakest link functions lying below the minimum. At $D_1 = 1$ or $D_2 = 1$ everything is attached to the axes at the top. In contrast, for the weakest link they are attached at the bottom.

Analogously to the weakest link, if one $D_i = 1$, then $f(D_i) = 1$ no matter what the values of the other $D_i$. The maximum (union or logical OR) constitutes the default best shot structure. One can define best shot aggregation functions, assuming a nondecreasing, continuous function, as

$$C = f(D_1, D_2, \ldots), \quad D_i \in [0, 1], \quad \text{where } C = 1 \text{ when any } D_i = 1.$$
$$(6.5)$$

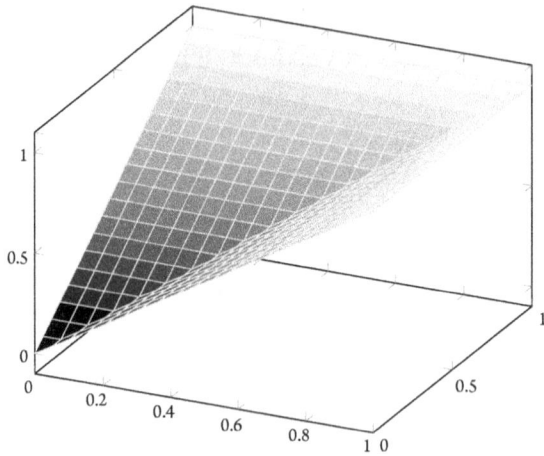

Maximum

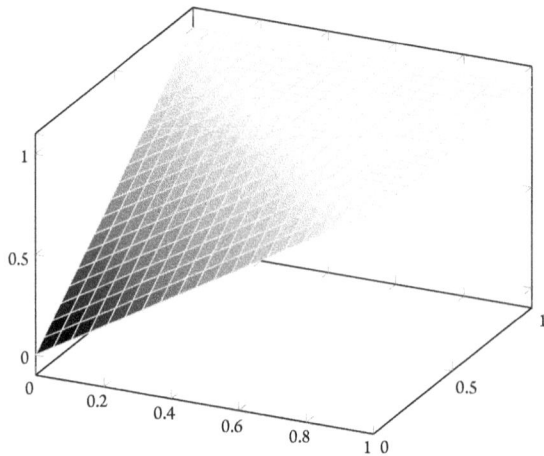

Best shot–sum threshold: $\min(D_1 + D_2, 1)$

FIGURE 6.3. Best shot concept structures and
aggregation functions.

Militarized international conflict and peace are my main substantive interests. The best shot is a common aggregation procedure in this substantive area. For example, "militarized disputes" (aka MIDs) are constituted by multiple militarized incidents. Thus, to arrive at a value for the severity of a militarized dispute one needs to aggregate over the severity of militarized incidents. The uncontested (as far as I can tell) procedure is to take the maximum level of severity of the incidents as the severity of the overall militarized dispute. Another common variable is military alliances: a country can have multiple military alliances with other countries; the strongest one is applied in statistical analyses. The same applies for multiple IGO memberships: the strongest one is used. These conventions in conflict research apply a best shot rule.

One thing to note about all these conventionalized decisions is that the sum is a plausible alternative to best shot aggregation, but the mean is not. The substantive logic is that, for example, multiple alliance commitments are stronger than one alliance commitment. If one were to take the mean then one would have the counterintuitive result that the overall alliance commitment is less than the strongest one.

Any concept for which the sum makes a lot of sense falls into the realm of best shot aggregation functions. One of my favorite examples is that of the welfare state. The concept of a welfare state refers to a set of services that the state provides to individuals and families. These constitute the secondary-level dimensions of the welfare state concept. Following the Usual Suspects Guideline these usually include traditional (i.e., dating back to the 19th and early 20th centuries) services–goods like unemployment insurance, healthcare, workman's compensation, and retirement benefits. In terms of measurement and data these goods are measured by the *sum* of government expenditures in these areas. A big welfare state is one that spends a lot *in total* for these services. Equivalent welfare states can spend a lot on health or a lot on retirement. At the extremes they can spend nothing on one service if they provide a lot on another. Typical of best shot aggregation, one dimension can completely substitute for another.

## Thresholds

The best shot structure is closely related to thresholds. A simple way this occurs is via family resemblance and *m*-of-*n* aggregation rules. The *m*-of-*n* rule says that if one has at least *m* of *n* possible features then it is a member of the concept C. This is a family resemblance approach because no dimension is necessary: the absence of any feature can be compensated for by the presence of other features. Chapter 9 discusses the family resemblance idea in more detail, particularly within philosophy where it was seen as challenging the necessary and sufficient condition, mathematical logic approach to concepts. In terms of substitutability, the $m$-of-$n$ rule ranges from high levels of substitutability, i.e., 1-of-$n$, to no substitutability when the rule is $n$-of-$n$.

For example, the EU utilizes the $m$-of-$n$ rule to assess whether someone is "materially deprived." This is part of the larger concept of the "risk of poverty and social exclusion."

> EU: Material deprivation rate
> Share of population living in households lacking at least 3 items among the following 9 items: The household could not afford: i) to face unexpected expenses, ii) one week annual holiday away from home, iii) to pay for arrears (mortgage or rent, utility bills or hire purchase installments), iv) a meal with meat, chicken or fish every second day, v) to keep home adequately warm, or could not afford (even if wanted to): vi) a washing machine, vii) a color TV, viii) a telephone, ix) a personal car. (European Commission 2009, 19)

Absence of one form of deprivation can be compensated for by another form of deprivation.

Equation (6.5) implies a 1-of-$n$ rule. This is a best shot rule. One can see how overall substitutability decreases as $m$ decreases. In the case of the EU and material deprivation this means that more and more people will be considered deprived as the number of deprivation items ($m$) decreases (this is the core issue of chapter 9 on the relationship between concept structure and empirical coverage).[6]

The EU uses the same $m$-of-$n$ strategy to aggregate the secondary-level dimensions to the basic-level "risk of poverty and social exclusion."

---

6. As an interesting terminology example, "severe" material deprivation requires 4 instead of 3 of the 9 (EU Social Protection Committee 2012).

If the individual has 1 of the 3 secondary-level dimensions then they pass the threshold and are considered at risk. While I have not searched too hard, I have seen no specific justification for the 3-of-9 rule for material deprivation or the 1-of-3 rule for the basic-level concept of risk of poverty and social exclusion.

Marks et al. (2017) constitute a population of "authoritative IGOs" with a relatively high threshold. They have 7 defining features of an authoritative IGO. To be included an IGO must have 6-of-7. Thus out of a candidate population of several hundred IGOs they end with only about 70. When one reaches the $n$-of-$n$ rule, one has in effect arrived at the weakest link end of the spectrum: each attribute is necessary and they are jointly sufficient for inclusion.

One way to link the $m$-of-$n$ rule to the best shot class is via the common fuzzy-logic OR-union rule

$$C = \min\left(1, \sum_{i=1}^{n} D_i\right), \quad D_i \in [0, 1]. \tag{6.6}$$

This illustrates how the sum often fits within a best shot logic. The intuition is that once we have "enough" then one is over the threshold and $C = 1$.

This should look familiar since it is the way consumption measures of poverty work: one adds up each consumption dimension, i.e., $D_i$, and when it reaches the poverty line [i.e., 1 in equation (6.6)] then it is not-in-poverty for all values above the threshold.

Mahoney and I used exactly this idea in our discussion of the causal logic of Skocpol's *States and social revolutions* (see chapter 10 of the previous edition of this book). The causal logic was that there needed to be a sufficient causal impact of the "data–indicator" variables to produce the secondary-level variables—peasant revolt or state breakdown. However, for each case it was a different combination of causal factors that did the job of generating a causal impact above the threshold for the secondary-level causal variables.

The concept of a welfare state illustrates this approach. There is no one service that a state *must* (necessarily) provide to be a welfare state, but if the state produces "enough" of these services we classify it in the welfare state category. Operationally, Hicks (1999) defines a welfare state circa 1930 as one that provides at least 3 of the 4 following services: (1) unemployment compensation, (2) old age pensions, (3) health insurance, or (4) workman's compensation.

In the context of decision-making, Herbert Simon's famous concept of satisficing implies a threshold of a "sufficient" alternative:

> An alternative "satisfices" … if it meets aspirations along all dimensions (attributes). If no such alternative is found, a search is undertaken for new alternatives. Meanwhile, aspirations along one or more dimensions drift down gradually until a satisfactory new alternative is found or some existing alternative satisfices. (Simon 1996, 30)

Thresholds for inclusion in the philosophy approach follow the logic of sufficient conditions. QCA can be seen as a threshold methodology that determines what combination of conditions is sufficient for the outcome to occur.

There is one rule of thumb that often seems to connect the number of defining features to the choice of a family resemblance rule on the substitutability continuum. It seems in practice that when the number of constituting dimensions is small, e.g., 2–5, then one uses the strict weakest link rule: one must have all $n$ attributes present. But as the number of constituting features increases, one is more likely to allow some modest level of substitutability. One can see the logic of this. A rule with many dimensions and using the strict weakest link rule may end up excluding "too many" cases from the population. One relaxes this by allowing modest substitutability: the Marks et al. (2017) 6-of-7 rule for authoritative IGOs illustrates this.

Notice that both the best shot and weakest link classes have threshold variants as illustrated in figures 6.2 and 6.3. Obviously, these thresholds can be varied as well as the functions above or below the threshold. For example, one could have curvilinear (e.g., power functions) variation above or below the threshold.

Clearly, whether the threshold should be high or low depends on the theoretical, substantive, normative, causal, and empirical considerations. The choice of a threshold will usually influence causal inference and statistical analyses. One can think of increasing thresholds as populations that are subsets of each other. The population with a high threshold is a subset of the population with a lower threshold.

## Mean Structures

The middle class of aggregation procedures involves variation on the mean. In many areas, e.g., global indices, some version of the mean is a common aggregation procedure. Since it is so common my discussion will be brief.

As with the weakest link and best shot, mean aggregation is a class of aggregation procedures. This is best thought of in terms of the generalized mean. The generalized mean of the positive real numbers $D_1, \ldots, D_n$ is defined by

$$C = \left( \frac{1}{N} \sum_{i=1}^{N} D_i^{\beta} \right)^{1/\beta}, \quad \beta \in [-\infty, +\infty]. \tag{6.7}$$

This becomes the simple average when $\beta = 1$ and ordinary least squares with $\beta = 2$.

Figure 6.4 graphically shows the two most common mean aggregation functions: the simple average and the OLS–Euclidean distance.

As shown by equation (6.7), $\beta = 1$ and $\beta = 2$ lie in the middle of the generalized mean class. In terms of substitutability they have neither high nor low levels of substitutability. The extremes of the generalized mean touch the neighboring class. When $\beta = -\infty$ one gets the minimum–weakest link and when $\beta = \infty$ it is the maximum–best shot. Because the quadratic mean ($\beta = 2$) moves in the best shot direction, that curve in figure 6.4 lies above the mean curve (or is identical when all dimensions have the same value).

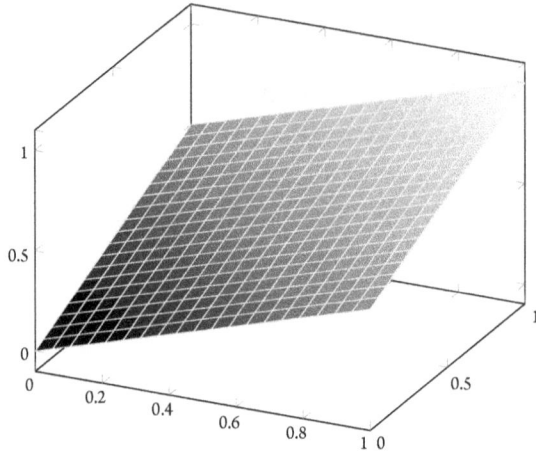

Mean, $\beta = 1$, $((D_1^1 + D_2^1)/2)^1$

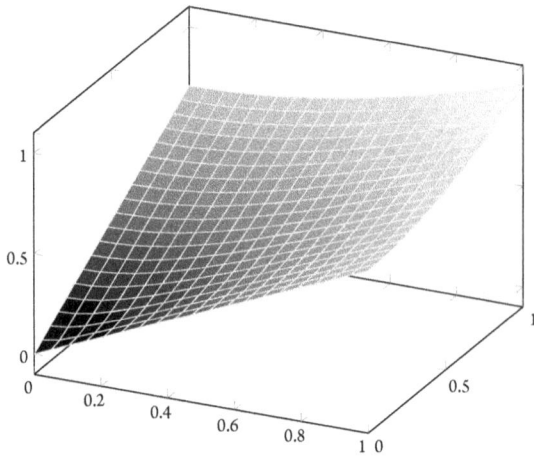

Quadratic mean (least squares), $\beta = 2$, $((D_1^2 + D_2^2)/2)^{1/2}$

FIGURE 6.4. Mean concept structures and aggregation functions.

The V-Dem project illustrates the connection between the mean and moderate substitutability in their measure of democracy: "Assuming that the extent to which the chief executive and the legislature are elected work as partial substitutes, we average the two" (Teorell et al. 2019, 79).

In contrast, it is hard to find examples in global indices where scholars have moved in the best shot direction, e.g., using $\beta \geq 2$. The most obvious choice there would be $\beta = 2$ with its connection to least squares OLS. In fact, options moving toward $+\infty$ are typically not presented at all as plausible options in practice (as opposed to theoretically possible options) when aggregation is discussed.

One of the generic concerns with OLS as a statistical technique is the influence of "outliers." The idea is that these outliers have "too much" influence over the final parameter estimate. This is because, as one is moving in the best shot direction, larger values substitute more and more for smaller ones and have a bigger and bigger impact over the final value. While this is seen as negative in an OLS context, the best shot logic suggests that it might be quite reasonable, depending on the substantive content of the concept.

No surprise, different substantive domains and traditions have different defaults on aggregation. When aggregation is seen as a distance then Euclidean distance becomes the norm. This would be true in the literature on ideal point estimation in political science. Euclidean distance is a value of $\beta = 2$ for the generalized mean, i.e., $C = (D_1^2 + D_2^2)^{1/2}$. This is a nice example because it links the mean class to linear aggregation in general. But it also emphasizes that Euclidean distance is only one among many other distance possibilities discussed in the ideal point–preference estimation literature.

What is less common is a discussion about the measurement logic behind the mean. The mean makes sense when one has *indicators of the same thing*. The mean is basically a unidimensional aggregation operation. One can see this clearly in latent variable approaches. If the indicators are not correlated, the whole methodology does not work. Highly correlated indicators are interpreted to be indicators of one concept.[7]

---

7. There does exist a class of latent variable models where the indicators are considered the cause and which are known generally as "formative" models. Here high correlations are no longer required and in fact these models are used when correlations are low between the indicators; see the appendix to chapter 2.

A good way to see the unidimensional logic of the mean is via the history of measurement and the role of the mean in that history. Classic measurement theory, e.g., in physics, dealt with situations where scientists were trying to measure descriptive features, such as the position and brightness of stars. Multiple *independent* physicists would make measurements of the same star. The question was how to aggregate those measurements into one best estimate of the true value. Assuming independent measurements, the classic theorem in statistics states that the mean of those independent measurements was the best estimate of the true (unmeasured) value.

If one had some measure of the accuracy of each astronomer, one would naturally weight the more accurate observations more heavily. In latent variable analyses those indicators most closely correlated with the unmeasured factor get larger weights. This is exactly the same logic.

An important general misconception is that the mean implements "perfect substitutability." The UNDP says, "Using the arithmetic mean allows perfect substitutability between mean years of schooling and expected years of schooling" (UNDP 2018b, 2) or "The twentieth Human Development Report introduced a new version of the HDI. The main change is that the authors relax the HDI's past assumption of perfect substitutability between its three components" (Ravallion 2016, 85). It is not clear what perfect substitutability means in this literature. Substitutability varies along a continuum: the mean is not "perfect" in any usual sense because it is in the middle of the substitutability continuum. Because of this use of the term "perfect substitutability," I use the term "complete substitutability." The mean offers in fact limited substitutability for reasons discussed above.

At the secondary-dimension level, one often wants nonredundancy between dimensions. However, for the data–indicator level we often want exactly the opposite: we want multiple, redundant, indicators, where redundancy means highly correlated. At the data–indicator level we are basically in a unidimensional setting: we want indicators of a single secondary-level dimension.

When one is using mean aggregation the indicators themselves are basically substitutable. And all things being equal, the more indicators the better, because that will reduce standard errors.

This comes out most clearly in the latent variable approach to measurement. Often one has many indicators of the latent concept, e.g., votes or survey questions regarding the ideology of politicians, voters, or judges. None are essential and the more good ones the better. The underlying logic is that if these are all indicators of the same thing, they should be highly correlated.

What is much less clear is the extent to which the mean makes sense for aggregation at the secondary level. Core to the semantics of definitions is that they are separate constitutive, defining dimensions. Latent variable models can be used to produce individual secondary-level dimensions, but one is still faced with how to aggregate the various latent secondary-level variables into a basic-level score.

In short, the mean along with linear (Euclidean) distances and linear semantic transformations all belong together as a closely related set of techniques for thinking about concepts, aggregation, and measurement. They can be and often are used for aggregation across multiple dimensions or indicators.

## Conclusion

This chapter has provided an overview of the three main aggregation classes for structuring concepts. Figure 6.5 gives a final summary comparison of the three concept-structure classes. The three meet when all the observations have the same value, i.e., on the diagonal; then the maximum, minimum, and mean have the same value. The figure illustrates that as observations begin to vary, these aggregation classes begin to diverge. While not so obvious in the figure, the mean plane cuts through the top ridge of the weakest link and the bottom ridge of the best shot. It really is in the middle between the other two classes.

The weakest link and best shot figures 6.2 and 6.3 also illustrate that one can have threshold versions of them. The global indicator industry

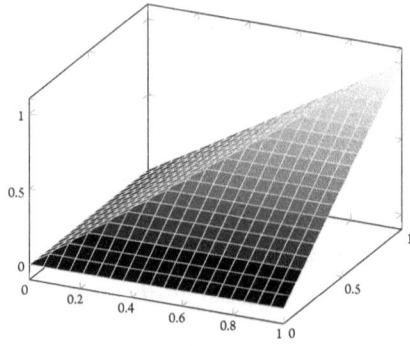

Weakest link: minimum

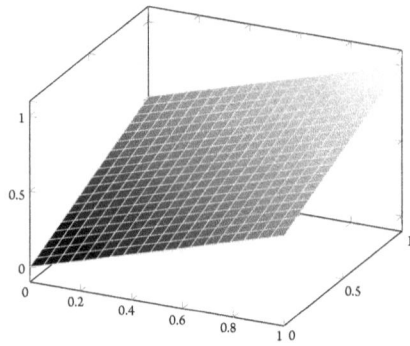

Mean

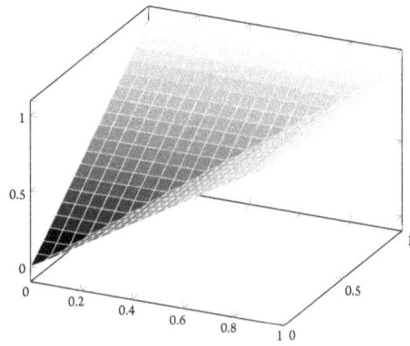

Best shot: maximum

FIGURE 6.5. Three classes of concept structure:
weakest link, mean, best shot.

typically uses best shot threshold functions based on the sum, which produce a ceiling. Weakest link threshold functions are not common, but illustrate a floor threshold.

Different substantive areas as well as academic disciplines—philosophy, political science, sociology, psychology, economics—have different norms about what makes sense in terms of concept structure. A lot depends on the substantive features of the concept in question. The exercises I have developed over the years explore a variety of issues and illustrate the diversity of approaches.

In the basic framework one can use different concept structures for different levels, e.g., best shot at the data–indicator level and weakest link at the secondary level, or the mean at both levels. In practice, some combinations appear particularly popular or make more sense than others. For example, best shot at the secondary level with weakest link at the data–indicator level is rare for concepts (chapter 10 briefly discusses causal models with this structure which are standard in QCA).[8]

A few general tendencies can be described regarding concept structure and aggregation at various levels. At the secondary level—the semantic, ontological level—the two clearest aggregation techniques and often most appropriate structures are the weakest link and best shot. They both apply the Redundancy and Completeness Guidelines.

In contrast, the mean aggregation class makes most sense at the data–indicator level where one is clearly looking for multiple indicators of *one* secondary-level dimension. The second quite common approach to the data–indicator level is to use best shot–threshold aggregation techniques. In contrast, the weakest link often does not make much sense at the data–indicator level.

It is not uncommon to see means used all the way up and down the basic framework. From a semantic and ontological perspective this typically reflects a lack of serious reflection and thought about the

---

8. Wuttke et al. (2020) provide a nice analysis of the same issue where the concept in question is populism, which is typically conceptualized using necessary and sufficient conditions and which is measured using various latent variable models. While the motivation for their analysis is the same as mine, the content is quite different and provides a nice complement.

semantics of the concept and how that relates to aggregation and concept structure. This practice almost always says that the levels are really not very important because the mean is used throughout.

The Multidimensional Poverty Index (MPI; Alkire et al. 2015) illustrates the natural use of threshold–best shot at the data–indicator level. For each of the 10 core indicators there are a variety of different lower-level indicators that are aggregated via the logical OR, maximum, best shot. The 10 core indicators themselves are summed to provide the basic-level index. Here we see the two variants of the best shot—the maximum and the sum—used within one concept and measurement structure.

It should be stressed that these are general tendencies and certainly there are exceptions. The biggest warning is against an unthinking and default use of the mean, when really something else would make more sense.

The previous edition of this book provided a couple of concrete examples of how aggregation decisions can play a key role in causal and statistical analyses. One chapter, on the democratic peace, looked at aggregation options from the weakest link to the best shot, passing through the mean and the geometric mean. In this literature, most were convinced by Dixon (1994) when he argued for weakest link aggregation in order to establish the democracy value for the relationship between two states. Here the aggregation problem was combining the democracy scores of two states into a relationship variable between the two states. Dixon made a convincing theoretical argument that one should use the weakest link. The chapter in the previous edition explored how these aggregation decisions for an independent variable can and did influence the statistical results in a typical liberal peace analysis.

Another chapter in the previous edition looked at the implications of aggregation decisions on the dependent variable of international dispute severity. Often, aggregation decisions produce subset relationships. The empirical example there explored the extent to which choosing a more restrictive conceptualization of the dependent variable, toward the weakest link direction, changes the results compared to a conceptualization more in the direction of the best shot. This produces effects similar to selecting on the dependent variable.

Not surprisingly, as one moves from the weakest link to the best shot, statistical results can quite dramatically change in both settings. Hence, concept-structure decisions are absolutely central and will usually have important impacts on statistical and other kinds of empirical analyses, for both dependent variables as well as independent variables.

The next chapter is devoted to the impact that concept structure and aggregation have on what might be called empirical coverage. Empirical coverage means the number of cases with nonzero membership in the concept. Using exactly the same data, if one uses a weakest link structure there will be fewer empirical cases, while using the best shot will generate more empirical cases. Thus the empirical description of the world can vary dramatically depending on concept structure.

Finally, the choice of concept structure can have massive normative implications. If a given dimension is of central normative importance then one will almost certainly tend to make that a necessary condition in the concept structure. Conversely, if there are substitutes for a given dimension, that almost inherently makes it less important. As opposed to the mean class, the other two classes dramatically give uneven weight to individual dimensions and indicators. This can be driven by normative concerns as with poverty. Conversely, equal treatment suggests other kinds of concept structures. In short, to choose a particular structure is to make a normative choice: there is no "objective, neutral" concept structure.

It would be folly to think that one can make general recommendations that cover the normative, descriptive, and causal uses that concepts serve. More important is that one should construct concepts and use aggregation rules that make sense in the particular substantive, causal, empirical, and normative context. One needs to critically examine defaults and standard operating procedures to see how well they fit the core criteria for conceptualization and measurement.

# 7

# Gray Zone and
# Hybrid Concepts

## Introduction

Chapter 3 stressed that conceptualization should always include a gray zone. While there may well be pragmatic reasons for dichotomization, such as case selection, one should as a default always include a gray zone in concepts. Once the gray zone exists then it can become an object of theoretical and empirical analysis. This chapter explores a variety of issues regarding the ontology, semantics, structure, and measurement of gray zone concepts.[1]

Hybrid concepts often go hand-in-hand with gray zone concepts. Hybridity as discussed in this chapter takes two basic forms. The first form is semantic hybridity: this means that two or more different semantic domains are used to construct the list of defining features.

---

1. One way scholars have thought about the gray zone is via "diminished subtypes." As always, careful attention to terminology can reveal problems. This term is triply problematic: (1) diminished, (2) sub, and (3) types. As discussed at length in chapter 8, the use of nominal typologies is problematic on a variety of dimensions. If one follows the guideline about conceptualizing key concepts specifically, the gray zone is not a "sub" type, but a concept in its own right. The same sort of issue arises with "diminished." For example, the gray zone is more democratic than autocracy and less democratic than full democracy. Using this terminology it could be an "augmented autocracy" as well as "diminished democracy." In short, the diminished subtype methodology is flawed on a variety of dimensions. I do not discuss it further in this volume; for an extended analysis see the previous edition of this book.

Hybridity is much discussed in anthropology and cultural studies as the combination of two different cultures in cultural and postcolonial theory (e.g., Kraidy 2005) or the interaction of international and local in critical peace studies (e.g., Mac Ginty 2010). This chapter discusses as an example hybrid political regimes, e.g., competitive–authoritarian regimes, that have features of autocratic regimes and features of democratic regimes, as well as "semipresidential" which are hybrids of the concept pair parliamentary–presidential.

This chapter argues that there is a very close connection between the gray zone and hybrid concepts. However, it is not a symmetric relationship. Gray zone concepts are often hybrid concepts, and hybrid concepts can be ideal types at a pole of a concept pair. In short, gray zone usually means a hybrid concept structure, but the implication does not run in the other direction.

The hybridity of the gray zone comes out most clearly when the gray zone is in the middle of a concept pair. A core example in this chapter is "semipresidential" political systems. These are a hybrid of parliamentary and presidential systems, which constitute the concept pair. Semipresidential regimes have features of both sides of the concept pair. This is why the gray zone is frequently a hybrid zone: it combines some features, but not all, of each side of the concept pair:

> If we think of parliamentary and presidential government as Weberian ideal types, we must acknowledge that there are numerous regimes that contain some elements of one and some elements of the other, and are thus hybrids. However, not all combinations of these elements qualify a regime as "semipresidential," unless that term is nothing more than a synonym for "hybrid." (Shugart 2005, 325)

The gray zone is then that area between ideal types:

> For our set of cases, we classify countries with popularly elected presidents as taking one of three regime types that capture fundamental differences in presidential authority: the parliamentary (a weak presidency), the mixed (a moderately powerful

presidency), and the true presidential (a powerful presidency)....
Presidential power increases on average from parliamentary to
mixed regimes, as well as from mixed to presidential regimes.
Nevertheless, the index of presidential powers reveals variation
in the size of the presidential prize within each type of regime,
especially true presidential regimes, that the simple trichotomy
obscures. (Hicken and Stoll 2012, 299–300)

Thus the parliamentary–presidential continuum varies on the degree
of presidential powers from zero in the parliamentary system (where
there is no president or the president has basically no power) to the
presidential system where the president has extensive powers.[2]

The second form of hybridity consists of structural hybridity. The
previous chapter focused on homogeneous aggregation operations.
This chapter defines structural hybridity as using some mixture of
different aggregation techniques. This could be different aggregation
techniques at the secondary level or at the data–indicator level. It could
mean using ANDs and ORs together or multiplication and addition
together to aggregate.

The DSM provides a huge number of hybrid concepts in terms of
concept structure. While I have not made a systematic analysis, it is very
normal in the DSM for a disease to have a certain number of required
symptoms and then have an $m$-of-$n$ rule for determining the sufficiency
threshold for the mental disorder.

Gray zone concepts and hybrid structures naturally go together. The
DSM provides a whole set of examples where the positive pole—a
mental disorder—is conceptualized in a hybrid manner. This will be
a key example in illustrating that hybrid structures do not necessarily
imply gray zone concepts.

---

2. Elgie makes the same point: "There is, though, a second definitional controversy. Even
the briefest of glances at the list of countries with semipresidential constitutions based on
the now standard post-Duvergerian definition reveals that it includes some countries with
very strong presidents (e.g., Russia), some with very weak presidents (e.g., Slovenia), and
some where the president has relatively strong but still limited powers (e.g., Romania)" (Elgie
2016, 52).

So in addition to talking about the gray zone, this chapter continues the discussion of the previous chapter on concept structure and aggregation. It assumes the basic ideas discussed in the previous chapter about the features and properties of different concept structures and aggregation techniques.

One interesting feature of the gray zone is the extensive and normal use of negation in the list of defining features. This arises because by definition the gray zone is *not* the positive pole AND *not* the negative pole. Gray zone concepts are often hybrid structures because between these two *nots*, one might use family resemblance structures.

While it is common to think of the gray zone in terms of hybrid concept structures one does not need necessarily to do that. Within each aggregation class one can formulate criteria for the gray zone. For example, using necessary and sufficient conditions, the gray zone appears when some of the necessary conditions are missing, but some are present. For example, if there are three necessary conditions for a "state" then one has gray zone states when one but not all of the necessary conditions is missing. If the territorial-control defining feature is missing then it becomes a *de jure* state. If the state has effective control but not does have international recognition (usually United Nations membership) then it becomes a *de facto* state. All of these cases missing one necessary condition end up in the gray zone.

One of the most important guidelines in chapter 3 was that if the research uses a concept in a hypothesis, then that concept is the positive pole. For example, there are many hypotheses about competitive–authoritarian regimes. Most think that they are at greater risk of civil war than autocratic or democratic regimes. Ideally then, one needs a clear conceptualization of the hybrid concept as a positive pole in its own right instead of an—often linear—interpolation between the poles. In short, one applies the guidelines in chapter 3 to the gray zone concept.

It cannot be stressed too much that while I have associated the gray zone with hybrid concepts, these are really separate issues. In particular, one needs to add hybrid structures to the concept-building toolkit. While the most common practice by far is to use the same aggregation rule for all attributes at a given level, one should always keep the possibility of hybrid structures in mind. In a variety of settings I think that hybrid structures are very good ideas for doing ideal type conceptualization. For example, one could easily have a number of necessary conditions for a low level of democracy and then have a variety of conditions that work in family resemblance style to get to higher levels of democracy. This is exactly the model used by the DSM. Again, the basic framework figure provides a guide for how to think about structural decisions.

## What Is a Hybrid Concept?

### Semantics and Terminology

One form of hybridity involves taking features from two different semantic domains and combining them somehow. In short, it is an important form of hyphenated concept because the terminology includes reference to two concepts. One canonical example of this is "competitive–authoritarian" regimes. "Competitive" refers to democratic, competitive elections, while "authoritarian" indicates features of autocratic regimes that are not democratic.

With hyphenated concepts we have the problem of how to combine concepts on either side of the hyphen. Chapter 3 discussed when adjectives are used to accentuate or attenuate a concept. For example, one might have hypotheses about "very wealthy" countries. "Quality of" concepts are used to push the positive pole further in the ideal type direction. With gray zone hyphenated concepts, the pull is in the opposite direction: the hyphen pulls the concept toward the middle.

I am sometimes tempted to call these hybrid, hyphenated concepts oxymoronic concepts because they include concepts that are semantic opposites, such as competitive–authoritarian. One can see this with terminology that pushes away from the positive pole. This is a common part of natural language, such as "lukewarm" water, which can be defined as "between warm and cool" (Wikipedia).

We can also have a separate term for the gray zone, such as tepid water.

The example of lukewarm is relevant when one thinks about the gray zone in terms of movement away from the positive pole toward the middle. We have the term lukewarm, but not lukecold. One possible terminology for gray zone democracy uses alternatives such as "illiberal democracy."

Another interesting semantic phenomenon involving concept pairs is which side of the pair is chosen for the hybrid. An important example in this chapter as well as the typology chapter is the concept pair of parliamentary–presidential. So what does one call the hybrid regime? The standard term is "semipresidential." Another alternative would be to choose the parliamentary side and have "semiparliamentary," something no one does.

Things are worse with the negative peace gray zone. Here one chooses the peace side of the war–peace concept pair. However, conceptually one is negating war. So in terms of what is actually going on, the more accurate term would be "negative war."

Hence the terminology guidelines of chapter 3 become even more important in the gray zone and with hybrid concepts. Sometimes things are relatively symmetric like with competitive–authoritarian, but often they are asymmetric and even misleading as in the case of negative peace.

One signal that a concept is problematic is that people debate the actual terms to be used. Not surprisingly, with the gray zone this problem is exacerbated. Sometimes the gray zone does not exist as a concept in its own right, hence it is not clear what to call it.

## Hybrid Structures and Aggregation

A good place to start discussing hybrid concept structures is via the opposite of "hybrid." Structurally "homogeneous" concepts use the same structure and aggregation rule for the whole concept structure. A number of examples from chapter 2 illustrate this in action. For example, the use of mean at both the data–indicator level as well as the secondary level is not uncommon. Often when money is the metric, scholars use the sum at both levels. These are nonhybrid concepts in structural terms.

If one thinks about the different concept structures and aggregation, the gray zone appears in different ways depending on the character of the aggregation structure.

The DSM provides a situation where hybrid aggregation structures are extremely common. This is completely compatible with following the Ideal Type Guideline. For example, here is how schizophrenia is conceptualized in the DSM:

1. Delusions
2. Hallucinations
3. Disorganized speech (e.g., frequent derailment or incoherence)
4. Grossly disorganized or catatonic behavior
5. Negative symptoms (i.e., diminished emotional expression or avolition)

Two or more of the above symptoms must be present over a one-month period. At least one of the symptoms (1), (2), and (3) must be present. If one has all of the symptoms, this is the maximum level of schizophrenia. The DSM examples illustrate that while the gray zone often uses hybrid concept structures, one can certainly use them for the positive pole as well.

In general, the gray zone for this kind of hybrid is situations where (1) one of the necessary conditions is absent but the facilitating conditions are present, or (2) the necessary conditions are present but not enough facilitating conditions to reach sufficiency.

By itself the $m$-of-$n$ rule produces a natural gray zone where some of the features are present but not enough to pass the sufficiency bar. The gray zone ranges from 1 feature present to $m - 1$ attributes, just below the sufficiency bar of $m$.

In this chapter I focus on hybrids that combine logical AND with logical OR, or using linear algebra, that combine addition and multiplication. This is perhaps the simplest kind of hybrid. It uses aggregation classes to define structural hybridity. For the purposes of this chapter structural hybridity uses two or more different aggregation strategies. The canonical example will be using logical ANDs and ORs at the same level in the basic framework.

These can be used for ideal type conceptualization, but I focus in this chapter on their close linkage to conceptualizing the gray zone.

## Disagreement in the Gray Zone

When comparing various concepts and measures one usually finds that correlation coefficients are used to assess similarity. This procedure often dramatically underestimates the dissimilarity of measures. One reason for this is that observations at the ends of the spectrum usually have more weight (in statistical terms more leverage; Belsley et al. 1980) than those in the middle. It is often the case that concepts and measures agree on the extreme cases since they are clear-cut and easy to code, while at the same disagreeing frequently on cases in the middle. Points in the middle often have a "half fish, half fowl" character that makes them hard to categorize and classify.

Democracy is a concept where the gray zone often plays a large role in various theoretical contexts, ranging from the war-proneness of transitional democracies (e.g., Mansfield and Synder 2002) to successful democratic transitions (e.g., Linz and Stepan 1996).

Bowman et al. (2005) focus on democracy concepts and measures for the five Central American countries 1900–99. They start out with the conventional wisdom that most democracy measures are highly correlated. This is true in general but not for this group of countries for the 20th century. Correlations between three standard measures (Polity, Vanhanen, and Gasiorowski) are often below 0.50, only once above 0.80. So what explains these low correlations between democracy measures for this set of country-years?

This section suggests that it is in part because of the high percentage of gray zone cases among these Central American countries. The discussion of "semidemocratic" regimes constitutes a large part of their discussion of individual cases. In fact they note the following:

We would suggest two explanations. First, high agreement among existing scales is a product of important numbers of stable autocracies and democracies. There is little disagreement that most advanced capitalist countries have been democratic and many African and Asian countries have been consistently authoritarian. Agreement about a large percentage of the cases fuels the high correlations, suggesting higher levels of scale reliability than actually exist. Second, existing indices get the facts wrong for an important set of cases that contain quite a few countries whose regimes are often in "purgatory"—regimes with often shifting authoritarian and democratic characteristics. (Bowman et al. 2005, 945–46)

When they say that existing indices get the facts wrong they are suggesting that these are not easy cases (one cannot trust graduate research assistants to code them correctly) and they might well be debatable.

They discuss the example of Nicaragua in the 1920s and early 1930s:

Nicaragua during the 1920s and early 1930s ... [is] a case that possesses characteristics of both dictatorship and democracy. The Polity IV data set codes the entire 1920s and early 1930s in Nicaragua as at least partially democratic, whereas the Gasiorowski index sees the same period as completely authoritarian. For its part, Vanhanen's scale classifies the period as exhibiting very low levels of democracy until the elections of 1928, after which semidemocracy exists until 1935. (Bowman et al. 2005, 947)

Nicaragua is nice for the purposes of this chapter because it had by far the highest correlations among the three measures of democracy. Part of the explanation is that it was clearly an autocratic regime for much of the 20th century. One might suspect that disagreements between data sets would start again in the 1980s when Nicaragua was transitioning toward democracy.

When there is a significant number of cases in the gray zone, using the correlation coefficient as a measure of similarity can wildly underestimate discrepancies between measures. For example, using the

TABLE 7.1. Systematic disagreement in the gray zone.

|  |  | $X_2$ |  |  |  |  |  |
|---|---|---|---|---|---|---|---|
|  |  | 1 | 2 | 3 | 4 | 5 | 6 |
| $X_1$ | 0 | 50 | 10 | 0 | 0 | 0 | 0 |
|  | 1 | 0 | 50 | 40 | 40 | 0 | 0 |
|  | 2 | 0 | 0 | 50 | 50 | 40 | 0 |
|  | 3 | 0 | 0 | 0 | 50 | 40 | 0 |
|  | 4 | 0 | 0 | 0 | 0 | 50 | 10 |
|  | 5 | 0 | 0 | 0 | 0 | 0 | 50 |

Polity democracy data, if one takes the cases at extreme values (i.e., $-10$ and 10) as given, which consist of 23 percent of the data, and then replaces all the observations in between with *independent, random*, and *uniform* data, one still gets a correlation coefficient of almost 0.50. In short, there can exist extensive disagreement between measures in the gray zone and one can still get quite respectable correlation coefficients.

Suppose that the relationship between the two measures is like that of table 7.1 (see chapter 3 in the previous edition of this book for an extended analysis with real data). There is excellent agreement on the extremes but some substantial disagreement in the middle. Yet a high correlation of 0.87 masks large differences between the two. Notably, measure $X_1$ is always less than measure $X_2$. This means that one measure is a subset of the other, which can be interpreted as meaning that one is a stricter measure. This then can have a significant impact on causal inference. But because a large percentage of observations do lie on the diagonal, one will get substantial correlations. This example suggests that there may not only be disagreement in the middle zone but there is a pattern to that disagreement.[3]

Patterns of disagreement like those of table 7.1 suggest that the *variance* between two measures changes systematically as one moves away from the extremes and toward the middle. The change in variance is driven by agreement at the ends and disagreement in the middle.

---

3. Teorell et al. (2019) have some examples where one measure lies below another, which could be a consequence of different aggregation procedures, since some use weakest link.

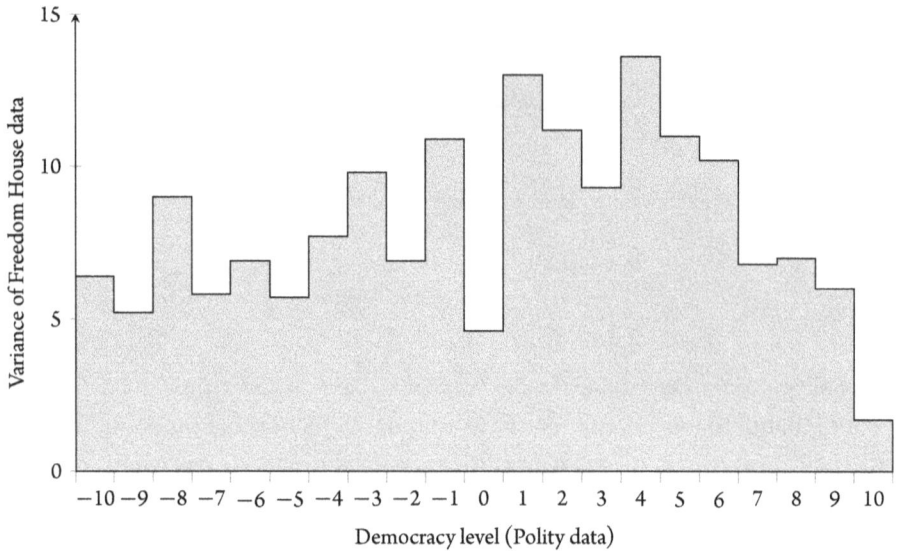

FIGURE 7.1. Variance and disagreement in the gray zone.

Figure 7.1 charts the changes in variance when comparing the Polity concept and measure of democracy (Jaggers and Gurr 1995) with Freedom House's concept and measure (Karantycky 2000). To do this I added the scores of the Freedom House variables "political rights" and "civil liberties," which each have range 1–7; the Freedom House scale is then 2–14. I then converted them to a −10 to 10 scale, which matches the Polity scale (unfortunately there is not a nice match between the Freedom House 2–14 scale and the Polity −10 to 10 scale). Figure 7.1 gives the variance of the Freedom House scores for all cases where the Polity codes a nation-year at a certain level.

At the extreme of democracy (i.e., Polity=10) there is very little variance (1.7) in the Freedom House codings. Moving toward the gray zone in the middle, the variation in how Freedom House codes a given nation-year increases significantly; this happens already for the Polity $= 9$ cases where the variance jumps almost 4 times to 6.0. In the middle range of competitive–authoritarian regimes there is another significant jump where the variance is now usually around 12–13. There is more agreement at the autocratic end with variances around 6, but still nothing like the extreme democracies. In short, for good democracies there is relative consensus between Polity and Freedom House. Once one moves toward the middle zone, variances increase by a factor of about 8–10. They decline by 50 percent again at the autocratic end, but still with significant levels of disagreement.[4]

Another way to look at disagreement on coding democracy in the gray zone is to compare democracy data sets regarding the extent of regime changes. One might imagine that much of the shifting occurs in the gray zone. Probably, countries that are firmly autocratic or firmly democratic change less than those that are in the middle. Bernhard et al. (2017) look at different ways to conceptualize and code regime change using a wide variety of different data sets. In their analysis of the correlation between all these democracy measures they find (what everyone finds) that overall they are highly correlated: "We examine the pairwise correlations between our democracy indicators; they are all very strongly correlated. The lowest correlation is 0.866" (2017, 953).

However, once one moves to the correlation between changes in regime type in either the democratic or the autocratic direction, these high correlations disappear. Particularly notable are the extremely low correlations in regions that correspond to the gray zone, which in their context is incomplete autocratization or incomplete democratization. Here the correlations between the various change measures range between 0.1 and 0.3. As they note, "Despite very similar starting points, the variables generated are quite different. There is nothing in these correlations that indicate anything like a strong relationship between changes in these various democracy indicators" (Bernhard et al. 2017, 954). These analyses support the notion that there is large-scale disagreement in the gray zone, because when things change in the gray zone, different measures disagree about how much they change.

This chapter and chapter 8 discuss the parliamentary–presidential concept pair with semipresidential as a gray zone concept in the middle. Not surprising, the poles are pretty clear but there is significant

---

4. I leave it as an exercise to reevaluate Przeworski et al.'s (2000, 58–59) argument that their dichotomous coding of democracy produces less error than a continuous measure if error follows the variance as illustrated in figure 7.1 and the cut point between democracy and autocracy is 0.

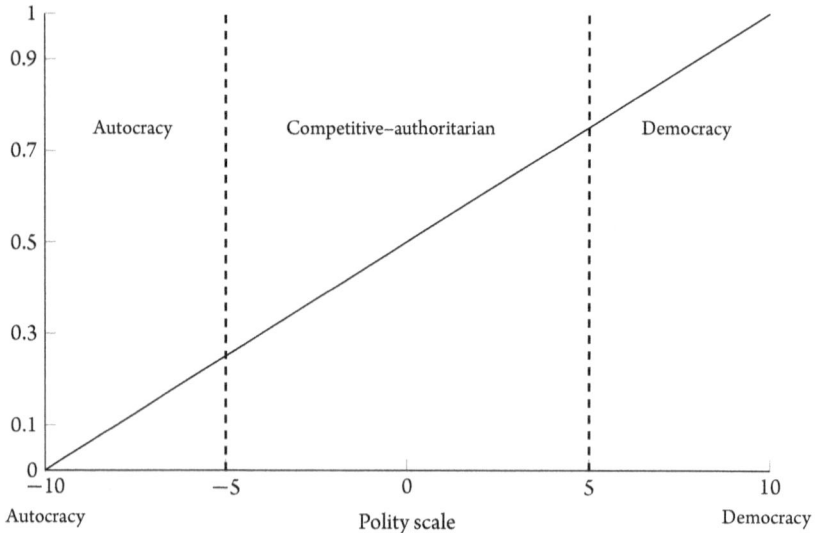

FIGURE 7.2. Linear interpolation for the gray zone.

disagreement about the middle: "One inference from these numbers is that scholars' understanding of presidentialism and parliamentarism may not be as consensual as one would expect. In fact, a major source of divergence has to do with how the scholars decide to treat intermediate cases" (Cheibub et al. 2013, 527).

Cumulatively, all of these analyses suggest that in spite of high levels of correlation between various democracy data sets, there is very low or at best mediocre correlation between them in the gray zone. This suggests that any analysis focusing on the gray zone is likely to depend a lot on the particular measure used.

## The Linear Interpolation Approach to the Gray Zone

One common way to think about the gray zone is as the linear interpolation between the positive and negative poles. The diagonal line in figure 7.2 gives the default linear semantic transformation. The gray zone is somewhere in the middle and is defined by the linear interpolation between the two ends.

The vertical dashed lines at −5 and 5 represent common boundaries used when the hypothesis focuses on the gray zone and dichotomous variables are used.[5] When conflict scholars use the Polity data to test hypotheses about the civil war–proneness of partially democratic regimes, they often choose −5 and 5 as defining the gray zone and create two dummy variables.[6]

The interpolation approach does not focus on the gray zone as a semantic and structural zone in its own right. It violates the Ideal Type Guideline. So while interpolation is common in practice, once one explores specifically the semantic content of the gray zone—usually a hybrid—linear interpolation no longer makes much sense as a conceptual and measurement methodology.

## Gray Zone and Hybrid Concepts

This and the following sections treat the methodological problem of conceptualizing gray zone concepts. This means thinking about the meaning and semantics of the gray zone as well as the formal, mathematical structures that one might use for these kinds of concepts. As my main example I use the gray zone of the democracy–autocracy pair.

One way to begin defining and conceptualizing this zone is via negation.

The gray zone is defined in part as not–positive pole AND not–negative pole.

Chapter 3 advised that conceptualizing via negation is rarely a good idea. The gray zone is one general situation where conceptualizing

5. These boundaries perhaps originated with the widely cited Fearon and Laitin (2003) analysis of civil wars.

6. The other option is to use the continuous Polity variable and hypothesize a U-shaped relationship by including a quadratic term.

involves the serious use of negation. When scholars have hypotheses about competitive–authoritarian regimes, they often trichotomize as in figure 7.2. Competitive–authoritarian regimes are conceptualized and measured as not-democratic AND not-authoritarian. While almost never thought of in these terms, this is another use of the necessary and sufficient condition concept structure. This is the beginning of the conceptualizing of the gray zone because one will typically need other defining features. Following the metaphor, not-white and not-black are necessary for gray but not sufficient (since other colors are also not-white and not-black).

The core methodological and semantic point is that, while not a complete methodology, conceptualizing the gray zone does require that one explicitly consider what "not–positive pole" and "not–negative pole" mean. Literally gray *means* not-black AND not-white.

The first step then in conceptualizing the gray zone is establishing the boundaries on either side. Gray zone concepts are likely to have two necessary conditions: (1) not–positive pole and (2) not–negative pole. This says nothing in particular about how the positive or negative poles are conceptualized; they could be both done via family resemblance. The key point is that not being at the poles are necessary conditions for the gray zone.

Not surprisingly, this volume suggests avoiding the sharp boundaries of figure 7.2. Figure 7.3 illustrates a general way to do semantic transformations for gray zone concepts.

There is no reason why the dividing zones need to be symmetric or semantic mirrors. This is clear in figure 7.3. The Polity concept of democracy–autocracy is not symmetric: it is heavily weighted toward the autocracy side of things. So while it is possible that the concept is symmetric, it is best to assume that it is not and to consider each boundary separately. This leads to a first guideline regarding gray zone concepts:

Gray Zone Guideline I: Conceptualize individually and separately the boundaries between white and gray and between black and gray.

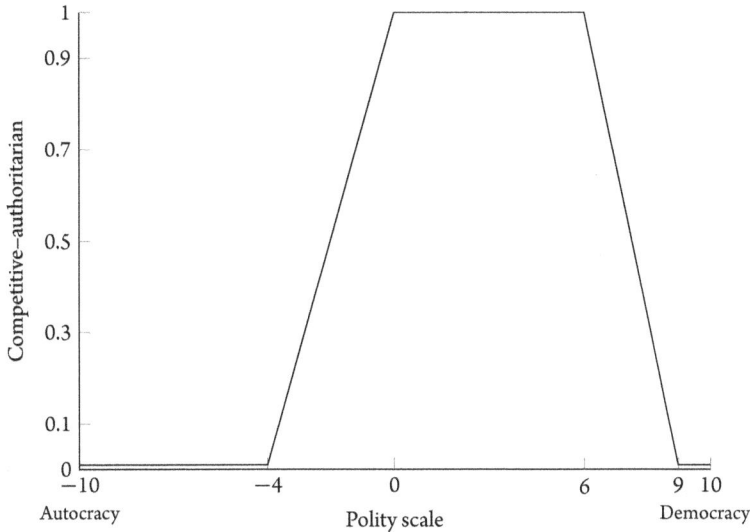

FIGURE 7.3. Gray zone concepts: competitive–authoritarian state.

For example, for competitive–authoritarian regimes one needs to conceptualize the boundary between competitive–authoritarian and autocracy as well as between competitive–authoritarian and democracy.

One of the most important guidelines in concept formation is to
conceptualize using ideal types. At first blush it might seem like a con-
tradiction to conceptualize an ideal type for the gray zone; in fact, it
is possible and it is a good idea. In the standard fuzzy-logic semantic
figure, e.g., figure 7.3, the top of the trapezoid is the ideal type region
for the gray zone.

The case of negative peace illustrates how terminology can easily
lead in the wrong direction. In spite of its name, negative peace is really
negative war in standard usage. Once it is realized that negative peace
is clearly between positive peace and war then it becomes clear that
negative peace is really not–positive peace AND not-war.

One method for thinking about this is to follow the gray metaphor.
The ideal type gray zone is where white and black are relatively evenly
balanced. Continuing with competitive–authoritarian this would mean
a relative balance of authoritarian and democratic characteristics. Using

a biological metaphor, it would be a hybrid that has some genetic balance between the two genetic parents.

Using fuzzy-logic semantics this would not be a point but rather a region where there is a relative balance, say the 40–60 percent range. This produces a trapezoidal-shaped membership function like figure 7.3 that constitutes a good default or starting point for thinking about gray zone concepts.

### *Conceptualizing between the Boundaries*

While one should always be cautious about generalizing from one or two examples, my intuition is that often there are lots of ways to be a competitive–authoritarian regime. More generally, one reason why data sets often differ on coding the gray zone is that there are lots of configurations of attributes in it. To use the Polity concept of democracy–autocracy, at the extremes there is only one way to be a complete democracy or complete autocracy, however there are many combinations that put a state in the middle.

One sees exactly the same phenomenon in the literature on the presidential–parliamentary concept pair, along with semipresidential in the middle. In this literature people talk about the wide variety of configurations that exist for semipresidential. This is exactly because they combine varying mixes of presidential and parliamentary features.

Levitsky and Way (2010) illustrate this nicely with their conceptualization of competitive–authoritarian (note that the subtitle of their book is *Hybrid regimes after the Cold War*). It should be noted that their conceptualization of authoritarianism and democracy is *much shorter* than that for the competitive–authoritarian regime type.

> Cases are scored as competitive authoritarian if:
> 1. The criteria for full authoritarianism are not met.
> 2. There exists broad adult suffrage.
> 3. The authority of elected governments is not seriously restricted by unelected "tutelary" powers.

4. *At least one* of the following criteria is met:

 ....

 (1) Unfair Elections:
 Evidence of any one of the following indicators is
 sufficient to score an election as unfair:

 ....

 (2) Violation of Civil Liberties:
 Evidence of any one of the following indicators is
 sufficient for civil liberties to be violated:

 ....

 (3) Uneven Playing Field:
 Evidence of any one of the following indicators is
 sufficient to score the playing field as uneven:

(Levitsky and Way 2010)

This is a hybrid structure in terms of positive and negative features. For example, it includes NOT–full authoritarianism along with the positive "adult suffrage."

It is also a hybrid structure. The first three items are joined by ANDs. Then there follows a relatively complicated family resemblance structure of ORs, "at least one of the following." Simplifying, the basic hybrid structure can serve as a beginning default concept structure for gray zone concepts,

$$X_1 \text{ AND } X_2 \text{ AND } X_3 \text{ AND } (Z_1 \text{ OR } Z_2 \text{ OR } \cdots \text{ OR } Z_N). \quad (7.1)$$

This equation is hybrid because of the combination of ANDs and ORs. One can easily produce a linear algebra version of this by substituting $*$ for AND and $+$ for OR.

Simplifying, there are three major categories for the family resemblance–OR part of equation (7.1): (1) unfair elections, (2) violation of civil liberties, and (3) uneven playing field. Within these three dimensions there about 11 criteria. If we treated these 11 as basically equal, then an ideal type competitive–authoritarian regime could be defined as one having 4–6 of these criteria present. Regimes that have only 1 present are thus weakly competitive–authoritarian on the democracy side and those with 10 are weakly competitive–authoritarian on the autocracy side.

The family resemblance ORs provide the variety of ways a regime can be not-democratic AND not-authoritarian. There are different mixes of democratic and authoritarian features that constitute a state which is competitive–authoritarian.

If one is looking for a template for gray zone concepts, equation (7.1) could be it. Roughly, one uses necessary conditions to work on the boundary delimitation problem and then within the boundaries one uses family resemblance structures.

Notice that equation (7.1) is exactly the hybrid structure described above that is so common in the DSM and which is used for ideal type mental disorders. The key feature that differentiates that ideal type use and its use for the gray zone is the fact that the necessary conditions are typically negations of the poles of the concept pair. So it is the combination of necessary conditions and negation of the poles that constitutes a common generic way of doing hybrid concept structures for the gray zone.

This leads to a general guideline for conceptualizing the gray zone for concept pairs:

> Gray Zone Guideline II: One should include characteristics from each concept of the concept pair.

This is why the gray zone is so often a hybrid: it combines features of each concept of the pair.

The literature on semipresidentialism provides a good example of balance between the two poles. Here features of each pole are used for the gray zone in the middle. So while the name and terminology might suggest imbalance toward the presidential side, in practice it is quite balanced and scholars understand that there is a range where a given regime might be more toward one pole rather than the other, but that the ideal type is a relative balance of the two polar types.

Lijphart (1984) argues that three criteria are essential to presidentialism, while a list of others are associated with but not necessary for presidential government. Lijphart's three essential criteria are that the chief executive shall (1) not be dependent on legislative confidence, but rather shall sit for a fixed term, (2) be elected by popular vote, (3) be a one-person executive. Here we see a hybrid conceptualization of the presidentialism pole as well. This is another example where hybrid concept structures and content are not limited to the gray zone.

One of the many challenging features of gray zone concepts is that they often appear in semantically unbalanced settings. By semantically unbalanced I mean extreme focus on one pole and lack of attention to the other. The democracy example illustrates this nicely. An example close to my interests and heart is "negative peace," which has been almost always conceptualized as not-war and rarely as not–positive peace. "Health" *in practice*, e.g., WHO, is defined as the absence of illness (and much more controversially as the absence of handicap, e.g., deafness is not-health): it has almost no positive health-defining features.[7]

Ideally, one must really take the hyphenated concept seriously. Semantically, competitive–authoritarian should be written as *competitive*–authoritarian because it is the competitive side that is leading the dance.

This section has outlined a hybrid structure for use with gray zone concepts. The hybrid concept structure of equation (7.1) and figure 7.3 provides a good starting point for explicitly conceptualizing gray zone concepts.

## Causal Hypotheses, Research Design, and Case Selection

In the civil war literature, when testing hypotheses about competitive–authoritarian regimes with the continuous Polity measure, the norm is to use a quadratic term to capture the inverted-U-shaped causal

7. The WHO defines health officially as "Health is a state of complete physical, mental and social well-being and not merely the absence of disease or infirmity," but in practice virtually all indices and measures are disease and illness related.

hypothesis. This inverted U is not that different from the trapezoid in figure 7.3. This suggests a contrast between getting the inverted U via a statistical estimate of causal effects versus having just a *one*-parameter estimate of a trapezoidal variable of competitive–authoritarian. This chapter suggests it is better and more straightforward to have a real measure of what the hypothesis is talking about. There is no reason why a gray zone variable like figure 7.3 cannot be used in statistical analyses.

It is important to separate the causal hypotheses regarding the gray zone from research design issues, notably the construction of the comparison or contrast cases. This involves choosing the category or comparison set of "not–gray zone" cases.

A core issue in research design is constituting the control or negative cases. When the concept lies at the positive pole the control cases are pretty straightforward: it is the negation of the positive pole. However, with gray zone concepts the construction of the research design becomes more complicated. Roughly, there are three options for the negative, control cases: (1) cases where the gray zone variable has value 0, i.e., "not-gray," (2) only cases of the positive pole, (3) only cases of the negative pole. Continuing with the competitive–authoritarian example, should the control group be (1) high-quality democracies only, (2) high-quality authoritarian regimes, or (3) both?

The default is just to do the negation of the gray zone, which means including both positive and negative pole cases in the comparison group. It is not obvious that this is always the right or best choice. Essentially one has the problem of heterogeneity of the comparison group. Imagine a standard statistical analysis where the gray zone variable is $X_1$. To give this content let's use the common hypothesis that competitive–authoritarian regimes are more prone to have civil wars. The question is, more prone than what? As understood in the literature it is both more war prone than democracies and more war prone than autocracies.

In this example the background discussions make it clear that the gray zone is contrasted with the concepts on either side of it. However, there might be situations (more common in my intuition) where the contrast is mostly in one direction. In this setting the statistical results are not informative at all. It could be the not-of-interest pole that is driving the results.[8]

In summary, a third guideline stresses the following:

Gray Zone Guideline III: In causal inference settings, e.g., statistical analyses, one must explicitly consider and justify the control or comparison cases.

For example, it might make sense for the population under analysis to include only the gray zone and one pole as the contrast. Including the other pole might just make the results harder to interpret and bring irrelevant cases into the causal contrast.

## Conclusion

This chapter has provided an introduction to the methodology of gray zone and hybrid concepts. These two topics do not exist as such in the literature on conceptualization and measurement. The chapter provides some beginning thoughts on the methodology for these two core aspects of conceptualization-measurement.

Just as genetic engineers take genes from different varieties of plants and animals to construct and design new biological entities, it is useful for those who create concepts to think about doing the same sort of thing. In genetic engineering there is no guarantee that the end result will be better; there is no guarantee that it will be worse.

The default, hybrid concept structure introduced in this chapter—equation (7.1) and figure 7.3—provides a good starting point for those thinking about gray zone concepts. It makes explicit the boundaries of the gray zone, which of course should be gradual and not abrupt (i.e., do not dichotomize). It embraces the diversity of the gray zone by using family resemblance strategies to define the threshold for full membership.

---

8. This issue of "compared to what" arises again in chapter 8 because with nominal typologies the comparison group is often multiple and not evident.

Hybrid structures are critical in the basic framework for concepts and measurement. The fact that many concepts are multilevel becomes dramatically important once one uses different structures at different levels. My default recommendation is to use best shot or weakest link at the secondary level and mean aggregation at the data–indicator level. Hence, one should probably start with hybrid concept-measurement structures.

Equation (7.1) and figure 7.3 are just a starting point. Much more could be done in terms of thinking about alternative conceptual structures for the gray zone as well as hybrid concepts.

While I have treated the gray zone and hybrid concepts together, it is important to remember that they are really separate methodological, conceptual, and theoretical issues. One can easily use hybrid concept structures for ideal types. One can define the gray zone for the philosophy approach as the absence of some but not all of the necessary conditions. Similarly, one can think about the gray zone for all the aggregation classes. A core recommendation is not to take arbitrarily just the middle as a gray zone, but to think specifically about it. What are its boundaries? What is the ideal type gray zone case? Once one begins to ask these kinds of specific questions it becomes clear that linear interpolation to construct the gray zone is a poor answer.

More importantly, gray zones are critical empirical phenomena in many research contexts. Often research does not really get going until concepts and data sets are available. I hope this chapter encourages those interested in gray zone phenomena to conceptualize, measure, and systematically gather data on them, not to mention develop causal theories involving them.

# 8

# Typologies

On those remote pages [of an ancient Chinese encyclopedia] it is
written that animals are divided into (1) those that belong to the
emperor, (2) embalmed ones, (3) those that are trained, (4) suckling
pigs, (5) mermaids, (6) fabulous ones, (7) stray dogs, (8) those that are
included in this classification, (9) innumerable ones, (10) those drawn
with a very fine camel's hair brush, (11) others, (12) those that have
just broken a flower vase, (13) those that resemble flies from a distance.

JORGE-LUIS BORGES

## Introduction

Typologies are incredibly popular. They are particularly common in
qualitative research. In some subfields like security studies they are
ubiquitous.

I define a typology as a set of concepts.[1] Therefore, the discussion of
concept methodology in other chapters is directly relevant. This chapter's analysis is a direct consequence of the methodology of concepts
outlined in this book.

---

1. This chapter discusses *conceptual* typologies and not causal ones. One often sees typologies constructed via 2 × 2 tables. Particularly if the piece is just about the typology it is
sometimes not clear whether there is a causal relationship between row and column. This
is clear when there are multivariate statistical analyses, less so in other settings. In conceptual typologies there is no causal relationship between row and column; it is ontological and
definitional.

There are two virtually uncontested rules for constructing typologies:

> If typologies are to meet the norms for standard categorical scales, the cells should be *mutually exclusive* and *collectively exhaustive*. For the purpose of classification, it is essential that these dual criteria be met; otherwise a given observed case might fit in more than one cell, or might not fit in any cell. (Collier et al. 2008, 157; emphasis is mine)

In spite of the wide-ranging popularity of typologies and these standard methodological rules, this chapter makes the following argument:

> The standard mutually exclusive and exhaustive rules for creating typologies are flawed.

This means that typologies constructed using these rules are problematic.

These are bound to be controversial claims. I illustrate the consequences of the standard typology methodology using the influential Geddes data set on types of autocratic regimes (Geddes et al. 2014). One might argue that one should not throw the typological baby out on the basis of one example. However, this chapter argues that these problems inevitably arise when doing typologies using the mutually exclusive and exhaustive rules.

In addition to typologies of autocratic regimes, I include as a second set of examples the bible for clinical psychology and psychiatry known under the acronym of DSM (American Psychiatric Association, *Diagnostic and statistical manual of mental disorders*; the current version is 5, in short DSM-5) which illustrates many of the same issues in a very different substantive context. The DSM is the authoritative reference, or in the context of this chapter, the typology of mental disorders. We will see the tension between following the two standard rules and the reality of mental disorders.

Much work on autocratic regimes has thought in terms of types of autocratic regimes. One of the most famous and earliest was Linz's typology of authoritarian regimes (1975). So while I focus on the

Geddes typology and data set, the critique applies to the whole literature on types of autocratic regimes. I use Weeks's typology of autocratic regimes (2014) to illustrate the potential confusion between nominal typologies and partially ordered ones, as well as the problems of statistical analyses with partially ordered typologies.

The DSM, along with other disease classification systems (e.g., the WHO's "International classification of diseases," https://icd.who.int /en) illustrates how typological thinking dominates theory and practice in the mental health area. There are many imperatives (e.g., medical insurance) to classify a person's disorder clearly into one type. The DSM is a nice example because I have found no justification of the methodological logic used to construct disorders. In general the DSM uses the $m$-of-$n$ rule along with some necessary conditions. Thus, most disorders constitute what this book calls hybrid concepts.

There is often a strong tension between nominal typologies and conceptual pairs with some underlying dimension. Often one can choose a nominal typology or think of it as a concept pair with an underlying continuum. For example, sticking with democracy, a standard typology is (1) parliamentary, (2) presidential, and (3) mixed or semipresidential. Should one think of that as a three-part nominal typology, or as a concept pair with parliamentary and presidential at the ends and mixed in the middle? I argue below that instead of it being a nominal typology, it is better thought of as a presidential–parliamentary concept pair with a gray zone in the middle for "mixed" or "semi."

Typologies come in two forms: one is a nominal typology, the second is a partially ordered typology. This chapter starts with the nominal and then moves to partially ordered typologies, which might eventually be completely ordered (i.e., ordinal). This is important because two-way typologies can easily be seen as just two concepts, each with its own underlying dimension, that interact. Viewed in this way the typology just disappears.

What is the recommendation if one should not do typologies? Recall that a typology is a set of concepts. The recommendation is to focus on the concepts themselves that form—or generate in the case of $2 \times 2$ tables—the typology. This is where the action should be; the typology is in fact distracting attention from in-depth analyses of the concepts that constitute the typology. If you are interested in "military regimes" as a type of autocratic regime then do a conceptual analysis of that, including hypotheses about its causes and effects.

## Scope Issues

It is quite common to propose a typology *of* S, e.g., a typology *of* autocratic regimes or *of* mental disorders. The Scope Guideline (chapter 3) requires that one give the population or scope of cases to which the concept can be applied. The terminology "typology of" suggests that S is the scope. This can be both problematic and misleading. The scope of concepts such as autocracy, military regime, or democracy is *all state-years*. Of course, there might be many state-years that have zero membership of the concept type: the key point is that they are codable.

The "typology of" creates a secondary scope. These are the observations that are in fact included in the data set, if there is one. It is a subset of the overall scope S. For example, autocratic states are a subset of all states.

Figure 8.1 illustrates the general issue. To make this more concrete, consider Geddes's typology of *autocratic regimes*. In terms of that figure, autocratic regimes are a secondary scope. Essentially, autocratic regime is a subset of the larger scope of all state-years independent of regime type.

Crucial then for Geddes is the initial dichotomization from all regimes to autocratic regimes, which creates her secondary scope as illustrated in figure 8.1:

> Autocratic regime starts when any one of the following occurs: An executive achieves power through undemocratic means…. "Undemocratic" is defined as any means other than a direct, reasonably fair competitive election in which at least ten percent of the total population (equivalent to about 40 percent of the adult male population) was eligible to vote; or indirect election by a body at least 60 percent of which was elected in direct, reasonably

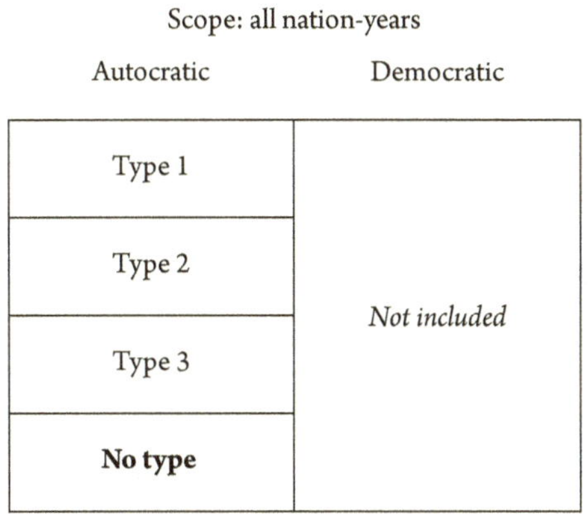

Scope: all nation-years

Autocratic                          Democratic

| Type 1 | |
| Type 2 | *Not included* |
| Type 3 | |
| **No type** | |

FIGURE 8.1. Standard typology methodologies:
types of autocratic regimes.

fair competitive elections; or constitutional succession to a democratically elected executive. (Geddes et al. n.d., 6)

Geddes codes all her democratic regimes as 0 on the various types of autocratic rule. However, as always the gray zone is present. For example, throughout European history there existed regimes that were partially democratic and partially monarchies. This was notably true for the UK and Germany. It was often the case that the monarchy over time had decreasing influence over policy; often it declined faster in domestic affairs than in foreign policy. In other cases, such as Japan, the monarchy was generally quite weak vis-à-vis either democratic, military, or shogun rule.

The alternative—recommended here—is to use the overall scope, which is all state-years, to code the data set. The rationale for this should be obvious by now. To draw a bright red line through the competitive–authoritarian gray zone is deeply problematic.

The key point is just a restatement in brief of the Scope Guideline in chapter 3:

Do not use secondary scope in conceptualization and measurement, and consequently in typologies as well. Follow the Scope Guideline, i.e., use S.

There are always cases that fall close to the dichotomization line: those on the autocratic side are coded, those on the democratic side are not. This is almost inevitably going to cause problems.

The DSM is a typology of mental disorders, to which figure 8.1 also directly applies. One needs just to replace the democracy terms with the relevant analogies from the DSM. So the left-hand side becomes mental disorder and the right-hand side is not–mental disorder. The types are the various kinds of mental disorders and as we will see, there is a big category "no type" that in the DSM becomes "not otherwise specified," which is a big problem for the DSM.

Thus to start one needs a concept of "mental disorder." Here is the official definition:

> Although no definition can capture all aspects of all disorders in the range contained in DSM-5, the following elements *are required*: A mental disorder is a syndrome characterized by clinically significant disturbance in an individual's cognition, emotion regulation, or behavior that reflects a dysfunction in the psychological, biological, or developmental processes underlying mental functioning. Mental disorders are usually associated with significant distress or disability in social, occupational, or other important activities. An expectable or culturally approved response to a common stressor or loss, such as the death of a loved one, is not a mental disorder. Socially deviant behavior (e.g., political, religious, or sexual) and conflicts that are primarily between the individual and society are not mental disorders unless the deviance or conflict results from a dysfunction in the individual, as described above. (DSM-5, 20; emphasis is mine)

It is worth noting in passing that these are the required conditions— necessary—for a disorder; in fact they do not give the sufficient conditions to be a disorder. It remains an open question whether in fact they are treated as sufficient.

It would seem that this boundary should be critical in the process of creating typologies of mental disorders. According to Cooper (2013), the current definition was inherited from previous editions and was not the topic of much discussion in revising for the fifth edition. But again, there are gray zone and controversial cases. As stressed in chapter 1, there are often very important normative issues in conceptualizing "disorder." Quite famously, homosexuality was a disorder until it was classified out of the DSM in the 1970s. In some prominent measures of health, deafness is considered not-healthy or "illness"; that is another critical boundary decision. There is probably a large gray zone between "physical" and "mental" diseases.

## The Mutually Exclusive Rule for Typologies

A standard and core part of the conventional wisdom on typologies involves making the typology *mutually exclusive*. This implies clear, sharp boundaries between categories. Standard typology methodology faces all the problems—and more—of dichotomous concepts discussed in earlier chapters.

With many concepts there is a long tradition of viewing questions in a certain manner (e.g., the importance of poverty lines in assessing poverty). For the concept of autocracy there is a long tradition, still going strong, of thinking of autocracy using typologies. There is an overlapping literature on "dictatorship" (e.g., Huntington 1968; Wintrobe 1990) and "totalitarian" regimes (e.g., Friedrich and Brzezinski 1965). The literature on types of autocratic regime dates back at least to Linz's influential discussion of authoritarianism using typologies. This got a big boost when the Democracy–Dictatorship group developed a typology of dictatorship, and has continued with Geddes's influential typology of autocratic regimes. Here are the most influential typologies of autocracy–authoritarianism–dictatorship in chronological order:

Linz (1975):
1. Totalitarian
2. Authoritarian
3. Post-totalitarian
4. Sultanism

Democracy–Dictatorship group (Cheibub et al. 2010):
1. Monarchy
2. Military dictatorship
3. Civilian dictatorship

Geddes et al. (2014):
1. Party-based regimes
2. Military regimes
3. Personalist regimes
4. Monarchical regimes

The tradition of treating mental illness and disorders via typologies goes back to the DSM-I published in the 1950s. This typological tradition continues unabated to the present. Of course, the various disorders have changed, and the number has greatly increased since the 1950s. But the basic typological and methodological framework has remained remarkably unchanged.

A core guideline from chapters 3 and 4 is that semantic neighbors should have overlapping membership functions: there are cases that are members (i.e., a nonzero membership function) of *both* concepts.

Typologies multiply the dichotomization problem because normally multiple dichotomizations are performed. Another way to view the mutually exclusive rule is that it denies the existence—and implicitly the importance—of the empirical fact that an observation belongs to two semantically near concepts. The overlap is that semantic area that the two types have in common.

Figure 8.1 illustrates the basic dichotomization scheme that lies underneath the mutually exclusive scheme, as well as procedures for doing typologies in general. The space is divided into the different nominal types. The vertical and horizontal lines in the figure symbolize the clear mutually exclusive boundaries dividing the types. One can contrast figure 8.1 with the overlapping mapping of neighboring concepts recommended in chapter 4. With multiple types—aka concepts—one has a multidimensional space of overlap, with each concept on its own dimension. The amount of overlap will be determined by the concepts as well as by the empirical distribution of cases for each concept.

To Geddes's credit she recognizes that there is overlap between the categories:

> I had to add intermediate categories to this classification scheme after discovering how many of the cases simply resisted being crammed into one or another of the original categories. (Geddes 2003, 51)

This leads to a set of hyphenated hybrids. Here is her complete typology of autocratic regimes:

1. Monarchy
2. Personal
3. Military
4. Party
5. Party–Personal
6. Party–Military
7. Military–Personal
8. Party–Personal–Military
9. Oligarchy
10. Indirect military

The hyphenated hybrids constitute roughly 25 percent of the total country-years. Hence, the degree of overlap between concepts is considerable.

This new typology is *incomplete*. There are quite a few possible hyphenated hybrids that are not on the list. A personal favorite is monarchy–military. In fact there are no hybrids involving monarchy. However, it is hard not to see traditional European monarchies as partially military regimes. Frederick the Great of Prussia was the head of the military, which was by far the biggest part of the Prussian state. In earlier periods monarchs were near the front lines during wars. In any case, there are quite a few missing one-hyphen cases, as well as all the other two-hyphen ones beyond party–personal–military.

Probably the reason for these missing types is that they do not appear or are extremely rarely empirically. However, this misses a key descriptive, theoretical, and causal point:

Why are there no cases of some hybrids such as oligarchy–military and monarchy–party?

As we saw in chapter 3, competitive–authoritarian regimes are relatively rare, i.e., democracy–autocracy data are quite bimodal. Similarly, if the percentage of a potential hyphenated hybrid case were near zero, one would wonder why it is so hard to create that hybrid. Often the gray zone is less populated than the poles. This poses many important theoretical and causal questions. However, if the conceptual framework does not "see" the hybrid then it disappears as a research question.

Of course, the problem with including all possible hyphenated types is that the typology becomes unwieldy. Typologies with "too many" types are generally not desired or desirable. In practice, when scholars use Geddes's data they follow her suggestions and collapse the hybrids back into one of the original four types. It would not be pretty to see a statistical results table with nine dummy variables.[2]

Following this mutually exclusive rule lies at the heart of some of the main problems with the DSM. Ideally, each disorder should be separate from any other disorder: each person should be clearly assigned to one and only one disorder. This leads to the demand for a "primary diagnosis" that clearly locates the individual in one disease category and not multiple disease categories. This is very clear in the DSM:

Although DSM-5 remains a categorical classification of separate disorders, we recognize that mental disorders do not always fit

2. "One convention for collapsing the regime type categories is the following:
- Party-based regimes: party-based, party-military, party-personal, party-personal-military, oligarchy.
- Military regimes: indirect military, military, military-personal.
- Personalist regimes: personal.
- Monarchical regimes: monarchy"
(Geddes et al. n.d.).

completely within the boundaries of a single disorder. Some symptom domains, such as depression and anxiety, involve multiple diagnostic categories and may reflect common underlying vulnerabilities for a larger group of disorders. In recognition of this reality, the disorders included in DSM-5 were reordered into a revised organizational structure meant to stimulate new clinical perspectives. This new structure corresponds with the organizational arrangement of disorders planned for ICD-11 scheduled for release in 2015. (DSM-5, xli)

At the same time there is a clear desire to have mutually exclusive categories:

Subtypes and Specifiers: Subtypes and specifiers (some of which are coded in the fourth, fifth, or sixth digit) are provided for increased specificity. Subtypes define mutually exclusive and jointly exhaustive phenomenological subgroupings within a diagnosis. (DSM-5, 21)

A statistical classification of diseases must be confined to a limited number of mutually exclusive categories able to encompass the complete range of diseases or morbid conditions. The categories are chosen to facilitate the statistical study of disease phenomena. A specific disease entity that is of particular public health importance, or that occurs frequently, should have its own category. (*International classification of diseases-11*, https://icd.who.int/en)

Cooper discusses this assumption or desire for mutually exclusive categories:

The idea that zones of rarity should separate valid disorders from other disorders and normality has a long history, championed most notably by Robert Kendell (with Jablensky). If one imagines plotting cases of disorder in multidimensional property space (as in cluster analysis), zones of rarity occur whenever sparsely populated space separates clusters. When classificatory boundaries align with zones of rarity then nature is cut at its joints, and the informational content of categories is maximized. If zones of rarity could be identified between disorders and normality then one may hope this could help avoid false positives. (Cooper 2013, 607)

As a philosopher, naturally Cooper thinks about these typologies vis-à-vis the massive literature and philosophy on "natural kinds" (e.g., Khalidi 2013).[3] These natural kinds imply a clumping of phenomena into the separate kinds. Often one sees the metaphor of "cutting up nature at the joints." Geometrically, it is the idea that these natural kinds cluster together in space and there is a significant amount of empty space between the kinds. It is of course possible that this cutting at the joints is a good empirical description of phenomena. However, with the DSM it is the tension between wanting to cut at the joints and the common fact that there is often much overlap among the categories.

Basically, the DSM recognizes that its basic methodological framework of mutually exclusive disorders does not work. My suspicion is that the DSM sticks with it because it lacks any clear alternative and because of the massive sunk costs in the existing typology.

The DSM methodology used to categorize disorders almost inevitably creates boundary issues. As a concrete example of a diagnostic category, consider the DSM's definition of schizophrenia, which requires that that two or more of a total of five symptoms be present and that at least one of them must in a short list of three from the five total (see p. 197 for a longer discussion). This is a typical hybrid with necessary conditions combined with a sufficiency rule of the $m$-of-$n$ sort.

---

3. "Mill places a further condition on natural kinds, in addition to those discussed in section 2.2—namely, that there should be an 'unfathomable chasm' (1843/1974, I vii §4) or 'impassable barrier' (1843/1974, IV vii §4) between them. There is a certain metaphorical vagueness to these formulations, but I will take them to imply that the distinction between one natural kind and another is clear and that there are no intermediate instances between any two natural kinds" (Khalidi 2013, 65).

When one is using the *m*-of-*n* rule it is clear that there will be debates about whether the threshold is really a clear threshold or not. Should one make a big difference between 3-of-7 versus 4-of-7? Inherently, this way of doing things creates a continuum from 0-of-*n* to *n*-of-*n*. Quite naturally one speaks of a more or less severe disorder.

Comorbidity can arise when an individual scores 2-of-5 on one disease while on another disease scores 3-of-5. The drive for mutually exclusivity strongly encourages one to ignore the weaker category and just go for the stronger one. It is the stronger one that presumably becomes the "primary diagnosis." This is exactly what happens with the typology of autocratic regimes: the hybrid, hyphenated types are collapsed back into one of the four main types.

Within the DSM the problem of overlapping disorders is quite massive. It is quite common that an individual person shows symptoms of multiple disorders. It is important to understand that this is both empirical as well as conceptual. The conceptual part comes in because the same symptom might be part of multiple disorders. This is what one might call "conceptual comorbidity," which means that the individual has both disorders at least partially *by definition*. "Empirical comorbidity" would be if the symptoms of each disorder are completely separate but the individual had the symptoms of both disorders. This means that the disorders might be highly correlated because the diseases themselves are related, probably causally.

In short, the reality of diseases as well as the methodology of classification produces all kinds of boundary problems. It is more realistic and probably better for the patient to be realistic about multiple disorders. It is quite possible that one disorder is a major cause of another related one. It could well be that the one that seems less important is actually causing the one that has a higher percentage of symptoms. Dichotomizing and using mutually exclusive categories serve no one very well, except perhaps for the practicalities of getting insurance, and perhaps as a timesaver for clinicians.

While it is probably impossible to know about the relative presence of multiple diagnoses for the DSM, in the case of the typology of autocratic regimes, 25 to 30 percent of the cases are hybrids and that is probably an underestimation given that the coders are probably hesitant to code hybrids. This percentage is certainly not trivial.

In summary, the mutually exclusive rule leads to numerous conceptual, descriptive, empirical, theoretical, and causal problems. This book claims that these are ubiquitous. Geddes and the DSM are not the exception; they are the rule. Often these issues are not even acknowledged, and scholars force cases on the border into one side or the other. By definition, mutually exclusive means ignoring, semantically and in the real world, that concepts overlap. The mutually exclusive rule thus faithfully represents neither the meanings of these concepts nor real-world cases that have membership in multiple neighboring concepts (aka types).

## The Exhaustive Rule for Typologies

The second standard rule for constructing and evaluating typologies is that they should be exhaustive:

> Every observation within the scope of the typology *must* be placed in some type.

Figure 8.1 has a "no type" section. What happens in practice is that as one begins to apply the typology through the population, there are cases that do not fit, i.e., lie in the no type section. To follow the exhaustive rule means that one needs to add a new type(s) to the typology. One keeps adding new types until every observation has a category. When Geddes stops with the hybrids above she is applying the exhaustive rule: if there are no regimes of the military–monarchy type then it is not added to the hybrid list.

This creation of types could be a good thing. New phenomena require names and conceptualizing. New biological species need description. So the exhaustive rule could lead to a whole new research agenda. *However*, in many situations the new types are just there to fulfill the exhaustive rule, and are not of any real interest to the researcher.

One can see this in the Geddes list above. She has added the new types of oligarchy and indirect military.[4] What are these concepts? One way to get a feel is to look at their definitions and the cases coded in these categories:

> Oligarchy identifies regimes in which leaders are chosen through competitive elections but most of the population is disenfranchised, e.g., South Africa before 1994. (Geddes et al. 2014, 316)

> Indirect military rule refers to regimes in which formal political leaders are chosen through competitive elections, but the military either prevents parties that would attract large numbers of voters from participating or controls key policy choices. (Geddes et al. 2014, 316)

Oligarchy seems like a competitive–authoritarian regime. Chile during its democratic transition sounds like indirect military rule.

One signal that these new types are there to meet the exhaustive rule requirement is that they often disappear from the scene in empirical and theoretical work. While I have not made a systematic search, I have not seen a single article using the Geddes data that focuses on these new types in the statistical analysis; even including them at all is quite rare.

In the DSM, the issue of exhaustiveness comes up frequently in discussions of the manual. Again, ideally, once one has the population of all people with mental disorders one should be able to categorize them all into some disorder. Almost always discussed in each revision is the problem of "not otherwise specified." These are people who do not fit well into the typology. As a result there is little guidance about what to do for these individuals, which is certainly a problem.

One can also see the exhaustiveness rule in action in the significant expansion of disorders in each edition of the manual. A major effort is to discover and describe new kinds of mental disorders.

The risk of course is that one has a proliferation of disorders, and it may be the case that there are few people that have a given disorder, which might imply diminished usefulness.

---

4. As discussed in chapter 9, "indirect" could be a subset of "military" but since the mutually exclusive rule is followed it is not.

The positive side of the exhaustiveness rule is thus an incentive to explore new phenomena. The downside occurs if one is doing this merely to fulfill the rule. Scholars are extremely hesitant to have observations that they cannot code. If the focus is on individual concepts in the typology this is not problematic because they are typically not members of the particular concept of interest, i.e., they have zero membership in the concept.

If one is focusing on the individual concepts rather than the typology, then the issue of exhaustiveness just disappears. Since a typology is a set of concepts then there is no reason to follow the exhaustiveness rule.

## Nominal Typologies versus Ordered Typologies

As we saw in chapter 5 on scaling, it is often not so clear what kind of scale is being used. In this chapter the tension is between nominal and ordinal. Concept pairs imply an ordinal scale. Typologies typically are nominal. While nominal is a scale type, the term "nominal scale" is virtually an oxymoron. The whole point of nominal typologies is that *there is no underlying continuum*. Some typologies are partially ordered (see below) or ordinal. Clarity on this point is important. Notably, if the typology contains only two types, they often can form a concept pair with an underlying continuum. Hence a critical question to ask of a typology is whether some of the types have an underlying continuum and hence are not nominal. The epigraph by Borges at the head of this chapter illustrates an ironic nominal typology of animals.

The key point about nominal scales is that they are not ordered. The big gulf lies between nominal and the other kinds of scales: ordinal, interval, ratio, and fuzzy. For the other kinds there is an underlying conceptual continuum: one can debate and move between the other kinds of scales because of this underlying conceptual continuum.

In short, one needs to be clear about whether the typology is ordered or not. We will see this tension again when discussing Weeks's typology of autocratic regimes as well as the question of whether president–mixed–parliamentary is a three-type nominal typology or a concept pair with a gray zone.

TABLE 8.1. Partially ordered typologies: a typology of autocratic regimes

|  | Nonpersonalist (elite-constrained leader) | Personalist (unconstrained leader) |
|---|---|---|
| Civilian audience | Machine | Boss |
| Military audience | Junta | Strongman |

Source: Based on Weeks (2014).

## Partially Ordered Typologies

A common procedure in creating typologies is via $2 \times 2$ tables. Each cell of the table is a type. Table 8.1 presents another typology of autocratic regimes. Here the tension arises between the "row" and "column" concepts vis-à-vis the concepts in the typology that are the cells of the table, i.e., $(1, 1)$, $(0, 0)$, $(1, 0)$, and $(0, 1)$.

This discussion also allows me to introduce the concept of a partially ordered scale. Some ordinal scales are not completely ordinal. The partial ordering is $(1, 1)$ at the top, $(0, 0)$ at the bottom, but no clear ranking of the $(0, 1)$ and $(1, 0)$ cells in the middle. This is intuitively obvious by performing the common procedure of adding the values of the row and column variables, which produces sums of 2, 1, and 0.

Critical to these $2 \times 2$ typologies—to give them a name—is the extent to which row and column are ordinal. As always, terminology is important. These are typically coded as 0 or 1: this already suggests an ordinal ranking. While 0 and 1 might be arbitrary, one needs to specifically discuss this. Things would be clearer if rows and columns were designated by arbitrary symbols (or even emojis!). In Weeks's case, already in the first column we see "unconstrained" (i.e., 0 on the column dimension) versus "elite constrained," (1, high levels of constraints) which implies an underlying dimension of degree of constraint. The row variable also seems to have an ordinal ranking by the size of the "audience" from small (i.e., military, 0) to large (i.e., civilian, 1). Her hypothesis is that the $(1, 1)$ cell is least likely to have a militarized dispute, while the $(0, 0)$ cell is the most likely. That row and column variables are ordinal becomes clear in Weeks's statistical analysis of them (see table 8.2).

TABLE 8.2. Partially ordered typologies and statistical analysis: autocratic regime type and militarized disputes

| Regime type | Parameter estimate | Standard error |
| --- | --- | --- |
| Junta | 0.46** | 0.20 |
| Boss | 0.67*** | 0.17 |
| Strongman | 0.93*** | 0.16 |

*Source:* Based on Weeks (2014). *Note:* Control variables left out.

There is a key methodological point:

If row *and* column are ordinal then the 2 × 2 table is minimally a partially ordered typology.

The next methodological question lies in the middle zone of $(1, 0)$ and $(0, 1)$. If there is a ranking between them then the 2 × 2 typology becomes ordinal. If they are equal then it is partially ordered. In practice, it is not common (in my experience at least) for authors to explicitly address this question. From the discussion one might interpret the typology as ordinal, but rarely is it made explicit.

Extremely common when using typologies as independent variables are hypotheses that type 1 is more likely than type 2 to score high on the dependent variable. Most of the literature using typologies of autocracy invokes hypotheses of this sort. For example, autocratic party regimes are longer lived than personalist regimes. In the case of Weeks we have hypotheses like the probability of initiating a militarized interstate dispute runs from machines at the lowest, to juntas, then bosses with strongmen as the most likely (Weeks 2014, table 1.3).

By making a hypothesis like this she suggests that there is an ordinal character to her typology. At the same time, the typology most often treated is nominal. This ambiguity appears in the statistical analyses; see table 8.2. With a four-category typology, one has three dummy variables and one excluded category. If the typology is partially ordered then the natural thing to do is to use the lowest category as the excluded category, which is exactly what Weeks does: "machine" types are the least likely to become involved in a militarized dispute and hence are the excluded category.

Because she treats the typology as nominal rather than ordinal she does not test a number of the hypotheses embedded in the partial ordering, but which she gives in her table 1.3. All that the statistics in table 8.2 tell you is, say, that strongman is significantly different from machine. However, the partial ordering also hypothesizes that (1) strongman is significantly more likely to be involved in a militarized dispute than junta or boss and (2) junta and boss are not significantly different from each other.

While it is hard to tell without actual statistical tests (which are possible; see Kim 2018 for an example), it does appear that strongman is significantly different from boss and junta. Thus, it is quite possible that the partial ordering is empirically an ordinal ordering since boss seems significantly more likely to be involved in disputes than junta based on the coefficients.

A key mythological issue is that there are two separate ways to do the ordering which often go together in practice. The first ordering might be called the conceptual ordering, where the aggregation procedures of the row and column variables produce the ordering. The second one is a causal ordering, where there is an order in the predicted probability or level of the outcome variable that determines the ordering.

If one considers the typology to be ordinal then *either row or column must be more important and influential, i.e., they are of unequal importance.* To say that the cell $(X_1 = 0, X_2 = 1)$ is greater than the cell $(X_1 = 1, X_2 = 0)$ means that $X_2 > X_1$.

The partial ordering arises only because row and column are considered of equal importance. Once this is no longer the case then the ordering in general will be complete, though this obviously depends on the exact weights one gives for each value of row and column. This becomes quite clear in the continuous version with an interaction term. The values for the four cells then are determined by formula $X_1 + X_2 + X_1 * X_2$. If this returns unique values for all cells then ordering is complete, if some cells have the same value then the ordering is partial.

TABLE 8.3. Underlying row and column concepts and statistical analysis

|  | Parameter estimate | Standard error |
|---|---|---|
| Personalism index | 1.08*** | 0.23 |
| Militarism index | 1.26*** | 0.28 |
| Personalism * Militarism | −0.81*** | 0.31 |

Source: Based on Weeks (2014). Note: Control variables left out.

This reinforces the point made in the scaling chapter: one must decide whether row and column are ordinal or not. If they are really nominal it would be better (following the terminology guidelines) to give values that do not suggest ordinality, hence the suggestion about emojis.

We can state the key takeaway guideline:

Partially ordered typologies imply a series of hypotheses that need to be tested empirically, particularly if statistical analyses are conducted. Depending on the outcome of the statistical tests the typology might be ordinal empirically.

The larger conceptual and theoretical issue lies in the relationship between the row–column concepts and the cells of the typology. The cells are really a function of and generated by the underlying row and column variables. One has two options: (1) treat the cells as a nominal or partially ordered typology or (2) just use the underlying row and column variables. Theoretically and empirically it is the underlying row and column concepts that are doing the work. As such, these should be the center of analysis. Weeks in her statistical analysis actually does this; see table 8.3, which illustrates that one does not need the typology at all; the analysis can proceed with the underlying row and column variables.

Weeks raises the interesting question of whether there should be an interaction term between row and column variables. Implicit in the whole typologizing idea is that each cell constitutes a different type. Hence it would be quite appropriate to include an interaction term as Weeks does.

A core issue with the DSM is that of comorbidity (see Richards and O'Hara 2014 for a long discussion in the context of depression). This is the fact that often there are multiple diseases that a person has. The DSM constructs and conceptualizes mental disorders using a continuum of more or fewer symptoms. One can take the $2 \times 2$ table and think of it as a way to deal with the comorbidity problem. The row variable is one disorder; the column variable is another related disorder. The various cells in the table are one way to think about how there are various configurations of the relation between the two diseases.

This example raises a core question about the causal relationship between the row and column diseases. The varieties of democracy and autocracy are mostly a descriptive literature. However, for comorbidity a crucial question is the causal relationship between row and column diseases. This would be a natural question to explore and the empirical data patterns might suggest causal relationships between the two diseases. This produces a core guideline for $2 \times 2$ table typologies:

Causal Relationships in Typologies Guideline: Examine for possible causal relationships between the row and column variables.

There should be a clear and explicit theoretical and empirical discussion about whether or not one includes an interaction term. The typology strongly suggests that one should, but practice is probably not at all uniform on this point. Thus in a $2 \times 2$ typology there is an inherent tension between the typology of the cells and the row and column concepts. It is completely reasonable to ask about the interaction of two concepts. As Weeks illustrates, one can do that independent of the typology.

In short, this creates the following recommendation:

Focus on the underlying row and column concepts and their interaction.

The Weeks example illustrates the tension between what seems to be a nominal typology, but which is minimally partially ordered, and might well be completely ordinal. This then coexists with the underlying row and column variables—which are continuous—that generate the typology to begin with. These problems will almost inevitably arise with 2 × 2 typologies, unless it is made completely clear that row and column themselves are really nominal without any underlying continuum. Otherwise, all the issues just discussed will arise with force.

If the typology is partially or completely ordered, the recommendation is to focus on the row and column concepts, their underlying continua, and their interaction. The row and column concepts are doing the heavy conceptual work. If one follows the recommendation then the typology disappears and we are left with the core, two concepts and their interaction. The typology distracts attention from what is most important: the two concepts.

### Nominal Typologies or a Concept Pair with an Underlying Continuum?

We have seen that 2 × 2 typologies are in fact easily ordinal or partially ordered. This is potentially a common problem with typologies. In terms of guidelines, one should always clearly ask whether some of the types or all of the types in fact have a continuum and perhaps constitute a concept pair. In this short subsection I illustrate how a nominal typology in fact is, or can easily become, a concept pair with an underlying continuum. Of course, if one ends up with a concept pair and continuum then the typology has in fact disappeared.

Schmitter's famous concept of corporatism (1974; see p. 90 in this book) illustrates this tension between nominal typologies and concept pairs. The scope of his concept was all states. Following the exhaustive rule, he created a typology of regime types with corporatism as the focal type. For almost all, the opposite of corporatism is pluralism (e.g., the USA). To fill out the population he included the types "syndicalist" and "monist." The typology of the four types was clearly nominal, but embedded in it was a concept pair. Once the two unimportant types—syndicalist and monist—disappeared (which they did almost immediately), the concept pair corporatism–pluralism was left. Because one was now left with corporatism and its opposite of pluralism, it was easy to generate data sets, almost all at the interval level, for the corporatism–pluralism concept pair.

The main example in this section involves the typology of democracy that dominates the literature with typically three types: parliamentary, semipresidential, and presidential. This is usually treated as a nominal typology but with serious ambiguity about it. Chapter 7 treated semipresidentialism as a gray zone concept in its own right. However, it has usually been seen as part of a nominal typology of democratic regimes. This section explores these ways of framing that concept: (1) as part of a nominal typology of democratic regimes versus (2) as a gray zone concept of the parliamentary–presidential concept pair.

One way to view this typology is as a concept pair with presidential regimes at one end and parliamentary at the other. This would be presidential–parliamentary, just like democracy–autocracy. Semipresidential is in the middle, just like competitive–authoritarian. This approach is strongly supported by table 8.4.[5] Of course, the gray zone of semipresidential is worthy of attention and there have been whole books devoted to it (Elgie 2011).

Table 8.4 gives a very clear and accepted view of the three concepts and their defining or important features and attributes. If there is a concept pair then one would expect the positive pole, parliamentary, to have exactly the opposite attributes of its opposite, presidential. Not surprisingly, if mixed were in the middle it would have a combination of attributes from both sides, but would lack the complete set for either side. As table 8.4 shows, this is exactly the case. If one side has yes on an attribute then the other has no on that attribute, e.g., "assembly confidence."

---

5. It is interesting to note in line with Geddes that there is a strong motivation to get rid of the hybrid type. For example, in Cheibub's influential book (2007) he collapses the mixed to parliamentary, just as Geddes collapses all of her hybrids into one of the pure types.

TABLE 8.4. Nominal typology or concept pair? Attributes of executive-legislative systems

| Attribute | Presidential | Parliamentary | Semipresidential |
|---|---|---|---|
| **Defining attribute** | | | |
| Assembly confidence | No | Yes | For head of govt |
| Popularly elected head of state | Yes | No | Yes |
| **Elective attributes** | | | |
| Executive decree | No | Yes | Depends |
| Emergency powers | Strong | Weak | Strong |
| Initiation of legislation | Legislature | Executive | Depends |
| Legislative oversight | Yes | No | Depends |
| Executive veto | Yes | No | Depends |
| Cabinet appointment | Executive | Legislature | Depends |
| **Other attributes** | | | |
| Assembly dissolution | No | Yes | Depends |

*Source:* Based on Cheibub et al. (2014).

With a concept pair one needs to discuss the underlying continuum. Here it is quite clear: the strength and autonomy of the president that varies from one end of the spectrum to the other.

The literature on varieties of democracy has various typologies of various sizes. There appears to be a process by which a typology of say, eight types, becomes a concept pair with an underlying continuum. So it is not only three-part typologies that become a concept pair, but it can happen with significantly more types in typology.

Part of this process seems to be that types at either end of the continuum are often considered essentially the same. Shugart (2005) and Siaroff (2003) provide examples with typologies of five types and eight types respectively. Siaroff nicely illustrates how this works. He starts with eight types and then loses a couple through consolidation at the poles: "Overall, though, Category 6 basically replicates the conditions of Category 2" (p. 306); this is the presidential pole.

One can then divide the continuum into parts according to some underlying dimension. Siaroff then explicitly develops a measure of presidential power, which is the continuum between the two poles. Thus at the negative side one has parliamentary systems, as well as mixed systems where the president has little or no power. At the other end are presidential regimes where presidents are powerful and not responsible to parliament at all, and not selected by parliament.

Siaroff then divides the gray zone into three parts depending on the size of presidential power: "I would argue that such systems [gray zone] should be divided into three categories, based on their total score [of presidential power], with the breakpoints set at three and six" (p. 307). Quite interestingly, he notes that there is much more heterogeneity in the gray zone than at the ends. As we saw in chapter 7, this is a common feature of gray zones.

It is of course hard to say how common it is that typologies can be represented by a concept pair with an underlying continuum. The example in this section illustrates just how this can happen in one important substantive area. So while it might seem unlikely that a typology with five or more types could be reduced to a concept pair, these examples show that it is certainly possible. In general, when faced with typologies it is worth asking the concept pair question. This can make the typology much more tractable once one begins to formulate causal hypotheses and create research designs.

## Latent Variables and Typologies

This chapter has explored typologies in a top-down fashion. One creates the typology and then applies it to individual observations and cases. This is quite typical of much qualitative research. However, one can do it bottom up in a statistical fashion. One has a variety of indicators, and one applies a latent trait or variable model which then produces latent variables that constitute the typology. There are numerous statistical techniques, e.g., clustering methods, for creating typologies. It goes way beyond the scope of this short section to discuss the many and varied statistical techniques, but in the context of this discussion of typologies a few remarks are in order.

The appendix of chapter 2 outlined the latent variable approach to conceptualization-measurement. These methodologies are commonly used to produce inductive typologies based on a set of indicators.

Recall that most often the methodology produces more than one latent variable. These different latent variables then become a typology.

For latent variables of democracy one can take dozens of indicators, plug them into the latent variable methodology, and then generate a typology. Ziaja and Elff (2015) illustrate how this can work for regime type. They include a variety of indicators of democracy from various democracy projects. Unlike Geddes and others, they use all nation-years, so it is not a typology of autocracy but a typology of political regimes. The empirical analysis (using a finite mixture methodology) discovers seven types.

In general, latent variable methodologies involve significant researcher input in determining the number of types. In latent variable methods there is no obvious break as the types get weaker and weaker. Ziaja and Elff could have gone with six or eight types but they opted for a typology of seven regime types: (1) transitional regimes, (2) presidential democracies, (3) defective presidential democracies, (4) (absolute) monarchies, (5) one-party regimes, (6) parliamentary democracies, (7) personalistic autocracies. It is clear that there are democratic types (presidential versus parliamentary), gray zone types (e.g., defective presidential democracies), and autocratic types.

In the statistical literature on typologies one does not always find explicit discussions of the mutually exclusive or exhaustive rules. However, they are often present in various ways. It is assumed in some techniques. For example, Rupp in his survey in an Oxford handbook illustrates this: "Hierarchical clustering techniques are prototypically designed to sequentially partition a set of $N$ cases into $K$ mutually exclusive clusters [a typology] based on the joint information contained in the $J$ outcome variables. (Rupp 2013, 522). Other techniques, such as latent class, are similar: "The $K$ classes are exhaustive and mutually exclusive such that each individual in the population has membership in exactly one of the $K$ latent classes" (Masyn 2013, 552). Sometimes the rule is implicitly present. When choosing latent variable types, a clear guiding principle is that they should be as different as possible. In practice this means, ideally, that they are not highly correlated with each other. The mutually exclusive rule becomes the goal of zero or low correlation, and hence low overlap, between the types.

The exhaustive rule means that every country-year is assigned to a type. There are no "missing data" for any country-year in terms of the typology. However, there are likely to be observations that fit no type very well; they are placed into the highest scoring type in order to fulfill the exhaustiveness rule. It is also possible and normal that an observation might have significant membership in multiple types, but it is placed into just one in order to fulfill the mutually exclusive rule.

The nature of the latent variable methodology means that the reality of overlap is present. Because there is overlap between empirically nearby categories, there are observations that cannot be neatly put into just one category. Typically, this messiness is ignored and a given observation is put into the category where it fits best, though perhaps not well.

## Conclusion

This chapter argues that following the standard guidelines for typologies will almost inevitably lead to serious problems, theoretical and empirical. Mutually exclusive categories ignore that observations can be partial members of multiple concepts. The exhaustive rule leads to the creation of new types that are often of little interest to the researcher: they are just there to fulfill the exhaustive rule.

To its credit, the DSM has slowly recognized that the mutually exclusive and exhaustive rules just do not work. Just like Geddes, when applying the rules in practice—the DSM is very much oriented toward practitioners—one finds that in the real world, people have multiple disorders at the same time and the boundaries between having the disorder and not having it are often not clear. Following the exhaustive rule means the proliferation of disorders, which is clearly not desirable and makes it harder for practitioners to make diagnoses because there are so many disorders: this then generates even more problems about boundaries and people having multiple disorders. It probably is best for the patient if the doctor admits that the patient does not fit neatly into any one category. This would be better than trying to force patients into some diagnosis, with potentially significant drug treatment issues, that are not appropriate for them.

> Structural problems rooted in the basic design of the previous DSM classification, constructed of a large number of narrow diagnostic categories, have emerged in both clinical practice and research. Relevant evidence comes from diverse sources, including studies of comorbidity and the substantial need for not otherwise specified diagnoses, which represent the majority of diagnoses in areas such as eating disorders, personality disorders, and autism spectrum disorder. (DSM-5, 12)

One can see the problems of the standard rules in the procedures for putting and coding typologies into spreadsheets. By far the most common procedure is to have one column that gives which type the observation is coded as, often from 1 to the maximum number of types. This implies, virtually by definition, that one should be doing things in a mutually exclusive fashion. When that becomes problematic, often research teams will add a second column for "secondary coding" for a second type for each observation. Following the recommendations of this chapter, the procedure should be to have one column for each concept or type and then the degree of membership of the observation for that particular type or concept. This explicitly allows for membership in multiple types with no limit to the number or amount of overlap. If a new concept is relevant then it becomes a new column in the spreadsheet and each observation is coded on that concept, independent of what's going on in the other columns.

The solution to the problems of typologies is to focus clearly on the concepts and ignore the typology. These concepts should be applied to all the observations in the scope independently. It might be the case that there is little overlap between the concepts in the data, but there might be significant overlap: this is an empirical as well as conceptual question.

With $2 \times 2$ typologies one should focus on the underlying row and column concepts that generate the typology. There might be important interactions between the two underlying concepts that generate interesting theories and hypotheses.

For all nominal typologies one needs to ask whether there are in fact one or more underlying concept pairs that are really driving the whole thing. If so, focus on them and not the typology.

Going full circle, a typology is a set of concepts. Each of those concepts merits a detailed examination and development. For example, all the guidelines of chapter 3 apply, and $2 \times 2$ tables that have partial ordering have underlying continua that need to be analyzed and described following the guidelines in chapter 3. Typologies require no additional methodology—i.e., rules like mutually exclusive and exhaustive—beyond those required for conceptualization-measurement in general.

# 9

# Intension–Extension

## CONCEPT STRUCTURE AND
## EMPIRICAL DESCRIPTION

## Introduction

This chapter discusses the relationship between concept structure, the number of secondary-level dimensions, and the empirical coverage of a concept. "Intension" is the meaning or definition of the concept; "extension" is its empirical coverage. For example, Skocpol's definition is that "social revolutions are rapid, basic transformations of a society's state and class structures; and they are accompanied and in part carried through by class-based revolts from below" (1979, 4–5). The extension, within her scope conditions, consists of Russia 1917, China 1950, and France 1789. Within larger scope conditions, Foran (1997) has added other cases such as Iran 1979 and Mexico 1910.

The issue of the relationship between intension and extension comes from the philosophy of concepts–definitions and its use of mathematical logic—necessary and sufficient conditions—to structure concepts. This intension–extension language from philosophy is quite foreign to the social sciences. Sartori (1970) imported this set of issues into political science and reformulated them in terms of "traveling" and "stretching."

One of the most important guidelines set out in chapter 3 is to conceptualize via ideal types. In common usage, an ideal type has very small extension. One conceptualizes so that extension is narrow or zero. To conceptualize via ideal types thus focuses already on the methodological issue of how intension relates to extension.

Extension *does not* mean the scope of the concept, but rather it means the number of cases with nonzero membership in the concept. So the ideas of traveling and stretching do not apply to scope but rather to the number of cases lying at the positive pole.

It is quite possible that ideal types do not always have low extension. Chapter 7, on hybrid concepts, explored ideal type, gray zone democracy, which might be relatively common. However, frequently ideal types do have few exemplars. The prototypical ideal type usually does have small extension. In the next section I discuss the most famous and most explicit ideal type definition of democracy, developed by Dahl. It is explicitly a zero-extension ideal type because there are no actual empirical examples of democracy in its ideal state.

My discussion of ideal types leads naturally then to a general discussion of the relationship between concept structure (intension) and empirical coverage (extension). With the mathematical logic approach to concepts there is a clear relationship between concept structure and extension, which is the weakest link aggregation class:

> As one increases intension in the sense of increasing the number of necessary defining characteristics, the extension—number of empirical cases—must stay the same or go down.

This is a mathematical fact linked to the use of necessary conditions. Once one moves to other methods of aggregation it no longer applies. Adding new secondary-level dimensions may result empirically in more or fewer cases.

In the history of philosophy it was Wittgenstein who introduced the notion of family resemblance, exactly as a contrast with the Aristotelian, necessary and sufficient condition approach to conceptualization. In contrast to the classic Aristotelian approach, family resemblance specifically denies that any feature is necessary. One only has sufficiency requirements. In terms of substitutability, the absence of one feature can be compensated for by the presence of another.

Cartwright and Runhardt illustrate this natural use of family resemblance in their discussion of *Ballung* concepts:

> In order to describe this fuzziness we find in concepts like civil war, we call them *Ballung* concepts: concepts that are characterized by family resemblance between individuals rather than by a definite property.... Neurath worried about the role that *Ballung* concepts can play in "proper science" since it seems there can be no strict universal relations of the kind typical in physics (and perhaps other natural sciences) between concepts that have neither strict boundaries nor whose instances share any essential features in common. (Cartwright and Runhardt 2014, 268–69)

Most of the discussion in philosophy, political science following Sartori, and much of cognitive psychology, has assumed the weakest link approach to concept structure. One must start there when discussing the semantics of adjectives and other hyphenated concepts. However, one can contrast this well-known view about the relationship between intension and extension with the almost completely ignored principle that with the best shot, maximum, OR, or union as the concept structure, extension increases:

> As one increases intension in the sense of increasing the number of best shot defining characteristics, the extension—number of empirical cases—goes up.

If we replace AND in the classic relationship between intension and extension with OR then the number of empirical cases must remain the same or go up. Obviously, adding a new feature to the union must increase, or not change, its size. The same is true with the sum (assuming again that everything is in [0, 1]): the sum must go up if you add another secondary-level dimension.

To illustrate how this can work I discuss the example of the gender critique of the traditional concept of the welfare state. The purpose of the gender critique is to *increase* the extension of the welfare state to cover circumstances that are common to women (e.g., single mothers).

One might ask about the mean aggregation class. As one might imagine, there is no clear automatic relationship between adding dimensions and extension. This is intuitively obvious by thinking about the average: if you add a new dimension the average might go up or might go down depending on the specific values for each observation.[1]

As discussed throughout this volume, terminology is critical. Often one has hyphenated concepts, my generic term for multiple concept concepts. Often with hyphenated concepts the adjective (which can also be a noun) modifies another concept. For example, "parliamentary democracy" consists of the core concept of democracy modified by the adjective concept parliamentary. This has direct implications for extension, because one has increased the number of dimensions. So how should one interpret this hyphenated concept?

This chapter also discusses another common semantic practice whereby the adjective does not add a dimension but rather restricts the value on a given dimension. Typically this occurs when one or more secondary-level dimensions are given the value 0. The concept of the Weberian state illustrates this. If a state has value 0 on territorial control, then it is often referred to as a *de jure* state. If it has control but no international recognition, it is often called a *de facto* state. If it has all the defining features it is just a state *tout court*. We will see that these kinds of concepts have no clear implication for extension: it can go up or down.

In summary, this chapter treats the classic issue of concept structure and its relationship to empirical coverage. It covers the standard inverse relationship between intension and extension and weakest link aggregation. Ideal type concepts enter into the discussion because again they are interpreted—almost always implicitly—using the assumption of the necessary and sufficient condition concept structure. The chapter briefly contrasts that with the opposite principle for the best shot

---

1. Because mean aggregation does not really exist in the discussion about intension–extension (and much semantic practice) I do not discuss it at length. This is a direct consequence of the fact that the debate arrives from philosophy and logic where the mean is not in the discussion.

concept structure. Finally, it deals with the semantics of hyphenated concepts and adjectives.

## Ideal Types: Zero Extension

One concept-building strategy known to most social scientists uses the "ideal type" construction. This chapter focuses on concepts and their extensions; an ideal type usually has the empty set as its extension. It is an *ideal* type because it never or rarely can be found. In practice, the principle meaning of ideal type is that the concept has zero extension.

The ideal type concept traces its historical origins back to Max Weber (1949). Burger describes Weber's view: "Ideal types are statements of general form asserting the existence of certain constellations of elements which are empirically *only approximated* by the instances of the class of phenomena to which each type refers" (Burger 1987, 133–34; emphasis is mine). There has developed a small literature devoted to Weber and his methodology, including the ideal type. Unfortunately, these analyses and debates about Weber are conducted in a very abstract and philosophical way (e.g., Heckman 1983). There is very little in the way of guidelines that permit one to evaluate what a good (or bad) ideal type looks like, and hence very little guidance on how to construct an ideal type concept.[2]

More useful than the controversial subject of what Weber said about ideal types is what sociologists and political scientists have done when they have created ideal types. So my analysis may not capture Weber's thought, but it does attempt to be faithful to common practice when scholars make and use ideal types.

An ideal type in my framework would mean those cases that score 1.0 (i.e., the maximum) on all the secondary-level dimensions. In many ways this is the best way to think about ideal types. Inherent in the notion of an ideal type is that it lies at the extreme end of the continuum. There can be nothing, conceptually at least, that is better.

2. It is striking to notice how often ideal types are used and the almost complete absence of any discussion of them in methodology texts.

It is useful to think of ideal types in geometric terms. The ideal type (like the ideal point in spatial utility models) is the point where all dimensions are at the maximum. One can contrast, e.g., measure the distance between, any given empirical object and that ideal point (e.g., Gärdenfors 2000).

What seems to typify ideal types in practice is that while they do not necessarily differ from ordinary concepts on intension they do differ from them on extension. Typically, when scholars propose an ideal type, they are thinking that the extension of the ideal type is likely to be zero or very small: "I shall take it that a distinguishing characteristic of ideal type concepts is that they have no instances" (Papineau 1976, 137). The ideal is one that cannot be attained in practice. This certainly lies behind Weber's use of the term. Ideal types were useful as a means—really a standard—for thinking about a less-than-ideal reality.

An important part of concept design is whether one can find actual cases with the maximum values on the scale of the basic-level concept. The advice to the concept builder is to think seriously about this issue. One might want to stretch out the scale so that there are very few (if any) cases at either extreme. The underlying idea is that if there is a large clump of cases at the positive end, then in reality the end point is not the ideal type and one could go further (see the discussion of figure 3.1 in chapter 3).

Robert Dahl's concept of democracy and polyarchy serves as one very good example of an ideal type in action that clearly uses a necessary and sufficient condition structure. His conceptualization of democracy is perhaps one of the most famous ideal types in the literature.[3] Dahl developed the same basic view of democracy over forty years (1956; 1971; 1989; 1998). He is interesting because he clearly distinguishes between the ideal type "democracy," which no country has ever achieved, and "polyarchy," the term he prefers for those states that are closest to the democracy ideal. Dahl is quite unusual in separating so clearly the ideal type from the lower levels; most scholars prefer to keep the same word for the ideal type and those phenomena that get

3. Max Weber's ideal type analysis of bureaucracy is another very famous example.

close. He quite clearly expresses his views on democracy in terms of ideal types:

> In this book I should like to reserve the term "democracy" for a political system one of the characteristics of which is the quality of being completely or almost completely responsive to all its citizens. Whether such a system actually exists, has existed, or can exist need not concern us for the moment. Surely one can conceive a hypothetical system of this kind; such a conception has served as an ideal, or part of an ideal, for many people. As a hypothetical system, one end of a scale, or a limiting state of affairs, it can (like a perfect vacuum) serve as the basis for estimating the degree to which various systems appropriate this theoretical limit. (Dahl 1971, 2)

Here we see most of the typical features of an ideal type. The extension of the concept may well be zero or near zero. The usefulness of the ideal type is as a standard against which one can compare existing objects.

It is worth noting that Dahl views democracy in a three-level fashion typical of complex concepts (1971):[4]

I. Formulate preferences
   A. Freedom to form and join organizations
   B. Freedom of expression
   C. Right to vote
   D. Right of political leaders to compete for support
   E. Alternative sources of information
II. Signify preferences
   A. Freedom to form and join organizations
   B. Freedom of expression
   C. Right to vote
   D. Eligibility for public office
   E. Right of political leaders to compete for support

---

4. See Dahl (1989, 222) for a different three-level model of democracy. I leave as an exercise whether it is a good idea to have the same lower-level attribute in different secondary-level dimensions, e.g., "Freedom to form and join organizations."

    F. Alternative sources of information

    G. Free and fair elections

III. Have preferences weighted equally in conduct of government

    A. Freedom to form and join organizations

    B. Freedom of expression

    C. Right to vote

    D. Eligibility for public office

    E. Right of political leaders to compete for support

    F. Alternative sources of information

    G. Free and fair elections

    H. Institutions for making government policies depend on votes and other expressions of preference

One way to build into the concept that its extension is likely to be zero is to use the necessary and sufficient condition structure for the concept. Dahl quite clearly uses AND at both levels of his concept of democracy. Everything at all levels is connected via AND (i.e., it is 100 percent nonhybrid). This makes it very difficult to find any real-world phenomenon that satisfies such exigent conditions. To make things even more difficult, Dahl says that the above structure is necessary but *not* sufficient: "These, [secondary-level dimensions] appear to me to be three necessary conditions for a democracy, though they are probably not sufficient" (Dahl 1971, 2).[5]

In short, democracy remains a pretty unattainable ideal: "Polyarchy is one of the most extraordinary of all human artifacts. Yet it unquestionably falls well short of achieving the democratic process" (Dahl 1989, 223). Polyarchy describes well those states that have made significant progress. Democracy is an ideal that we should strive for but which we are unlikely to ever achieve.

It is not hard to find others with a similar take on ideal types, for example in the context of concepts of political parties:

---

5. Schmitter and Karl adopt the Dahl list of prerequisites and add two more necessary conditions: "Popularly elected officials must be able to exercise their constitutional powers without being subjected to overriding (albeit informal) opposition from unelected officials [e.g., army].... The polity must be self-governing; it must be able to act independently of constraints imposed by some other overarching political system" (1991, 81).

It is important to note that the models of political parties that we describe below are ideal types, in the strictest Weberian sense of that term. As such, they are heuristically useful insofar as they give easily understandable labels that will help the reader more easily comprehend otherwise complex, multidimensional concepts. Moreover, they facilitate analysis insofar as they serve as baselines for comparisons involving real-world cases, or as extreme endpoints of evolutionary processes that might never be fully attained. As with all ideal types, however, one should not expect that real-world political parties fully conform to all of the criteria that define each party model; similarly, some parties may include elements of more than one ideal type. Perhaps most importantly, individual parties may evolve over time, such that they may have most closely approximated one party type in an earlier period, but shift in the direction of a different type later on. (Gunther and Diamond 2003, 172)

Given the framework for concept construction in this book, thinking in terms of ideal types provides no additional benefits. From chapter 3 we have guidelines for thinking clearly about the positive pole of the basic level. The positive pole almost by definition provides a standard for comparison. In reality, when most scholars use the term "ideal type" all they really mean is that the extension is zero at the pole. Whether the extension is large or small at the end is an empirical puzzle that calls for a causal explanation. For example, there are good causal reasons why it is hard to achieve absolute zero temperature. The existence of few or zero cases *anywhere* along the continuum—for example in the gray zone between democracy and autocracy—generally poses questions worth examining.

## Necessary and Sufficient Condition Concept Structures and Concept Extension

The relationship between intension and extension has been a staple of philosophical logic for decades. It was introduced into the social sciences by Sartori (1970) and then implicitly analyzed by Collier and his students (e.g., Collier and Mahon 1993). Satori's choice of the term "ladder of abstraction" is unfortunate, while Collier's "ladder of generality" is only marginally better. A concept with four defining features is not necessarily more or less abstract or general than one with two.

Philosophers see definitions as involving necessary and sufficient conditions. It is useful to go to Sartori's main source, the classic philosophical logic textbook of the 1930s and 1940s by Cohen and Nagel:

"A 'definition,'" according to Aristotle, "is a phrase signifying a thing's essence." By the essence of a thing he understood the set of fundamental attributes which are the necessary and sufficient conditions for any concrete thing to be a thing of that type. It approximates to what we have called the conventional intension of a term. (Cohen and Nagel 1934, 235)

Gerring in his book on concepts gives a brief genealogy which ends with Sartori (see also Adcock and Collier 2001):

The classical approach to concept formation [necessary and sufficient conditions] may be traced back to Aristotle and the scholastic philosophers of the Middle Ages. For later variants, see Chapin (1939), Cohen and Nagel (1934), DiRenzo (1966), Dumont and Wilson (1967), Hempel (1952, 1963, 1965, 1966), Landau (1972), Lasswell and Kaplan (1950), Lazarsfeld (1966), Meehan (1971), Stinchcombe (1968, 1978), Zannoni (1978) and most important Sartori (1970, 1984), and Sartori et al. (1975). (Gerring 2001, 66)

In principle, intension determines the extension. In good social science, theory should drive the choice of cases. It is the theory of social revolution that should determine which cases are selected, not necessarily the everyday use of the term "revolution," or informal ideas about which cases fit.

If one increases the number of secondary-level attributes in the intension *and if*—this is the big if that Sartori does not mention—one uses the necessary and sufficient condition structure then there is an inverse relationship between intension and extension. Again quoting from Sartori's source:

The law of inverse variation must, therefore, be stated as follows: *If a series of terms is arranged in order of increasing intension, the denotation of the terms* [extension] *will either remain the same or diminish.* (Cohen and Nagel 1934, 33)

In short, we can increase the coverage (i.e., extension) of a concept by reducing its intension (i.e., number of attributes). More specifically, and more accurately, we can increase the extension by reducing the number of necessary attributes in the intension. "Conceptual stretching" thus means in operational terms eliminating necessary dimensions.

When scholars talk about "how far a concept travels" what they in fact mean is increasing extension. This traveling metaphor is actually quite misleading. For example, the concept of "military coup" applies to Western European states, e.g., they would be included in a data set on military coups as zero cases. The extension issue is that since World War II there have been almost no cases (except, e.g., Greece 1968) of military coups in this region.

This becomes pretty clear once one begins to think about the mathematical operations that typify the necessary and sufficient condition structure in contrast with the family resemblance one. We can contrast the necessary and sufficient condition AND with the family resemblance OR. Clearly, if we add attributes with AND the extension can only go down (or remain the same in exceptional circumstances). However, if we use OR to add dimensions then the extension almost certainly goes up. This is visible if one imagines Venn diagrams; the intersection of two sets (representing two attributes) is almost always smaller than either set individually. In contrast, the union is almost always larger than the individual sets.

Figure 9.1 illustrates how extension goes down as intension goes up with the well-known Democracy–Dictatorship group concept

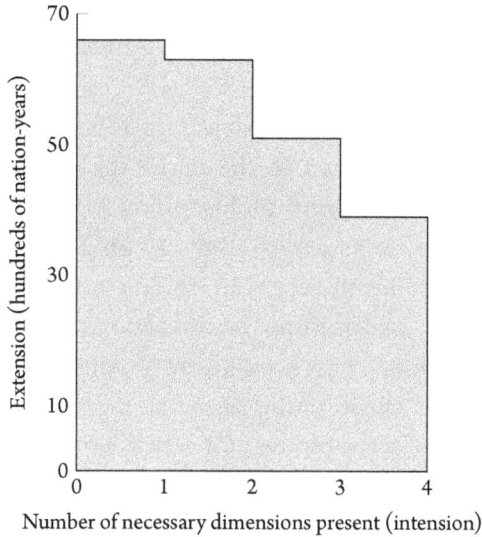

FIGURE 9.1. Intension–extension relationships:
Democracy–Dictatorship group concept of
democracy, 1946–2008.

and data set on democracy (Cheibub et al. 2010).[6] There are four necessary secondary-level dimensions that are jointly sufficient for democracy:

> A regime is classified as a democracy if it meets the requirements stipulated in *all* of the following four rules:
> 1. The chief executive must be chosen by popular election or by a body that was itself popularly elected.
> 2. The legislature must be popularly elected.
> 3. There must be more than one party competing in the elections.
> 4. An alternation in power under electoral rules identical to the ones that brought the incumbent to office must have taken place.

(Cheibub et al. 2010, 69)

6. I've added the new dimensions in the order given below.

As one can see from figure 9.1, increasing the intension of democracy by adding new required definitional dimensions means that the extension must go down.

The family resemblance approach was made famous by Wittgenstein (1953) exactly as a contrast to the necessary and sufficient condition essentialism of traditional philosophical logic. The contrast was that there were no necessary conditions, only a sufficiency condition. Classic family resemblance is an "$m$-of-$n$" concept structure: possessing $m$ of the $n$ total features is sufficient to be a member of the family (i.e., extension). This means substitutability for each individual dimension. It is worth noting that the $m$-of-$n$ rule means *at least* $m$-of-$n$, so $(m+1)$-of-$n$ counts, e.g., for a 2-of-3 rule, cases of 3-of-3 are included.

The clearest example linking the $m$-of-$n$ rule to the best shot is the 1-of-$n$ rule: if one of the dimensions is present then it is a member of the family. The presence of one substitutes for the absence of all the others. At the other end of the spectrum, to require $n$-of-$n$ means that each is necessary.

Philosophers focused on the family resemblance as involving no necessary conditions. This means looking at the $m$-of-$n$ structure toward the weakest link end. If one has a rule of $n$-of-$n$ for membership then one is at the weakest link end of the spectrum. Once one has $(n-1)$-of-$n$ then there are no longer any necessary conditions. Not surprisingly, philosophers and others of the Sartori tradition paid little attention to the other end of the spectrum, the 1-of-$n$ rule, which is complete substitutability and the best shot.

Figure 9.2 illustrates the relationship between intension and extension moving between the weakest link $n$-of-$n$ rule to the best shot 1-of-$n$ rule. With the dimensions of democracy of the Democracy–Dictatorship group, concept, data, and measure of democracy (Cheibub et al. 2010) we can explore the spectrum between the 1-of-3 rule (best shot) and the 3-of-3 (weakest link) concept structure and the extension using each rule.[7]

---

7. Because of the special nature of rule 4, I have used just the main three: "An alternation in power takes place when the incumbent occupying the chief executive office is replaced through

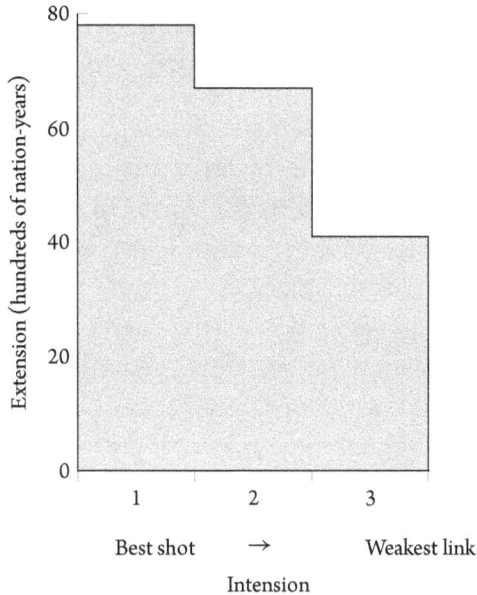

FIGURE 9.2. Best shot to weakest link rules:
Democracy–Dictatorship group concept
of democracy, 1946–2008.

It is important to realize that unlike figure 9.1, in figure 9.2 the intension has not changed in terms of the number of defining dimensions.
What has changed is the concept structure. In figure 9.1 intension was
changing as one added new defining features. So while the two figures
show the same pattern, we get there in very different ways: one by
changing the intension but keeping structure constant, the other by
keeping intension the same and changing the structure.

The possibility that OR might be used in concept structure does not
appear in the literature on intension and extension. As far as I can tell it
is extremely rare for an adjective or hyphen to mean OR in terms of concept structure. However, as the next section illustrates, one can want
to increase extension by adding secondary-level dimensions and hence
implicitly use a best shot concept structure.

---

elections that were organized under the same rules as the ones that brought him to office. The
alternation issue becomes relevant only in the cases where the first three rules apply" (Cheibub
et al. 2010, 70).

## Adding Dimensions and Increasing Extension:
## The Gendered Welfare State

As we have seen in the context of the philosophy, logic, and Sartori tradition, increasing intension decreases extension because of the use of AND to structure concepts. One could use OR or + as the structural principle. In this case, quite obviously, to increase intension increases extension. This section illustrates this with the concept of the welfare state and gender critiques of it. Recall that the size of the welfare state is the *sum* of spending on all categories (i.e., secondary-level dimensions) considered to constitute the welfare state. The point of the gender critique is to extend the conceptualization of the welfare state to include special concerns of women.

A major development in the literature on the welfare state over the last decades has involved the analysis of the gender bias both in the welfare state itself and in the scholarly literature on it which has reproduced that bias.

In these few pages I cannot cover all the ramifications of the gender critique of the welfare state literature (for reviews see Orloff 1996 and Pierson 2000). Of direct concern here is how gender issues modify our concept of the welfare state and the implications for both theory and methodology, in terms of both the concept itself and its links to theories about the welfare state.

The classic idea of a welfare state at its core involves the provision of goods and services to some large part of the population. One can reasonably ask (independent of gender really), (1) Who are the main target populations? (2) What kinds of goods and services get delivered? Virtually all social welfare programs targeted male workers in nonagricultural occupations, typically an industrial employee. Implicit in welfare state policies was a typical recipient who was male, married, and head of a household with children. Clearly, the wife/mother provided (unpaid of course) childcare, healthcare, and often services to aged parents, in addition to household duties.

If you examine the list of services typically included in the operationalization of the welfare state, they reflected quite faithfully the concept; almost all deal with problems of the working man. What happens if there is an accident on the job? What happens when he is unemployed? What happens when he gets old? Historically, the goods and services for the household/family were funneled through the principal (male) wage earner.

One can then ask what kinds of goods and services would be appropriate for a female head of household to keep her and her family alive and well. In addition to worker compensation, she would need maternity leave. To maintain her income (i.e., remain employed) she would need childcare. She would need a pension plan tied not just to the income of her spouse (not just survivor benefits). Thus to really take into account the concerns of women in the population, particularly as (single) heads of households, we need to reconceptualize the welfare state.

This gender analysis moves the concept of a welfare state in the ideal type direction. Just as a better concept and data for democracy should include women's and minority suffrage, so too should a good concept of welfare state include women and issues that are particularly relevant to their lives. A good concept of the welfare state includes all people in a country not just a subset of them. This clearly involves a normative analysis of the ontology of the welfare state.

Orloff argues that to take into account gender one must *add* two dimensions to the Esping-Andersen three dimension concept of the welfare state.[8] The first additional dimension requires that in addition to maintaining the basic wage of (male) workers, the strength of

---

8. The initial three dimensions from Esping-Andersen involve

    1. "A fundamental dimension that varies across welfare states concerns the 'range, or domain, of human needs that are satisfied by social policy' instead of by the market," that is, "how state activities are interlocked with the market's and the family's role in social provision" (Orloff 1993, 310);

    2. "A second dimension of policy regimes is stratification.... Power resources analysts [e.g., Esping-Andersen] argue that systems of social provision have stratifying effects: some policies may promote equality, cross-class solidarity, or minimize economic differences, while others may promote social dualism or maintain or strengthen class, status, or occupational differentiation" (Orloff 1993, 311);

a welfare state should depend on the degree to which it supports paid labor by women:

> Thus, the decommodification dimension must be supplemented with a *new* analytic dimension that taps into the extent to which states promote or discourage women's paid employment—the right to be commodified. I call this fourth dimension of welfare-state regimes *access to paid work*.... Thus, I contend that the extent to which the state ensures access to paid work for different groups and the mechanisms that guarantee jobs (e.g., reliance on private employment, creation of tax incentives, legal regulation of private employment, or public jobs programs) are dimensions of all policy regimes. (Orloff 1993, 318)

The second new gender dimension argues that one needs to extend the range of concern from individual men or women to the household and family. Most dramatically, the group of people most excluded from the traditional model was single-mother families. In the traditional system, all monies and services to the family, wife/mother, and children were funneled through the working father. One thus needs to think about what services would be appropriate to keep a *household* headed by a single woman going:

> If decommodification is important because it frees wage earners from the compulsion of participating in the market, a parallel dimension is needed to indicate the ability of those who do most of the domestic and caring work—almost all women—to form and maintain autonomous households, that is, to survive and support their children without having to marry to gain access to breadwinners' income. (Orloff 1993, 319)

---

3. "The third dimension of the welfare state concerns the character of social rights of citizenship. Some benefits are *universal*, that is, they are available to all citizens of a certain age or condition (e.g., sickness, unemployment, parenthood); some benefits depend on *labor market participation and financial contributions*; and some benefits are *income-tested*, that is they are available only to those with incomes assets below a certain level" (Orloff 1993, 311).

Most conceptualizations of the welfare state use the logic of the sum for conceptualization and measurement. This is not surprising when money is used as the quantitative measure of the welfare state. The aggregation function is thus the sum. If we conceive of the welfare state along these new lines then there are important downstream implications for measures of the welfare state.

Most quantitative studies of the welfare state use spending data [usually from the International Labor Organization (ILO)] for programs typically part of the male welfare state. ILO spending data (International Labor Organization 1949–) do cover "family allowances" and hence in part include programs that form part of Orloff's two additional dimensions. But Orloff argues that we also need to include all spending categories for programs that support (1) paid women's work and (2) women's capacity to maintain an autonomous household.

A gendered analysis thus includes new spending dimensions that should be included in the sum. However, a gendered analysis of the welfare state suggests a more radical reconceptualization of the welfare state, along with common quantitative measures. With rare exceptions, all post–World War II analyses of the welfare state use spending data.[9] However, the gender analysis of the welfare state often focuses quite explicitly on *rights*. For example, O'Connor et al. (1999) in their analysis of Australia, Canada, Great Britain, and the United States include abortion rights as a central dimension of comparison. Rights to divorce, contraception, and abortion are absolutely fundamental to women's welfare. In addition to the spending dimensions of the welfare state, one could well add a series of rights as new secondary-level dimensions.

This is exactly the sort of issue we have already seen when contrasting consumption concepts and measures of poverty with human well-being ones. Once one begins to include nonmonetary factors, such as

9. Welfare spending is defined by the ILO as government spending related to schemes, transfers, or services that (1) grant curative or preventive medical care, maintain income in case of involuntary diminution of earning, or grant supplementary income to persons with family responsibilities, (2) are legislatively sanctioned, and (3) are administered publicly or quasipublicly.

rights, then staying within the sum approach to conceptualization and measurement becomes difficult.

The gendered welfare state also illustrates how normative issues lie at the core of conceptualization. The classic welfare state was built on a view of women's and men's roles in the workplace and home such as "a woman's place is in the home." It also included an empirical description of how families work that lacked descriptive accuracy because it did not include single-parent families managed by women.

In terms of intension and extension, the point of adding new gender dimensions to the welfare state concept is to increase the coverage of the welfare state. With this example in mind it might be more common than one might imagine for scholars to want to increase the extension of a concept. One way to do this is to remove a necessary condition (i.e., the classic, Sartorian way) but another is to adopt a best shot or hybrid best shot concept structure.

## Hyphenated Concepts I: Necessary and Sufficient Condition Structure

The intension–extension rule for the necessary and sufficient condition concept structure defines what happens when the dimensions of the concept are added or removed. Perhaps the most common way to add dimensions is by attaching adjectives to the concept. As a first cut, when adjectives are used the default interpretation should be following the weakest link concept structure. Not surprisingly, however, semantic usage in social science practice—not to mention ordinary language practice—does not follow the rules of philosophical logic. The next sections explore some of the issues regarding the semantics of hyphenated concepts, concept structure, and extension.

Generally, there is the linguistic and semantic fact that we often attach adjectives to concepts. For example, a bewildering array of adjectives has been used to modify the concept of democracy. Corporatism has been modified by "liberal," "societal," or "democratic," among others. What is not clear is how adding an adjective modifies the structure of concepts. Often the adjective is a secondary-level dimension. This section explores the "classic" or "logical" semantics of what I call "hyphenated concepts." Whether there is in fact a hyphen depends on tradition and usage. The key thing is that hyphenated concepts involve two or more concepts, so sometimes there is a hyphen, e.g., "competitive–authoritarian," sometimes not "parliamentary democracy." The V-Dem project has different varieties of democracy, which means attaching the seven adjectives electoral, liberal, participatory, majoritarian, consensual, deliberative, or egalitarian to democracy.[10]

The classic hyphenated concept from philosophy and logic means semantically that *we are adding a new necessary dimension to the existing ones.* For example, "presidential" when modifying democracy adds a new attribute to those already existing for democracy. Hence the structural principle uses AND to conjoin the attribute presidential to the concept democracy. The basic principle is that "all noun modifiers are to be treated via conjunction" (Lakoff 1987, 14). Stepan and Skach on parliamentary and presidential democracy illustrate this:

> A pure parliamentary regime in a democracy is a system of mutual dependence: (1) The chief executive power must be supported by a majority in the legislature and can fall if it receives a vote of no confidence. (2) The executive power (normally in conjunction with the head of state) has the capacity to dissolve the legislature and call for elections. A pure presidential regime in a democracy is a system of mutual independence: (1) The legislative power has a fixed electoral mandate that is its own source of legitimacy. (2) The chief executive power has a fixed electoral mandate that is its own source of legitimacy. These necessary and sufficient characteristics are more than classificatory. (Stepan and Skach 1993, 3–4)

Notice that the intension of both definitions is limited by democracy, e.g., "a pure parliamentary regime *in a democracy.*" At the end, the

10. https://www.v-dem.net/en/about/

authors explicitly see the "parliamentary" adjective as adding two necessary conditions that are jointly sufficient. I refer to this practice as
AND-hyphenated concepts.

As we have seen, the fuzzy logic of necessary and sufficient conditions uses the minimum. So a continuous AND-hyphenated concept
would be interpreted in that fashion:

> They [Osherson and Smith 1982, a classic article] now consider
> three concepts: *apple, striped,* and *striped apple.* They correctly
> observe that within classical fuzzy set theory there is only one way
> to derive the complex category *striped apple* from the categories
> *apple* and *striped,* namely, by intersection of fuzzy sets—which is
> defined by taking the minimum of the membership values in the
> two component fuzzy sets. (Lakoff 1987, 140)

Sometimes there is a semantic hierarchy between the two concepts,
sometimes they are semantically equivalent. Mathematically the end
result is the same: one uses the logical AND to aggregate or structure
the concept. In short, AND-hyphenated concepts invoke the subsetting operation as well as the intersection of two concepts. "Pet fish" suggests a straight intersection, while "parliamentary democracy" invokes
subsetting.

## Hyphenated Concepts II: Nested Concepts

AND-hyphenated concepts often mean that one has a subset and superset relationship. When one has nested concepts, terminology needs
to be developed to distinguish betweem these nested concepts. The
concept of revolution illustrates this nicely.

Table 9.1 gives a modified survey of the concept of revolution
(Kotowski 1984). The names that appear on this list constitute many of
the key contributors to the literature on revolution over the years before
1984. Kotowski is quite explicit about the fact that the characteristics
listed in the table are necessary conditions for a revolution.

TABLE 9.1. Concepts with adjectives: nested concepts of "revolution"

| Scholar | Violence | Popular involvement | Change in governing body | Minor political structural change | Major political structural change | Stratification changes |
|---|---|---|---|---|---|---|
| *Social revolution* | | | | | | |
| Skocpol | Y | Y | Y | Y | Y | Y |
| Moore | Y | Y | Y | Y | Y | Y |
| *Political revolution* | | | | | | |
| Huntington | Y | Y | Y | Y | N | N |
| Johnson | Y | Y | Y | Y | N | N |
| Davies | Y | Y | Y | Y | N | N |
| *Rebellion* | | | | | | |
| Gurr | Y | Y | N | N | N | N |

*Source:* Adapted from Kotowski (1984, 422).

Clearly, Moore and Skocpol have the most restrictive concept of revolution since theirs contains the most necessary conditions. Their concepts—which are necessary and sufficient condition ones—will have the least extension of any of those in the table. The first thing that any knowledgeable reader of Skocpol will exclaim is that her book is not about revolutions per se but about *social* revolutions. Voilà. We see that an adjective "social" has been added to the concept of revolution.

If we subtract two attributes, (1) changes in systems of stratification and (2) major political structural change, we arrive at the concepts of revolution of Huntington, Johnson, and Davies. We have subtracted the adjectives, if you will, that deal with system-wide changes, the "social" part of Skocpol's definition. We now have what for Skocpol and Moore would be *political* revolutions, e.g., the American Revolution. Here again we see an adjective appearing.

If we continue to remove dimensions—those dealing with (1) minor political structural change and (2) change of governing body—we arrive at the concept of Gurr. Taking the lead from the title of his book we might call them "rebellions," since they do not necessarily involve social or political change.

Because the attributes used to define revolution can vary so widely, one needs adjectives to fix the meaning of the concept for the author. Skocpol had to affix "social" or some other term to revolution because she had to distinguish her dependent variable from other common uses of the term revolution. From Skocpol's perspective "political revolution" subtracts the system-wide and societal dimensions from the social revolution concept. From the other side, "social revolution" works classically by adding new attributes to the view of revolution as working only on government structures.

Subsetting is often associated with increasing the level on some continuum. For example, Tir and Karreth (2017) are interested in "institutionalized" IGOs, which are often thought to be more influential than noninstitutionalized ones. Marks et al. (2017) are interested in "authoritative" IGOs, a relatively small subset of all IGOs. In both these cases, the adjective functions as a subset of the superset of all IGOs. As seen in chapter 4, when one adds adjectives such as "very," one is involved in subsetting.

In the previous edition of this book I discussed the implications of this kind of subsetting on the dependent variable in a series of statistical analyses. If one has two possible dependent variables and one is the subset of the other, then one can get something that looks very much like selection on the dependent variable. One can think of this in terms of thresholds: the subset variable essentially has a higher threshold and hence the statistical results might be quite different for a high threshold than for a low one.

As far as I can tell, almost no one has explored subsetting relationships on the independent variable side. If one independent variable is a subset of the other it might still have only a modest correlation with it. However, all of the variability in the subsetted variable is taken by the superset independent variable. Hence in terms of causal information, the subset variable provides no information in the statistical analysis other than removing the subset cases from the analysis.

There are a whole series of causal issues related to two variables that have a subset–superset relationship. These are separate from problems of multicollinearity. Multicollinearity comes into play only when the subset is close in size to the superset. As illustrated in the previous edition of this book, this can quite dramatically change the statistical results. Usually there is no theoretical or statistical analysis of changing causal relationships when contrasting supersets with subsets. However, these must be considered if there are issues of subsets within dependent or independent variables.

## Hyphenated Concepts III: Nonstandard Semantics

No surprise, actual semantic, linguistic practice does not always conform to the canons of mathematical and philosophical logic.[11]

One core semantic practice that does not accord with standard logic is where the adjective suggests that the secondary-level dimension is absent. A key factor to keep constantly in mind is that the adjective *does not remove the secondary-level dimension*. Instead of removing it, the value on this secondary-level dimension becomes 0. As such, the basic conceptualization does not change, but instead of using an ideal type where all secondary-level dimensions have value 1, some of them have value 0.

In terms of the intension–extension issue, the question is whether extension is increasing or decreasing:

Fixing the value on a secondary-level dimension does not necessarily increase or decrease the extension of a concept.

The basic situation is illustrated in figure 9.3. One is moving toward the gray zone and the hybrid zone by requiring that certain secondary-level dimensions have value 0. Within my framework then, to "remove" a dimension—code it as 0—is to move left along the autocracy–democracy continuum. In figure 9.3, as we remove attributes we have

11. There is a huge cognitive psychology literature on concepts and adjectives. It is clear that people's—including social scientists'—manipulation of concepts and adjectives often does not conform to the classic necessary and sufficient condition logic; for a good review see Murphy 2002.

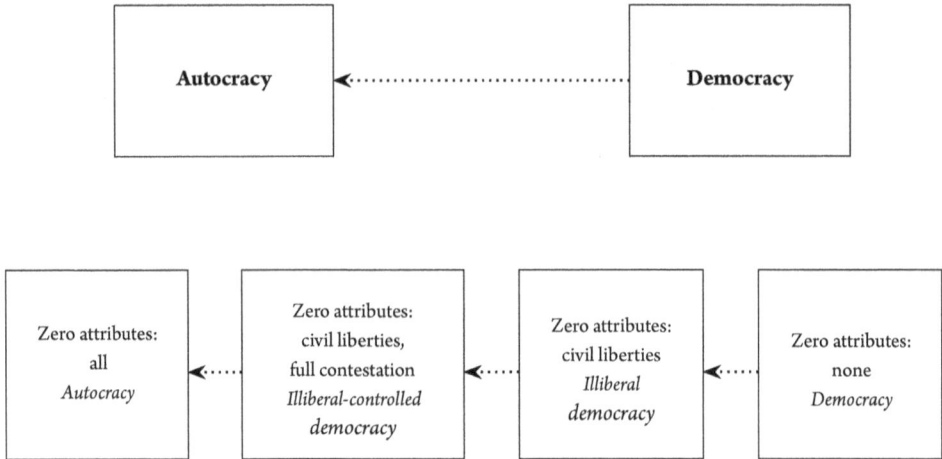

FIGURE 9.3. Nonstandard adjective semantics: the autocracy–democracy continuum.

regimes that are less and less democratic. Movement is horizontal from democracy to autocracy.

To see how this can work in practice, I continue with the Democracy–Dictatorship group view of democracy. Figure 9.4 illustrates what happens to extension when we fix the value of some of the defining dimensions as 0. One can see that, depending on which dimension one makes 0, the result can be fewer or more cases than the number of democracies. The number of cases and the extension can vary dramatically when one of the defining dimensions has value 0. This illustrates very clearly that there is no principle about the relationship between 0 on a given dimension and extension.

This kind of analysis is very useful for getting an empirical sense of how important different dimensions might be. One might assume that, when it is easy to achieve the highest level on a dimension, that dimension is more common and perhaps less important. This empirical fact could play an important role in causal analysis where the concept is a dependent or independent variable. So instead of talking about a diminished subtype, one conducts an analysis of the role and importance of a given dimension of the complex concept.

The whole terminology of "diminished subtype" is quite misleading. The member of defining dimensions remains the same in all of the

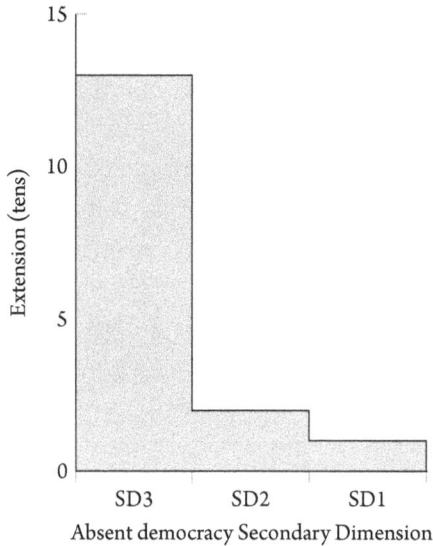

FIGURE 9.4. Intension–extension when a
secondary-level dimension is absent (others
present): Democracy–Dictatorship data.

circumstances: what is changing is whether a given dimension is coded
0 or 1. So one might call these different kinds of democracies, but the
notion of subtype is really not very useful. It distracts from descriptive
and causal analyses.

The key point in the context of this chapter is that fixing a secondary-
level dimension as 0 has no clear implications for extension: it can go
up or down. This is true for necessary and sufficient conditions, as well
as the family resemblance concept structures. The general principle is
that fixing any given defining dimension as 0 (or 1) has indeterminate
effects on the extension of the concept.

## Conclusion

I have argued throughout this volume that how we conceptualize a
phenomenon has deep and intimate links with causal theories. One
of the important, if not the most important, signs of this in welfare

state literature is how gendered analyses have moved the welfare state variable from the dependent variable side of the equation to the independent variable side. Before the nonsilent revolution in the literature of the 1990s, the welfare state often appeared as the dependent variable: one explained the causes of its origin or expansion. In contrast, much of the gender literature looks at the impact (or not) of the welfare state on women's quality of life. A core question is the influence of the welfare state, not its causes. Not surprisingly, this is one area where rights play a key role. For women it is not just spending, but control over their bodies, that determines many aspects of their well-being (back to Nussbaum again). We add new secondary-level dimensions to the concept of the welfare state because we know that they have important causal powers in the lives of women (and of course men). We add these new dimensions to the concept because we cannot understand how the welfare state works for 50 percent of the population without them.

It is not surprising that when the welfare state was viewed through the male model, one of the key independent variables was labor union strength. Because we see the welfare state dependent variable in a new light we can then look to new kinds of independent variables, such as the strength of women's movements. Going back to the chemical metaphor, finding out about the nuclear structure of copper means we understand better the properties of copper. Now that we understand better the gendered character of the welfare state, we can understand better its policies, their causes, and effects.

The impact of concept structure on extension is worth keeping on the checklist for concept analysis. Clearly, concept structure influences extension and empirical coverage. It is directly related to the core goal of empirical description at the heart of conceptualization and measurement. While most of the discussion of the intension–extension relationship has assumed the weakest link, philosophy approach to conceptualization, it is clear that the other aggregation classes are relevant as well. As illustrated by the gender welfare state critique, there may be situations where one wants to increase extension, perhaps because of normative concerns. In short, intension–extension issues arise in descriptive, causal, and normative analyses of conceptualization and measurement. Hyphenated and multiword concepts require a clear structural analysis of the semantics and meaning of the new complex concept and how that connects with descriptive and causal research goals.

# 10

# Two-Level Theories

COMPLEX CONCEPTS IN COMPLEX
CAUSAL THEORIES

Every one may observe how common it is for names to be made use
of, instead of the ideas themselves ... especially if the ideas be very
complex, and made up of a great collection of simple ones. This makes
the consideration of *words* and *propositions* so necessary a part of the
Treatise of Knowledge, that it is very hard to speak intelligibly of the
one, without explaining the other.

JOHN LOCKE

## Introduction

Concepts play an important role in the research enterprise as constituent parts of theories.[1] Much of this volume has focused on the
ontological, descriptive, and normative aspects of concept construction. It is appropriate to end this volume with how concepts play a role
in causal theories.

Secondary-level dimensions in explanatory variables play a key
causal role in the larger theoretical enterprise. If one takes core hypotheses, they consist of basic-level concepts. Putting multilevel and

---

1. The core role of concepts in case selection is covered by chapters 6–8 of the previous
edition of this volume, deleted here for space reasons.

multidimensional concepts into these variables produces multilevel theories, which I call two-level theories. I call them two- and not three-level *theories* because the third level of concepts, indicator data, deals with measurement and data. This level rarely comes into play in the description of causal mechanisms and explanations at the basic level. In contrast, secondary-level dimensions frequently appear—or should appear—as part of the theoretical framework. Many quantitative as well as qualitative models are two-level theories because of the causal hypotheses embedded in concepts. The exercises I have developed over the years (available on request from me at ggoertz@nd.edu) contain many examples of how two-level theories have been used in a variety of domains.

Putting multilevel concepts into hypotheses and propositions generates a complex theoretical edifice. Not only does one need to decide how to construct concepts, but also how the basic-level concepts are "put together" and structured to form some kind of theory or model. Of course, by now this is a fairly familiar problem. It is one that the researcher faces in aggregating from the data–indicator level to the secondary level, and from the secondary level to the basic. This chapter focuses on theory and concept structure using the logical AND and OR, using the weakest link and best shot aggregation classes.

Just as one can use AND and OR to structure concepts, one can use them to model the relationship between independent and dependent variables. Many influential scholars have used mathematical logic for their theories. They have claimed that some factor $X$ is a necessary condition for the outcome $Y$ (using boldface fonts for basic-level variables). For example, in Skocpol's theory of social revolution, state crisis is a necessary condition for social revolution. Many of the issues about concept structure and aggregation discussed in chapter 6 apply to the basic-level model as well as the secondary-level dimensions.

As examples of concepts in theories I will be revisiting some familiar friends: concepts such as social revolution, welfare state, and democracy. These concepts appear as key independent and dependent variables in major social theories. While previous chapters have analyzed these concepts in isolation, it is useful to see how these core concepts of political science and sociology appear when surrounded by other complex concepts.

This volume has stressed the importance of ontology, substitutability, and causality in building concepts. I have focused more on the ontological-semantic aspects because they are generally recognized as constituting an approach to concepts. However, two-level theories often involve causal relationships between levels.

The latent variable approach usually models indicators as effects of basic-level causes. Here I explore the converse pattern, how basic-level factors are effects of secondary-level causes. Using Skocpol I show how basic-level factors like state breakdown are produced by some secondary-level causes like international pressure. In this kind of two-level model the causal arrow goes from the secondary level to the basic level. One can think of this relationship between levels in terms of causal mechanisms. The secondary level provides various causal mechanisms for the production of basic-level phenomena.

One *noncausal* relationship between the secondary and the basic levels takes the form of substitutability. Typically, this refers to different means to attain a given end (e.g., foreign policy substitutability; Most and Starr 1989). A principle example of this will be Ostrom's (1991) theory of common pool resource institutions. For example, an important basic-level factor is the ability to monitor compliance with institution rules. However, depending on the characteristics of the society and the resource itself there are various *means* of achieving successful monitoring. These means do not stand in a causal relationship to monitoring; they are different ways to do it.

John Kingdon's (1984) famous work on agenda setting illustrates other features of substitutability and the two-level model. Kingdon reformulated the garbage can model into one with three "streams"—problem, solution, and political context—which are individually necessary and jointly sufficient for agenda success. He emphasized how contingent and nonlinear the process is by which these three factors occur at the same time. He also stressed substitutability in the various ways in which the three streams can be filled.

I use Downing's (1992) well-known historical-comparative work to discuss the ontological version of the two-level theory. This example will be short because this material is explored extensively in other chapters.

Two-level theories constitute an outline of more complex causal mechanisms. Part of the motivation for my book (2017) on causal mechanisms came from the analysis of the variety of two-level theories. The final substantive section takes an example from my causal mechanism book that moves beyond the two-level framework but incorporates many features of it. Grzymała-Busse's (2007) causal mechanism analysis of the nonexploitation of the state by political parties illustrates more generally how this volume intersects deeply with causal mechanism analysis.

The power of the two-level framework comes out in how famous scholars have implicitly used this structure. It is quite clear that the two-level structure has been repeatedly and independently discovered and used (I have used it myself on several occasions, e.g., Goertz 2003 and Schenoni et al. 2020). By the end of the chapter we will have seen a march of famous social scientists who have used the framework.

## The Structure of Two-Level Theories

In this section I describe the basic structure of two-level theories, using the basic level and the secondary level. I also review the different causal and ontological structures that can exist at the two levels, and the different kinds of relationships that can exist between the secondary and the basic levels.

### Basic Level

In a two-level theory, the basic level contains the main causal variables and the outcome variable of the theory as a whole. Variables at the basic level form the building blocks of two-level theories, but there are different logical relationships with which these variables can be put together to form theories. I find that much qualitative and comparative work uses two logical structures at the basic level: (1) a set of causal factors that are individually necessary and jointly sufficient for an outcome and (2) a set of causal factors that are collectively sufficient but not necessary for an outcome. I refer to the first structure as a "conjuncture of necessary causes," to highlight the fact that a combination of necessary conditions are sufficient for an outcome. I refer to the second structure using the term "equifinality," which means that there are various conditions that are sufficient to produce the same outcome and hence *multiple paths* to the same end (Ragin 1987). For example, a classic example of equifinality is Barrington Moore's (1966) argument that there are three independent routes to the modern world.

The underlying logical structure of a conjuncture of necessary causes can be specified simply as

$$X \text{ AND } Z \rightarrow Y. \qquad (10.1)$$

In this equation, I have two necessary conditions ($X$ and $Z$) that are jointly sufficient for $Y$. The $\rightarrow$ in equation (10.1) has two meanings. The first is the standard interpretation in mathematical logic: "is sufficient for." The second is the standard interpretation in figures: "is a/the cause of." I refer to this basic structure as characterized by AND.

As we have seen, there are linear algebra analogues to AND and OR in the form of multiplication and addition. I do not use these because the examples all explicitly use mathematical logic, e.g., necessary and sufficient conditions. In addition, the extent to which one could model or test two-level theories with off-the-shelf statistical methods is not clear. As a result, this chapter remains firmly in the realm of mathematical logic and set theory.

The second logical structure is equifinality. In contrast to equation (10.1), there are no necessary conditions in this structure. Instead, there are multiple paths by which $Y$ can occur:

$$X \text{ OR } Z \rightarrow Y. \qquad (10.2)$$

Hence, equifinality is a logical structure characterized by OR.

These two types are not the only options for representing causal structures at the basic level. For example, one could have a basic-level theory that simply focused on individually necessary causes. Likewise, one could easily formulate more complex hybrid structures such as

$$(U \text{ AND } X) \text{ OR } (U \text{ AND } Z) \rightarrow Y. \qquad (10.3)$$

Equation (10.3) has both a necessary condition (i.e., $U$) and equifinality [i.e., $(U \text{ AND } X) \text{ OR } (U \text{ AND } Z)$]. These kinds of models are what QCA (qualitative comparative analysis) generates as a default, and as such could be called QCA-INUS models. For purposes of contrast, I briefly describe Hick's QCA of the early welfare state.

### Secondary Level

Variables at the secondary level are less central to the core argument and refer to concepts that are less easily remembered and processed. Nevertheless, these variables play a key theoretical role. For example, in theories about the causal impact of democracy, factors such as free elections, civil liberties, and broad suffrage often play a major role, even though they are still secondary compared to the basic-level concept of democracy itself.

Considering the explanatory factors in a two-level theory, there are three relationships that can exist between the secondary level and the basic level: causal, ontological, and substitutability. It bears emphasis that none of these relationships is simply one in which the secondary-level variables serve as indicators or measures of the basic-level variables. The role of the secondary-level variables is *not* to operationalize the basic-level variables. Rather, in a two-level theory, the secondary-level variables *always have a causal relationship to the main outcome variable*. Two-level theories are complex precisely because the way in which secondary-level variables affect the main outcome varies depending on how they relate to factors at the basic level.

First, there may be a *causal relationship* between secondary-level variables and explanatory basic-level variables; in this case, secondary-level variables represent "causes of causes." With a causal relationship between levels, the secondary-level variables affect the main outcome variable by helping to bring into being basic-level causal variables. Sometimes, when a causal relationship exists between levels, one can often speak about more remote causes (i.e., secondary-level causes) and more proximate causes (i.e., basic-level causes).

Second, an *ontological relationship* can exist between levels. In this case, the secondary-level variables represent the defining features that constitute the basic-level variables; the secondary-level variables literally *are* the elements that compose the basic-level variables.

Cartwright (1989) discusses the useful notion of "causal powers"; secondary-level dimensions in explanatory factors typically have causal powers. That is why they are chosen as key defining features of explanatory variables to begin with, as stressed by the Causal Powers Guideline discussed in chapter 3. For example, free elections, civil liberties, and broad suffrage are the ontological secondary-level variables that constitute the basic-level variable of democracy. I use the word "ontological" to describe this relationship because it stresses that the issue concerns the essential character, structure, and underlying parts of the phenomenon to which the basic-level concept refers.

The secondary-level variables play a key causal role in explaining why the basic-level causal variables have the effects they do. The institutional theory of the democratic peace invokes elections as a key part of the explanation for why democracies do not fight wars with each other. In this theory, the ontological secondary-level variable of elections has a causal impact on the main outcome variable of war.

Finally, I consider the *substitutable relationship* between the secondary and the basic levels. The secondary-level variables are neither causes nor constitutive features of the basic-level causal variables. Rather, each secondary-level variable is a substitutable means to a given basic-level variable. At the basic level is a concept such as "labor incorporation" (Collier and Collier 1991). Substitutability at the secondary level is an analysis of the different ways that labor can be or has been incorporated in different countries. In some countries this incorporation occurred via political parties, while in others it has been done by the state.

Cioffi-Revilla (1998) stresses that substitutability is related to redundancy in systems (e.g., Bendor 1985; Landau 1969). Systems are more stable if necessary components have backups and alternative sources. An example is US nuclear deterrence via the triad of air-, land-, and submarine-based weapons. If one or two legs of the system were to be taken out by attack, there is enough redundancy in the system to give the United States a second strike capability (Cioffi-Revilla 1998).

Two-level theories are thus distinctive and powerful precisely because secondary-level variables are systematically related to basic-level factors. The addition of the secondary-level variables not only adds complexity to the argument developed at the basic level, but also helps analysts empirically substantiate the argument at the basic level. To concretely test the claims at the basic level, analysts must draw on the information at the secondary level, which allows them to move down levels of analysis and examine factors that further elaborate the causal relationship.

On the dependent variable side of things, one has the standard multidimensional concept. The key difference is that unlike the explanatory factors, the relationship between the basic level and the secondary level is generally ontological. This ontology can use various alternative structures (aka aggregation techniques) and degrees of substitutability.

Not only do two-level theories provide a framework for future theorizing, I suggest that they are very useful in understanding existing theories. Many social theorists have implicitly thought in two-level terms. Much of the confusion around some theories, e.g., Skocpol (1979), arises from a failure to appropriately understand the levels and relationships between them. The sections below illustrate and discuss the features of two-level theories and their characteristics using some prominent social theorists: in order of presentation, Skocpol, Ostrom, Kingdon, Downing, Hicks, and Grzymała-Busse. Each example foregrounds specific characteristics of the general two-level model.

# Causal Relationships between Levels:
# Skocpol's Theory of Social Revolution

I begin with Skocpol's *States and social revolutions*, which seeks to explain the onset of social revolution in France, Russia, and China through a comparison with several other cases that did not experience social revolution. Despite all the attention surrounding this work, most analysts have failed to recognize its two-level structure. Figure 10.1 summarizes its theoretical and causal structure.

## *Basic Level*

At the basic level, *States and social revolutions* has the structure of a conjuncture of two necessary causes that are jointly sufficient for the outcome of social revolution. Skocpol summarizes these two basic-level causes as follows:

> I have argued that (1) state organizations susceptible to administrative and military collapse when subjected to intensified pressures from more developed countries from abroad, and (2) agrarian sociopolitical structures that facilitated widespread peasant revolts against landlords were, taken together, the sufficient distinctive causes of social-revolutionary situations commencing in France, 1789, Russia, 1917, and China, 1911. (Skocpol 1979, 154)

These two causes can be summarized simply as "state breakdown" and "peasant revolt." Because these variables are at the basic level, most (good) summaries of Skocpol's work have referred to them.

Skocpol is explicit that these two causes are jointly—not individually—sufficient for social revolutions. This is clear from her assertion that the two factors "were, taken together, the sufficient distinctive causes" and from her explicit remarks that state breakdowns would not have led to social revolutions without peasant revolts (1979, 112). Elsewhere, by examining cases of non–social revolution in which only one of the two conditions was present, she attempts to empirically

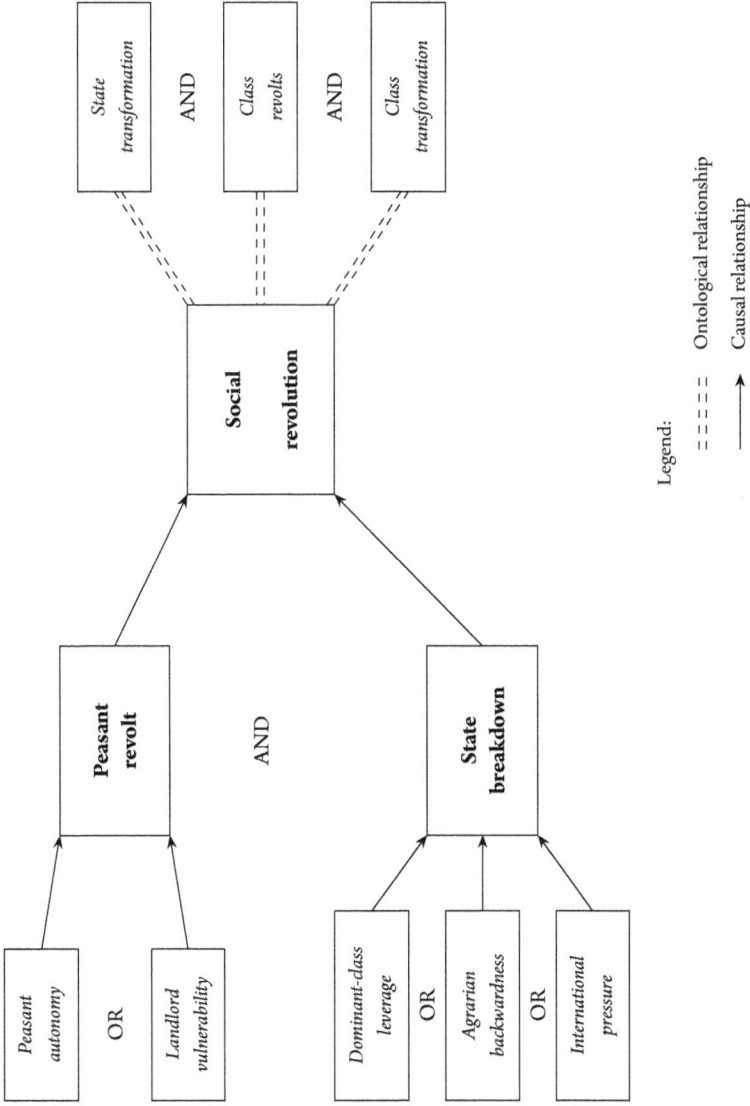

FIGURE 10.1. Two-level theories: *States and social revolutions*.

Legend:

= = = = =  Ontological relationship

———▶  Causal relationship

demonstrate that neither condition is by itself enough to produce social revolution.

It is harder to find explicit passages in *States and social revolutions* where Skocpol states that her key variables are *necessary* for social revolution. But there are passages that strongly hint at the necessary condition character of her two core variables, such as the following example:

> Nevertheless, peasant revolts have been the crucial insurrectionary ingredient in virtually all actual (i.e., successful) social revolutions to date ... Without peasant revolts urban radicalism in predominantly agrarian countries has not in the end been able to accomplish social-revolutionary transformations.... they [English and German revolutions of 1848] failed as social revolutions in part for want of peasant insurrections against landed upper classes. (Skocpol 1979, 113)

In addition, Skocpol has been widely interpreted as identifying necessary causes (e.g., Kiser and Levi 1996, 189–90; Dion 1998) and her work is used by Ragin as a central example of necessary conditions: "Consider the argument that both 'state breakdown' and 'popular insurrection' are necessary conditions for 'social revolution'" (2000, 219).

The basic-level argument of *States and social revolutions* therefore has the formal structure of equation (10.1), which I call a conjuncture of necessary causes. Succinctly, Skocpol's basic theory of social revolution at the basic level:

> State breakdown and peasant revolt are individually necessary and jointly sufficient for social revolution.

This proposition is bound by certain scope conditions, such as the presence of an agrarian-bureaucratic state that lacks a significant colonial history. Within the scope identified by Skocpol, state breakdown and peasant revolt represent a combination of individually necessary and jointly sufficient factors.

## Secondary Level

At the secondary level, Skocpol focuses on the different processes that can produce state breakdown and peasant revolt. There is a *causal relationship* between secondary-level variables and basic-level causes. The logical structure of this causal relationship is one of equifinality—i.e., the secondary-level variables are sufficient but not necessary for either state breakdown or peasant revolt. Formally, to characterize Skocpol's argument in this way, I use OR at the secondary level of the theory. Hence, whereas Skocpol's theory is built around a causal conjuncture of necessary conditions at the basic level, it is characterized by equifinality at the secondary level.

With respect to explaining the basic-level cause of state breakdown, Skocpol focuses her analysis on three secondary-level causes: (1) *international pressure*, which causes crises for regime actors, (2) *dominant-class leverage* within the state, which prevents government leaders from implementing modernizing reforms, and (3) *agrarian backwardness*, which hinders national responses to political crises. With respect to peasant revolt, Skocpol focuses on two secondary-level variables: (1) *peasant autonomy and solidarity*, which facilitate spontaneous collective action by peasants, and (2) *landlord vulnerability*, which allows for class transformation in the countryside.

In classic fashion, Skocpol defines social revolution using a necessary and sufficient condition structure: "Social revolutions are rapid, basic transformations of a society's state and class structures; and they are accompanied and in part carried through by class-based revolts from below" (1979, 4–5). This definition holds that social revolutions are the combination of three components: (1) class-based revolts from below, (2) rapid and basic transformation of state structures, and (3) rapid and basic transformation of class structures.[2] Skocpol is explicit that if any one of these three attributes is missing, the case

2. The first component is actually somewhat problematic given that it may be causally related to the other two, thereby raising questions of whether it should be on the independent variable side of the model.

in question cannot be considered a social revolution. In this sense, each of the three attributes is *necessary* for social revolution. Skocpol also strongly implies that the simultaneous presence of the three components is *sufficient* for an event to be classified as a social revolution: any case that contains her three components is definitely a social revolution.

Given that Skocpol uses a necessary and sufficient approach to defining the outcome variable, it is appropriate to use AND in specifying the relationship between Skocpol's three definitional components and social revolution. When the two-level structure of the outcome variable is added to the two-level structure of the causal variables, the full argument depicted in figure 10.1 emerges.

Much of the debate around Skocpol can be traced to confusion about which variables belong to which levels and the structural relationships between levels. Not surprisingly this has important ramifications for theory testing. For those interested in an empirical test of Skocpol's model, where all variables are coded and the logical structure of the theory subjected to empirical test, I refer the reader to the previous edition of this book, which contained a long and detailed empirical analysis of her model.

The Skocpol example illustrates some features of two-level models that have made them popular and useful:

1. Notice that the necessary conditions at the basic level are generally pitched at quite a high level of abstraction. This is because they are intended to be general theoretical and causal constructs. Importantly, they apply to a variety of different cases: they are cross-case concepts that travel.
2. The secondary level provides for sensitivity to local conditions and the specifics of causal mechanisms. Much of the book discusses how different cases showed causal mechanisms that were different combinations of these causal factors.
3. In terms of equifinality, there is no equifinality at the basic level but large degrees of equifinality at the secondary level.
4. The model is very nonlinear since the outcome is *not the sum* of the individual effects, as is the case in statistical models like

regression and event history. This is due to its highly interactive character.

Features (1) and (2) illustrate perhaps the core reason why comparative historical and multiple case-study scholars have found this model attractive. It combines clear general causal claims at the basic level with sensitivity to case-specific detail. The necessary and sufficient condition structure at the basic level is quite rigid; flexibility occurs at the secondary level.

# Substitutable Relationships at the Secondary Level: The Ostrom–Kingdon Model

The second main category of two-level theories uses substitutable relationships at the secondary level. To use the multiple roads metaphor, the various roads to Rome (since "all roads lead to Rome"[3]) are not causes of getting to Rome, but the alternatives available to travelers for getting to Rome. These roads can play a role in causal explanations. For example, the absence of some people from Rome might be explained by the absence of any road to Rome. So while the substitutable relationship is not itself causal, it can easily play a role in causal explanation of individual cases.

## Common Pool Resource Institutions: Ostrom

An excellent example of a two-level theory that uses a *substitutable* relationship between the secondary and the basic levels is the work of Ostrom (1991). Ostrom identifies eight conditions[4] that are necessary for her key outcome of "institutional functioning." Of these eight conditions, monitoring and sanctions stand out. In her American Political Science Association presidential address, she selects them

3. This phrase refers to the road system of the Roman Empire, in which Rome was positioned in the center, with every road attached to it.

4. These are (1) monitoring, (2) graduated sanctions, (3) clear boundaries and memberships, (4) congruent rules, (5) conflict resolution mechanisms, (6) recognized rights to organize, (7) nested units, and (8) collective-choice arenas (Ostrom 1991, 180).

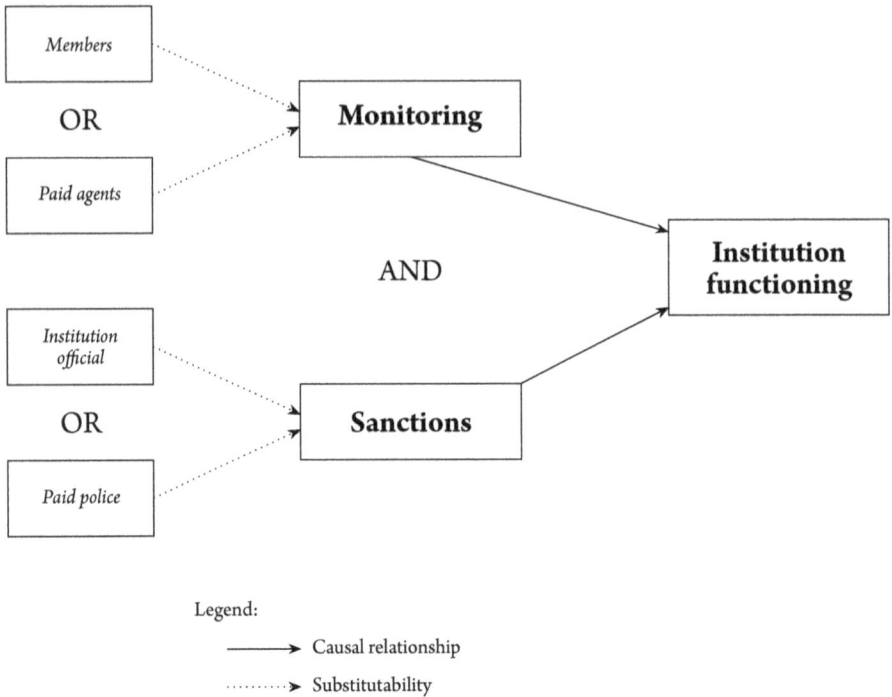

FIGURE 10.2. A two-level model of common pool resource institutions.
*Source:* Adapted from Ostrom (1991); see also Goertz (2003).

for special attention: "Most robust and long-lasting common-pool regimes involve clear mechanisms for monitoring rule conformance and graduated sanctions for enforcing compliance" (Ostrom 1997, 8). Thus, her argument emphasizes necessary conditions that form a conjuncture that is sufficient. In figure 10.2, I have represented this basic-level theory by focusing on how "monitoring" and "sanctions" are individually necessary and jointly sufficient for the outcome of institutional functioning (see Goertz 2003 for an elaboration of this model).

A key causal feature is that monitoring and sanctioning are key determinants of success. There are multiple ways to perform each of these functions. This is not to say that they are all equal in cost or effectiveness, but rather that they do fulfill the function.

At the secondary level, Ostrom identifies variables that are specific means of sanctioning and monitoring, thereby employing a substitutable relationship between levels. She describes two ways that monitoring can be accomplished: monitoring by an institutional member or monitoring by a paid agent. Clearly, these two types neither cause nor define the basic-level variable of monitoring. Analogously, the basic-level cause of sanctions can be arrived at in one of two ways: sanctions by institutional officials or sanctions by paid police. Again, the relationship is one of equifinality: institutional-official sanctions or paid-police sanctions are alternative paths to sanctions in general.

Here is a typical example of how the basic level focuses on a factor, e.g., monitoring, common to all successful common pool resource institutions. The secondary level is then an analysis of how different societies with different resource technologies go about implementing a monitoring system. At the basic level the key fact is that someone monitors; the secondary level shows the substitutable ways in which this can occur in different cases, or in other words, a situation of equifinality in which the secondary-level variables are sufficient for the basic-level variable, as represented by the OR in figure 10.2.

Ostrom's model illustrates some key features of two-level models:

1. The alternatives for monitoring and sanctioning are substitutable but play a role in causal explanations of individual cases.
2. Two-level theories provide a framework for functionalist theories and mechanisms. For an institution to work effectively it needs to perform certain functions. One important aspect of these models of institutions and collective goods is that they focus on *how* the collective good is *produced*. Using this language we can begin to think about economic production functions in the context of collective goods. One could then model international regimes or Ostrom's environmental institutions by replacing "labor" and "capital" by "sanctions" and "monitoring" (see chapter 6 for a discussion of aggregation functions including production functions).

## Kingdon's Agenda-Setting Model

In an extremely influential book, John Kingdon developed a model for explaining why certain issues made it onto the federal decision-making agenda in Washington, DC. Importantly he was also interested in explaining why certain, seemingly important issues, were *not* on the agenda.

His agenda-setting framework includes three "streams," which reflect key features of the agenda-setting process: (1) the existence of problems, created endogenously by powerful actors or which occur exogenously (e.g., ebola), (2) existence of solutions, and (3) a favorable political context. In terms of figure 10.2, we have three boxes instead of two, with a stream in each box.

Each stream is necessary for agenda success:

> If one of the three elements is missing—if a solution is not available [policy stream], a problem cannot be found or is not sufficiently compelling, or support is not forthcoming from the political stream—then the subject's place on the decision agenda is fleeting. (Kingdon 1984, 187)

Sufficiency is when the streams *happen* to occur at the same time:

> The rise of an item [on the agenda] is due to the joint effect of several factors coming together at a given point in time, not to the effect of one or another of them singly ... It was their *joint* effects that were so powerful. (Kingdon 1984, 188; this is followed by the ways one can express this idea such as "there was a confluence of streams")

Similarly, Kingdon stresses that there are various ways that the political stream condition can be fulfilled: political crisis, scheduled renewal of legislation, elections, etc. Problems can arise in a wide variety of ways. Solutions can come from various ideological positions.

Kingdon's model illustrates some other key characteristics of the two-level model in addition to those discussed above:

1. One of the things that Kingdon has stressed and which has generated a lot of criticism and praise is his emphasis on how *contingent* the process is. Only when the three streams "happen" to coincide does the item make it onto the agenda.
2. Window of opportunity models. If a theory makes frequent use of "window" metaphors it is likely to be at least partially a two-level theory. For example, the political opportunity structure in the social movement literature has this window characteristic.
3. Agent–structure or micro–macro. Many applications of the two-level model have two kinds of variables: (1) structural, background, contextual and (2) agency, motivation, individual-level factors. For Kingdon, the political stream and problem stream form the background/window factor and the political entrepreneurs and solution stream is the catalyst variable.
4. The absence of one stream explains why the item is not on the agenda and why it is hard to get items onto the agenda.

## Other Prominent Examples of Two-Level Theories

In this chapter, I have given some examples of prominent works that implicitly use two-level models. While I do not pretend to know all works that use two-level models (at least to a significant degree), other works that use this framework include Blake and Adolino (2001), Ertman (1997), Goertz (2003), Jacoby (2000), Linz and Stepan (1996), Marks (1986), Weede (1976), Wickham-Crowley (1991), and Schenoni et al. (2019) (see the two-level section of the exercises that accompany this book online for more examples).

In particular, I have found the literature on states, public policy, and social movements/revolution to be rich in applications of two-level ideas. One of the goals of this chapter is to make explicit explanatory theories that a number of researchers have intuitively found useful. Instead of reinventing two-level models each time, I hope that an explicit awareness of their structure and properties will help increase the theoretical and methodological rigor of future work.

Cioffi-Revilla (1998) and Cioffi-Revilla and Starr (1995) provide a mathematical and probabilistic analysis of a model with the same structure as Ostrom's. Most and Starr introduced the influential notion of foreign policy substitutability [Most and Starr 1984; see also the special issue of the *Journal of Conflict Resolution* 2002 39(1)]. They are also well known for the idea that opportunity and willingness are individually necessary and jointly sufficient for foreign policy action. If one puts opportunity and willingness at the basic level and foreign policy substitutability at the secondary level, one arrives at the model in figure 10.2. Cioffi-Revilla and Starr (1995) formally model this in ways that make clear the tight link with my analysis of two-level models and they do so in a completely probabilistic fashion. Bara's award-winning article (2014) uses the opportunity and willingness framework to integrate various factors in the causes of civil war literature via QCA.

## Ontological Relationships between Levels: Downing and Early Modern Democracy

Downing's (1992) *The military revolution and political change* offers a two-level theory of the origins of liberal democracy in early modern Europe (see figure 10.3). At the basic level, Downing identifies two main causes that are individually necessary and jointly sufficient for liberal democracy: (1) medieval constitutionalism, i.e., an institutional heritage that included representative assemblies and other constitutional features and (2) the absence of military revolution, i.e., little or no domestic mobilization of resources for war-fighting purposes during the sixteenth and seventeenth centuries. In his words, "To put the argument in its barest form, medieval European states had numerous institutions, procedures, and arrangements that, if combined with light amounts of domestic mobilization of human and economic resources for war, provided the basis for democracy in ensuing centuries" (1992, 9).

In the two-level theory, the medieval constitutionalism factor is constituted by four secondary-level variables that literally are "medieval

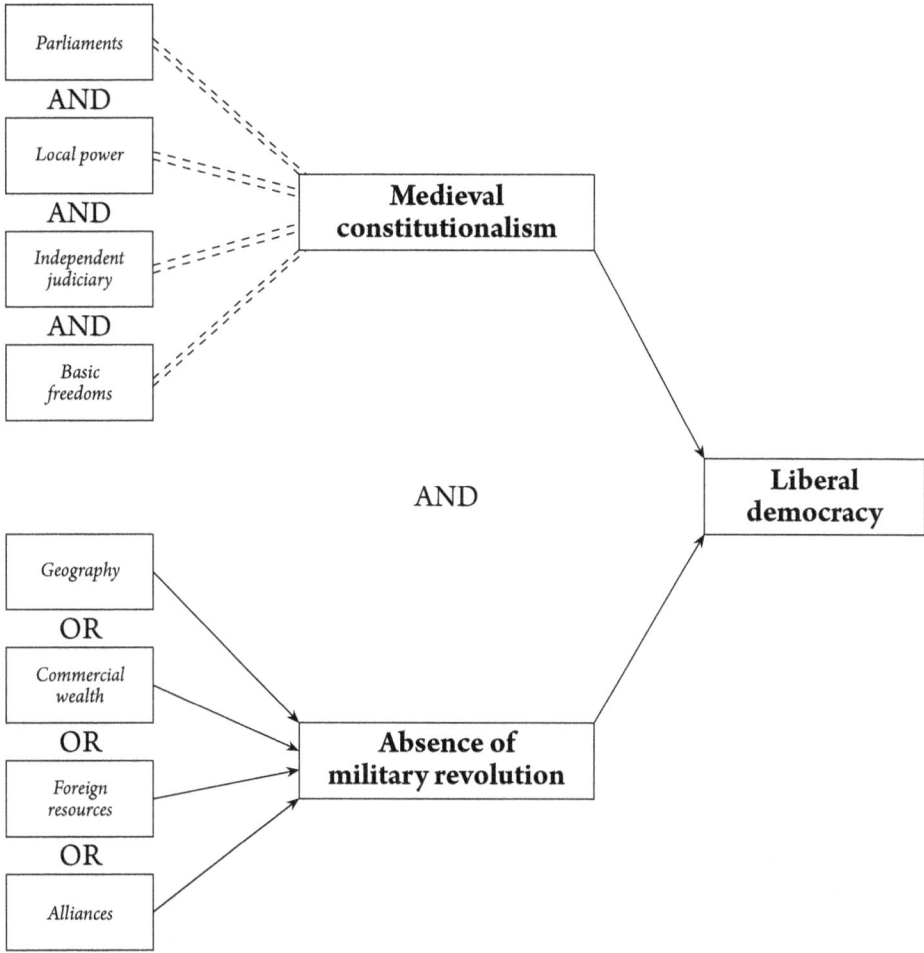

Parliaments

AND

Local power

AND

Independent
judiciary

AND

Basic
freedoms

Medieval
constitutionalism

AND

Liberal
democracy

Geography

OR

Commercial
wealth

OR

Foreign
resources

OR

Alliances

Absence of
military revolution

Legend:

⟶　　Causal relationship

= = = = =　　Ontological

FIGURE 10.3. A two-level model of the early modern roots of liberal democracy.
*Source:* Based on Downing (1992).

constitutionalism." Downing defines medieval constitutionalism as "parliaments controlling taxation and matters of war and peace; local centers of power limiting the strength of the crown; the development of independent judiciaries and the rule of law; and certain basic freedoms and rights enjoyed by large numbers of the population" (1992, 10). As figure 10.3 shows, Downing uses the classic necessary and sufficient condition approach to concept membership when modeling medieval constitutionalism (as indicated by the AND in the figure). These ontological secondary-level variables enter into the causal analysis because they affect the possibility of democracy. For example, if a country lacks one or more of the defining attributes of medieval constitutionalism (e.g., independent judiciaries), then that country will also lack an essential prerequisite (i.e., necessary condition) for democracy. Hence, ontological secondary-level variables are causally related to the basic-level outcome variable.

For the basic-level cause of "absence of military revolution," the relationship with the secondary level is one of equifinality. Four secondary-level variables are alternative causes of the absence of a military revolution. Thus, when faced with heavy warfare, a country can avoid a substantial mobilization of national resources for the military if one or more of the following causes are present: (a) a geography that provides a natural barrier to invading armies, (b) commercial wealth that allows the country to protect itself while mobilizing only a proportion of resources toward war, (c) foreign resource mobilization that takes place when war is conducted primarily outside a country's territory, and (d) alliances that reduce the extent of domestic resources that must be mobilized (1992, 78–79, 240). A key aspect of Downing's argument involves exploring the different ways that specific countries avoided a military revolution and stayed on a path leading to democracy.

Not much more needs to be said about the ontological two-level model since it has in many ways been the focus of much of this book. Virtually inherent in the multidimensional nature of complex concepts as causal factors lie arguments about how these ontological features play causal roles in theories.

## Two-Level Theories: INUS, QCA, and SUIN

QCA generates single-level models where there are multiple paths to the outcome variable. However, conceptualizing these models in terms of two levels can make the interpretation of the results more coherent, both formally and theoretically.

A not uncommon situation is when the final results of the QCA look like

$$Y = (A * B * C) + (A * B * D). \tag{10.4}$$

Often it makes much theoretical and empirical sense to think of $C$ and $D$ as substitutes for each other. Accordingly, one arrives at a two-level model such as

$$Y = A * B * E, \tag{10.5}$$

$$E = C + D. \tag{10.6}$$

Ragin's (1987; 2008; Ragin and Fiss 2017) discussions of QCA are centrally concerned with the following logical structure: substitutability at the basic level and necessary conditions at the secondary level. By contrast, the examples discussed so far tend to have the converse structure: a conjuncture of necessary conditions at the basic level and mostly equifinality at the secondary level. I do not believe that the model described here is more important than the typical QCA one, but rather that it needs to be recognized as powerful and common in its own right. In this section I consider the logical structure familiar from QCA.

I examine the two-level theory developed in Hicks et al.'s QCA (1995; see figure 10.4) of the creation of welfare states during the crucial period of social provision expansion in the 1920s. This outcome is conceptualized using the family resemblance approach to concepts. Thus, a country is coded as a "welfare state" if it adopts at least three of four classic welfare programs: (1) old age pensions, (2) health insurance, (3) workman's compensation, or (4) unemployment compensation. Here is an equifinality relationship between secondary-level variables and the outcome variable: no single condition is necessary; there are multiple paths to the welfare state.

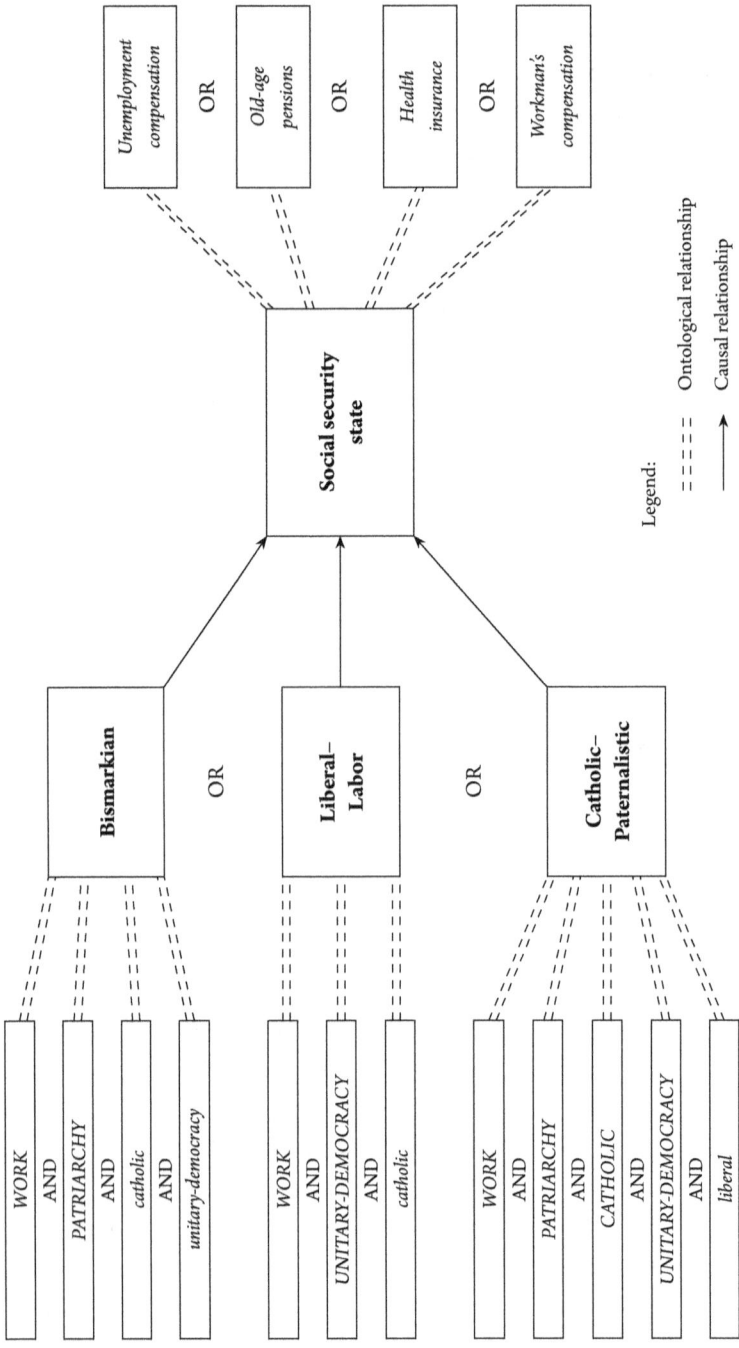

FIGURE 10.4. A two-level model of the development of the social security state. *Source:* Based on Hicks et al. (1995).

At the basic level, the structure of the causal theory is also one of equifinality. The main secondary-level variables are working-class mobilization, patriarchal state, unitary democracy, catholic government, and liberal government. The QCA results yield a relatively parsimonious model that is consistent with previous theory, yet enriches it in other ways. In the final model, there are respectively "three routes to the early consolidation of the welfare state ... (1) a 'Bismarckian' route, (2) a unitary-democratic 'Lib-Lab' [i.e., Liberal–Labor] route, and (3) a Catholic paternalistic unitary-democratic route" (1995, 344). The routes are represented by the following variable summaries: (1) WORK AND PATRIARCHY AND catholic AND unitary-democracy, (2) WORK AND UNITARY-DEMOCRACY AND catholic, and (3) WORK AND PATRIARCHY AND CATHOLIC AND UNITARY-DEMOCRACY AND liberal. In presenting these equations, I follow the standard QCA practice of designating variables that are present with capital letters and those that are absent with lowercase letters.

This QCA thus arrives at substantively important findings. Working-class mobilization is a necessary but not sufficient condition for all causal paths to a welfare state. In the Bismarckian path, working-class mobilization combines with a patriarchal autocratic regime to produce a welfare state. In the other two routes, welfare states emerge in democracies facing working-class mobilization, either under the support of Liberals or under the support of Catholics in a context of patriarchy. Though scholars have discussed the important role of Liberals in creating welfare states, Hicks and his collaborators suggest that the Catholic path to welfare consolidation was also critical.

To reconceptualize QCA results in this fashion, the analyst must identify the concept $E$ for which $C$ and $D$ function as substitutes. Typically, this will involve moving up the ladder of abstraction to a more general concept. For example, Amenta and Poulsen (1996) show that there are two necessary conditions for New Deal policies such as OAA pensions, voting rights, and absence of patronage politics. To achieve sufficiency, some mechanism for positively pushing reform through government must be present. This can happen in substitutable ways, e.g., "administrative powers" or "democratic or third parties" (see also Amenta et al. 1992). These substitutable means are variables $C$ and $D$, while the general idea of a mechanism for achieving reform is variable $E$.

A key point is that one can often reinterpret QCA in terms of two-level theories, particularly using substitutability relationships. This is another reason why two-level theories provide a rich set of methodological tools: they can help make sense of the results of single-level models by reinterpreting them as two-level models.

Mahoney introduced SUIN causes, which have the same basic structure as two-level theories: "A SUIN cause is, to make a parallel with Mackie's INUS cause, a *sufficient* but *unnecessary* part of a factor that is *insufficient* but *necessary* for an outcome. Here the constitutive attributes of a necessary cause are treated as causes themselves" (Mahoney 2008, 419). Mahoney (2008) uses Moore as an example: $X$ AND $Z \rightarrow Y$, where $(A$ OR $B) \rightarrow Z$ ($Y$ = democratic pathway, $X$ = strong bourgeoisie, $Z$ = politically subordinate aristocracy, $A$ = alliance between bourgeoisie and aristocracy, $B$ = weak aristocracy). In the terms of this chapter, SUIN causes are secondary-level causes of the basic level; they have a clear substitutability relationship in producing $Z$.

Often QCA, INUS, SUIN models and results are variations on the theme of two-level theories. The key feature is that all have two levels. Where they differ is in the kinds of relationships within levels and how the secondary-level factors combine to generate the basic-level factors.

## Concepts and Causal Mechanisms

Two-level theories have close connections to causal mechanisms. The combination of levels and the various ontological, substitutable, and causal relationships provide tools for sketching the outline of a causal mechanism. Figure 10.5 uses an important example from my causal mechanism book (2017).

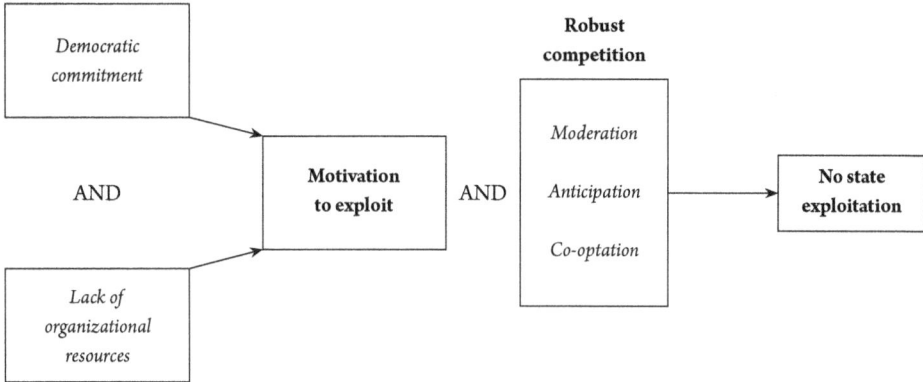

FIGURE 10.5. Causal mechanisms and two-level theories: constraints on state exploitation. *Source:* Based on Grzymała-Busse (2007) and Goertz (2017).

Grzymała-Busse's analysis of the causes of the exploitation of the state by political parties is a good example. At the basic level we see the core factors of "motivation to exploit" AND "robust competition," which are sufficient for "no state exploitation." At the secondary level, (1) moderation, (2) anticipation, or (3) co-optation constitute three mechanisms that in various combinations produce robust competition. On the explanatory factor side, "democratic commitment" AND "lack of organizational resources" are sufficient for the motivation to exploit.

Most of the causal mechanisms in my (2017) book can be cast as two-level theories. Some quite explicitly use mathematical logic (e.g., see my discussion of Mello's (2012) QCA of decisions to participate in the Iraq war by western democracies). Others occur within a statistical analysis framework. For example, Pevehouse's (2005) analysis of the impact of democratic IGOs on democratic stability occurs within a statistical, linear model framework. The causal mechanism becomes the weighted sum instead of the logical OR. In short, the structure of two-level theories provides a methodological and causal toolkit for exploring causal mechanisms.

More generally, multilevel and multidimensional concepts connect naturally to causal mechanisms. They move the researcher closer to connecting individual case studies to the analysis of causal mechanisms. They provide a framework for analyzing multiple case studies (e.g., in the 2017 causal mechanism book, see the discussion of large-$N$ qualitative analysis). Focusing on the secondary level forces the scholar to connect the choice of secondary-level dimensions to a theoretical outline of causal mechanisms. Decisions about concept structure and aggregation force researchers to think about interconnections across levels and within levels.

————

This book has approached conceptualization and measurement from a semantic perspective. This semantic perspective is also a causal one. Causal mechanisms are fundamentally more elaborate and more specified theories. Chapter 1 described the "conceptual juggling act" (figure 1.1) whereby concepts serve the role of accurate description and causal inference. Without accurate description, causal inference is meaningless. Causal inference and explanation require the elaboration of causal mechanisms. Concepts are a central building block of causal mechanisms. The normative dimension arrives in many situations because we want to change the world. Conceptualizing those goals is conceptualizing dependent variables, which constitute the ends of political action (e.g., Goertz 2020).

# REFERENCES

Adcock, R., and D. Collier. 2001. Measurement validity: a shared standard for qualitative and quantitative research. *American Political Science Review* 95:529–46.

Alexandrova, A. 2017. *A philosophy for the science of well-being.* Oxford: Oxford University Press.

Alkire, S., et al. 2015. *Multidimensional poverty measurement and analysis.* Oxford: Oxford University Press.

Allison, P. 1977. Testing for interaction in multiple regression. *American Journal of Sociology* 83:144–53.

Amenta, E., B. Carruthers, and Y. Zylan. 1992. A hero for the aged? The Townsend Movement, the political mediation model, and U.S. old-age policy, 1934–1950. *American Journal of Sociology* 98:308–39.

Amenta, E., and J. Poulsen. 1996. Social politics in context: the institutional politics theory and social spending at the end of the New Deal. *Social Forces* 75:33–60.

American Psychiatric Association. 1952. *DSM-I.* Washington, DC: American Psychiatric Association.

American Psychiatric Association. 1965. *DSM-II.* Washington, DC: American Psychiatric Association.

American Psychiatric Association. 1980. *DSM-III.* Washington, DC: American Psychiatric Association.

American Psychiatric Association. 1987. *DSM-III-R.* Washington, DC: American Psychiatric Association.

American Psychiatric Association. 1994. *DSM-IV.* Washington, DC: American Psychiatric Association.

American Psychiatric Association. 2000. *DSM-IV-TR.* Washington, DC: American Psychiatric Association.

American Psychiatric Association. 2013. *DSM-5.* Washington, DC: American Psychiatric Association.

Bara, C. 2014. Incentives and opportunities: a complexity-oriented explanation of violent ethnic conflict. *Journal of Peace Research* 51:696–710.

Beck, N., G. King, and L. Zeng. 2000. Improving quantitative studies of international conflict: a conjecture. *American Political Science Review* 94:21–35.

Belsley, D., E. Kuh, and R. Welsh. 1980. *Regression diagnostics: identifying influential data and sources of collinearity.* New York: John Wiley & Sons.

Bendor, J. 1985. *Parallel systems: redundancy in government*. Berkeley: University of California Press.

Bernhard, M., et al. 2017. Democratization in conflict research: how conceptualization affects operationalization and testing outcomes. *International Interactions* 43:941–66.

Blake, C., and J. Adolino. 2001. The enactment of national health insurance: a Boolean analysis of twenty advanced industrial countries. *Journal of Health Politics, Policy and Law* 26: 679–708.

Blalock, H. 1979. The Presidential Address: Measurement and conceptualization problems: the major obstacle to integrating theory and research. *American Sociological Review* 44: 881–94.

Blalock, H. 1982. *Conceptualization and measurement in the social sciences*. Beverly Hills: Sage Publications.

Bollen, K. 1989. *Structural equations with latent variables*. New York: John Wiley & Sons.

Bollen, K., and B. Grandjean. 1981. The dimension(s) of democracy: further issues in the measurement and effects of political democracy. *American Sociological Review* 46: 651–59.

Borges, J. 1960. *Otras inquisiciones*. Madrid: Alianza Editorial.

Borsboom, D. 2005. *Measuring the mind: conceptual issues in contemporary psychometrics*. Cambridge: Cambridge University Press.

Bowman, K., F. Lehoucq, and J. Mahoney. 2005. Measuring political democracy: case expertise, data adequacy, and Central America. *Comparative Political Studies* 38:939–70.

Brambor, T., W. Clark, and M. Golder. 2006. Understanding interaction models: improving empirical analyses. *Political Analysis* 14:63–82.

Braumoeller, B. 2004. Hypothesis testing and multiplicative interaction terms. *International Organization* 58:807–20.

Broome, A., et al. 2018. Bad science: international organizations and the indirect power of global benchmarking. *European Journal of International Relations* 24:514–39.

Brown, T. 2013. Latent variable measurement models. In T. Little (ed.) *The Oxford handbook of quantitative methods, vol. 2: statistical analysis*. Oxford: Oxford University Press.

Bueno de Mesquita, B. 1981. *The war trap*. New Haven: Yale University Press.

Burger, T. 1987. *Max Weber's theory of concept formation: history, laws, and ideal types*. Durham: Duke University Press.

Cartwright, N. 1989. *Nature's capacities and their measurement*. Oxford: Oxford University Press.

Cartwright, N., and R. Runhardt. 2014. Measurement. In N. Cartwright and E. Montuschi (eds.) *Philosophy of social science: a new introduction*. Oxford: Oxford University Press.

Cerioli, A., and S. Zani. 1990. A fuzzy approach to the measurement of poverty. In C. Dagum and M. Zenga (eds.) *Income and wealth distribution, inequality and poverty*. New York: Springer.

Chambers, R. 1988. *Applied production analysis: a dual approach*. Cambridge: Cambridge University Press.

Chang, R. (ed.) 1998. *Incommensurability, incomparability, and practical reason*. Cambridge: Harvard University Press.

Cheibub, J. 2007. *Presidentialism, parliamentarism, and democracy.* Cambridge: Cambridge University Press.

Cheibub, J., J. Gandhi, and J. Vreeland. 2010. Democracy and dictatorship revisited. *Public Choice* 143:67–101.

Cheibub, J., et al. 2013. Beyond presidentialism and parliamentarism. *British Journal of Political Science* 44:514–44.

Cioffi-Revilla, C. 1998. *Politics and uncertainty: theory, models and applications.* Cambridge: Cambridge University Press.

Cioffi-Revilla, C., and H. Starr. 1995. Opportunity, willingness, and political uncertainty: theoretical foundations of politics. *Journal of Theoretical Politics* 7:447–76.

Cobb, C., and P. Douglas. 1928. A theory of production. *American Economic Review* 18:139–65.

Cohen, M., and E. Nagel. 1934. *An introduction to logic and scientific method.* New York: Harcourt, Brace.

Collier, D., and J. Mahon. 1993. Conceptual "stretching" revisited: adapting categories in comparative analysis. *American Political Science Review* 87:845–55.

Collier, D., et al. 2008. Typologies: forming concepts and creating categorical variables. In J. Box-Steffensmeier, H. Brady, and D. Collier (eds.) *The Oxford handbook of political methodology.* Oxford: Oxford University Press.

Collier, R., and D. Collier. 1991. *Shaping the political arena: critical junctures, the labor movement, and regime dynamics in Latin America.* Princeton: Princeton University Press.

Cooper, R. 2013. Avoiding false positives; the role of zones of rarity, the threshold problem, and the DSM clinical significance criterion. *Canadian Journal of Psychiatry* 58:606–11.

Coppedge, M. 2012. *Democratization and research methods.* Cambridge: Cambridge University Press.

Coppedge, M., and J. Gerring. 2011. Conceptualizing and measuring democracy: a new approach. *Perspectives on Politics* 9:247–67.

Dahl, R. 1956. *A preface to democratic theory.* Chicago: University of Chicago Press.

Dahl, R. 1971. *Polyarchy: participation and opposition.* New Haven: Yale University Press.

Dahl, R. 1989. *Democracy and its critics.* New Haven: Yale University Press.

Dahl, R. 1998. *On democracy.* New Haven: Yale University Press.

Dasgupta, P. 2001. *Human well-being and the natural environment.* Oxford: Oxford University Press.

Davis, K., B. Kingsbury, and S. E. Merry. 2012. Introduction: global governance by indicators. In K. Davis et al. (eds.) *Governance by indicators: global power through quantification and rankings.* Oxford: Oxford University Press.

Deaton, A., and M. Grosh. 2000. Consumption. In M. Grosh and P. Glewwe (eds.) *Designing household survey questionnaires for developing countries, vol. 1.* Washington, DC: World Bank.

Dion, D. 1998. Evidence and inference in the comparative case study. *Comparative Politics* 30:127–45.

Dixon, W. 1994. Democracy and the peaceful settlement of international conflict. *American Political Science Review* 88:14–32.

Downing, B. 1992. *The military revolution and political change: origins of democracy and autocracy in early modern Europe.* Princeton: Princeton University Press.

Dul, J. 2016. Necessary condition analysis (NCA): logic and methodology of "necessary but not sufficient" causality. *Organizational Research Methods* 19:10–52.

Dusa, A. 2018. *QCA with R: a comprehensive resource.* New York: Springer.

Duverger, M. 1980. A new political system model: semi-presidential government. *European Journal of Political Research* 8:165–87.

Elgie, R. 2011. *Semi-presidentialism: sub-types and democratic performance.* Oxford: Oxford University Press.

Elgie, R. 2016. Three waves of semi-presidential studies. *Democratization* 23:49–70.

Elkins, Z., et al. 2009. *The endurance of national constitutions.* Cambridge: Cambridge University Press.

Ertman, T. 1997. *Birth of the leviathan: building states and regimes in medieval and early modern Europe.* Cambridge: Cambridge University Press.

EU Social Protection Committee. 2012. *Social protection performance monitor (SPPM) methodological report by the indicators sub-group of the social protection committee.* Brussels: EU.

European Commission. 2009. *Portfolio of indicators for the monitoring of the European strategy for social protection and social inclusion, 2009 update.* Brussels: EU.

Eurostat. 2005. Tools for composite indicators building. Luxembourg: EU.

Fagerberg, J. 2001. Europe at the crossroads: the challenge from innovation-based growth. In B. Lundvall and D. Archibugi (eds.) *The globalizing learning economy.* Oxford: Oxford University Press.

Fearon, J., and D. Laitin. 2003. Ethnicity, insurgency and civil war. *American Political Science Review* 97:75–90.

Fischer, C., et al. 1996. *Inequality by design: cracking the bell curve myth.* Princeton: Princeton University Press.

Foran, J. (ed.) 1997. *Theorizing revolution.* London: Routledge.

Fraassen, B. 2008. *Scientific representation: paradoxes of perspective.* Oxford: Oxford University Press.

Friedrich, K., and Z. Brzezinski. 1965. *Totalitarian dictatorship and autocracy.* Cambridge: Harvard University Press.

Friedrich, R. 1982. In defense of multiplicative terms in multiple regression equations. *American Journal of Political Science* 26:797–833.

Fukuda-Parr, S., et al. 2015. *Fulfilling social and economic rights.* Oxford: Oxford University Press.

Gärdenfors, P. 2000. *Conceptual spaces: the geometry of thought.* Cambridge: MIT Press.

Geddes, B. 2003. *Paradigms and sand castles: theory building and research design in comparative politics.* Ann Arbor: University of Michigan Press.

Geddes, B., J. Wright, and E. Frantz. 2014. Autocratic breakdown and regime transitions: a new dataset. *Perspectives on Politics* 12:313–31.

Geddes, B., et al. n.d. Autocratic regimes code book, version 1.2. Manuscript. UCLA.

Gerring, J. 2001. *Social science methodology: a criterial framework.* Cambridge: Cambridge University Press.

Gerring, J. 2017. *Case study research: principles and practices,* 2nd edition. Cambridge: Cambridge University Press.

Gilman, A., and J. Hill. 2007. *Data analysis using regression and multilevel/hierarchical models.* Cambridge: Cambridge University Press.

Gleditsch, K., and M. Ward. 1999. A revised list of independent states since the Congress of Vienna. *International Interactions* 25:393–413.

Goertz, G. 2003. *International norms and decision making: a punctuated equilibrium model.* New York: Rowman & Littlefield.

Goertz, G. 2006. *Social science concepts: a user's guide.* Princeton: Princeton University Press.

Goertz, G. 2017. *Multimethod research, causal mechanisms, and case studies: an integrated approach.* Princeton: Princeton University Press.

Goertz, G. 2020. Peace: the elusive dependent variable and policy goal. *Perspectives on Politics* 18:200–204.

Goertz, G., P. Diehl, and A. Balas. 2016. *The puzzle of peace: the evolution of peace in the international system.* Oxford: Oxford University Press.

Goertz, G., T. Hak, and J. Dul. 2013. Ceilings and floors: Where are there no observations? *Sociological Methods & Research* 42:3–40.

Goertz, G., et al. 2019. Conceptualizing and measuring civil negative peace (CNP): a modular approach. Manuscript.

Goodfield, J., and S. Toulmin. 1962. *The architecture of matter.* Hutchinson

Greene, W. 1993. *Econometric analysis,* 2nd edition. London: Macmillan.

Grzymała-Busse, A. 2007. *Rebuilding leviathan: party competition and state exploitation in post-communist democracies.* Cambridge: Cambridge University Press.

Gunther, R., and L. Diamond. 2003. Species of political parties: a new typology. *Party Politics* 9:167–99.

Gurr, T., K. Jaggers, and W. Moore. 1990. The transformation of the Western state: the growth of democracy, autocracy, and state power since 1800. *Studies in Comparative International Development* 25:73–108.

Harré, R., and E. Madden. 1975. *Causal powers: a theory of natural necessity.* Oxford: Basil Blackwell.

Haughton, J., and S. Khandker. 2009. *Handbook on poverty and inequality.* Washington, DC: World Bank.

Hausman, D. 2015. *Valuing health: well-being, freedom, and suffering.* Oxford: Oxford University Press.

Heckman, S. 1983. *Weber, the ideal type, and contemporary social theory.* Notre Dame: University of Notre Dame Press.

Herrnstein, R., and C. Murray. 1994. *Bell curve.* New York: Free Press.

Hicken, A., and H. Stoll. 2012. Are all presidents created equal? Presidential powers and the shadow of presidential elections. *Comparative Political Studies* 46:291–319.

Hicks, A. 1999. *Social democracy & welfare capitalism: a century of income security politics.* Ithaca: Cornell University Press.

Hicks, A., J. Misra, and T. Ng. 1995. The programmatic emergence of the social security state. *American Sociological Review* 60:329–49.

Huntington, S. 1968. *Political order in changing societies.* New Haven: Yale University Press.

Illari, P., and J. Williamson. 2011. Mechanisms are real and local. In P. Illari et al. (eds.) *Causality in the sciences*. Oxford: Oxford University Press.

Jacoby, W. 2000. *Imitation and politics: redesigning modern Germany*. Ithaca: Cornell University Press.

Jaggers, K., and T. Gurr. 1995. Tracking democracy's third wave with the Polity III data. *Journal of Peace Research* 32:469–82.

Jencks, S., et al. 2003. Change in the quality of care delivered to Medicare beneficiaries, 1998–1999 to 2000–2001. *Journal of the American Medical Association* 289:305–12.

Kaltwasser, C. 2019. How to define populism? Reflections on a contested concept and its (mis)use in the social sciences. In G. Fitzi et al. (eds.) *Populism and the crisis of democracy, vol. 1*. London: Taylor & Francis.

Karantycky, A. 2000. *The comparative study of freedom, 1999–2000: survey methodology*. Washington: Freedom House.

Karl, T. 1990. Dilemmas of democratization in Latin America. *Comparative Politics* 23:1–21.

Kaufman, D., et al. 2007. Growth and governance: a reply. *Journal of Politics* 69:555–62.

Kelley, J. 2017. *Scorecard diplomacy: grading states to influence their reputation and behavior*. Cambridge University Press.

Kelley, J. and B. Simmons. 2015. Politics by number: indicators as social pressure in international relations. *American Journal of Political Science* 59:1146–61.

Kelley, J., and B. Simmons. 2019. Introduction: the power of global performance indicators. *International Organization* 73:491–510.

Khalidi, M. 2013. *Natural categories and human kinds: classification in the natural and social sciences*. Cambridge: Cambridge University Press.

Kim, J.-O., and G. Ferree. 1981. Standardization in causal analysis. *Sociological Methods & Research* 10:187–210.

Kim, N. 2018. Are military regimes *really* belligerent? *Journal of Conflict Resolution* 62:1151–78.

Kingdon, J. 1984. *Agendas, alternatives, and public policies*. Boston: Little, Brown.

Kiser, E., and M. Levi. 1996. Using counterfactuals in historical analysis: theories of revolution. In P. Tetlock and A. Belkin (eds.) *Counterfactual thought experiments in world politics: logical, methodological, and psychological perspectives*. Princeton: Princeton University Press.

Kitcher, P. 1992. The naturalists return. *Philosophical Review* 101:53–114.

Kosko, B. 1993. *Fuzzy thinking: the new science of fuzzy logic*. New York: Hyperion.

Kotowski, C. 1984. Revolution. In G. Sartori (ed.) *Social science concepts: a systematic analysis*. Beverly Hills: Sage Publications.

Kraidy, M. 2005. *Hybridity, or the cultural logic of globalization*. Philadelphia: Temple University Press.

Krishnakumar, J. 2007. Going beyond functionings to capabilities: an econometric model to explain and estimate capabilities. *Journal of Human Development* 8:39–63.

Krook, M. 2009. *Quotas for women in politics: gender and candidate selection reform worldwide*. Oxford: Oxford University Press.

Kuhlmann, J. 2018. What is a welfare state? In B. Greve et al. (eds.) *The Routledge handbook of the welfare state*, 2nd edition. London: Routledge.

Kurtz, M., and A. Schrank. 2007. Growth and governance: models, measures, and mechanisms. *Journal of Politics* 69:538–54.

Lakoff, G. 1987. *Women, fire and dangerous things: what categories reveal about the mind.* Chicago: University of Chicago Press.

Landau, M. 1969. Redundancy, rationality, and the problem of duplication and overlap. *Public Administration Review* 29:346–58.

Laurent, E. 2018. *Measuring tomorrow: accounting for well-being, resilience, and sustainability in the twenty-first century.* Princeton: Princeton University Press.

Lazarsfeld, P. 1966. Concept formation and measurement in the behavioral sciences: some historical observations. In G. DiRenzo (ed.) *Concepts, theory, and explanation in the behavioral sciences.* New York: Random House.

Lazarsfeld, P., and A. Barton. 1951. Qualitative measurement in the social sciences: classification, typologies, and indices. In D. Lerner and H. Lasswell (eds.) *The policy sciences: recent developments in scope and method.* Stanford: Stanford University Press.

Leamer, L. 1978. *Specification searches: ad hoc inferences with nonexperimental data.* New York: John Wiley & Sons.

Levitsky, S., and L. Way. 2010. *Competitive authoritarianism: hybrid regimes after the Cold War.* Cambridge: Cambridge University Press.

Lijphart, A. 1984. *Democracies: patterns of majoritarian and consensus government in twenty-one countries.* New Haven: Yale University Press.

Linz, J. 1975. Totalitarian and authoritarian regimes. In F. Greenstein and N. Polsby (eds.) *Handbook of political science.* Reading: Addison-Wesley.

Linz, J., and A. Stepan. 1996. *Problems of democratic transition and consolidation: Southern Europe, South America, and post-communist Europe.* Baltimore: Johns Hopkins University Press.

Locke, J. 1959 (1690). *An essay concerning human understanding.* New York: Dover.

Loyle, C., and H. Binningsbø. 2018. Justice during armed conflict: a new dataset on government and rebel strategies. *Journal of Conflict Resolution* 62:442–66.

Lucas, S., and A. Szatrowski. 2014. Qualitative comparative analysis in critical perspective [symposium]. *Sociological Methodology* 44:1–159.

Mac Ginty, R. 2010. Hybrid peace: the interaction between top-down and bottom-up peace. *Security Dialogue* 41:391–412.

Machery, E. 2009. *Doing without concepts.* Oxford: Oxford University Press.

Mahoney, J. 2008. Toward a unified theory of causality. *Comparative Political Studies* 41: 412–36.

Mansfield, E., and J. Synder. 2002. Democratic transitions, institutional strength and war. *International Organization* 56:297–337.

Marks, G. 1986. Neocorporatism, and incomes policy in western Europe and north America. *Comparative Politics* 18:253–77.

Marks, G., et al. 2017. *Measuring international authority: a postfunctionalist theory of governance, vol. III.* Oxford: Oxford University Press.

Masyn, K. 2013. Latent class analysis and finite mixture modeling. In T. Little (ed.) *The Oxford handbook of quantitative methods, vol. 2: statistical analysis.* Oxford: Oxford University Press.

McNeill, D., and P. Freiberger. 1994. *Fuzzy logic.* New York: Simon and Schuster.

Mello, P. 2012. Parliamentary peace or partisan politics? Democracies' participation in the Iraq War. *Journal of International Relations and Development* 15:420–53.

Merry, S. 2016. *The seductions of quantification: measuring human rights, gender violence, and sex trafficking.* Chicago: University of Chicago Press.

Mill, J. S. 1905 (1859). *System of logic, ratiocinative and inductive.* London: Routledge.

Milligan, G., and M. Cooper. 1988. A study of standardization of variables in cluster analysis. *Journal of Classification* 5:181–204.

Mintz, A. 1993. The decision to attack Iraq: a noncompensatory theory of decision-making. *Journal of Conflict Resolution* 37:595–618.

Moore, B. 1966. *The social origins of dictatorship and democracy: lord and peasant in the making of the modern world.* Boston: Beacon Press.

Morgenbesser, L., and T. Pepinsky. 2019. Elections as causes of democratization: southeast Asia in comparative perspective. *Comparative Political Studies* 52:3–35.

Most, B., and H. Starr. 1989. *Inquiry, logic, and international politics.* Columbia: University of South Carolina Press.

Murphy, G. 2002. *The big book of concepts.* Cambridge: MIT Press.

Nussbaum, M. 1992. Human functioning and social justice: in defense of Aristotelian essentialism. *Political Theory* 20:202–46.

Nussbaum, M. 2011. *Creating capabilities: the human development approach.* Cambridge: Harvard University Press.

Nussbaum, M., and A. Sen (eds.). 1993. *The quality of life.* Oxford: Oxford University Press.

O'Connor, J., A. Orloff, and S. Shaver. 1999. *States, markets, families: gender, liberalism, and social policy in Australia, Canada, Great Britain, and the United States.* Cambridge: Cambridge University Press.

OECD. 2008. *Handbook on constructing composite indicators: methodology and user guide.* Paris: OECD.

OECD. 2011. *How's life? Measuring well-being.* Paris: OECD.

OECD. 2015. *How's life? Measuring well-being.* Paris: OECD.

OECD. 2017. *How's life? Measuring well-being.* Paris: OECD.

Orloff, A. 1993. Gender and the social rights of citizenship: the comparative analysis of gender relations and welfare states. *American Sociological Review* 58:303–28.

Orloff, A. 1996. Gender in the welfare state. *Annual Review of Sociology* 22:51–78.

Osherson, D., and E. Smith. 1982. Gradedness and conceptual conjunction. *Cognition* 12:299–318.

Ostrom, E. 1991. *Governing the commons: the evolution of institutions for collective action.* Cambridge: Cambridge University Press.

Ostrom, E. 1997. A behavioral approach to the rational choice theory of collective action. *American Political Science Review* 92:1–22.

Papineau, D. 1976. Ideal types and empirical theories. *British Journal for the Philosophy of Science* 27:137–46.

Paxton, P. 1999. Is social capital declining in the United States? A multiple indicator assessment. *American Journal of Sociology* 105:88–127.

Paxton, P. 2000. Women in the measurement of democracy: problems of operationalization. *Studies in Comparative International Development* 35:92–111.

Pevehouse, J. 2005. *Democracy from above: regional organizations and democratization.* Cambridge: Cambridge University Press.

Pierson, P. 2000. Three worlds of welfare state research. *Comparative Political Studies* 33: 791–821.

Pinker, S. 2011. *The better angels of our nature: the decline of violence.* New York: Viking Press.

Pinker, S. 2018. *Enlightenment now: the case for reason, science, humanism, and progress.* New York: Vintage Books.

Powell, J., and C. Thyne. 2011. Global instances of coups from 1950 to 2010: a new dataset. *Journal of Peace Research* 48:249–59.

Przeworski, A., et al. 2000. *Democracy and development: political institutions and well-being in the world, 1950–1990.* Cambridge: Cambridge University Press.

Ragin, C. 1987. *The comparative method: moving beyond qualitative and quantitative strategies.* Berkeley: University of California Press.

Ragin, C. 2000. *Fuzzy-set social science.* Chicago: University of Chicago Press.

Ragin, C. 2008. *Redesigning social inquiry: fuzzy sets and beyond.* Chicago: University of Chicago Press.

Ragin, C. 2014. Comment: Lucas and Szatrowski in critical perspective. *Sociological Methodology* 44:80–94.

Ragin, C., and P. Fiss. 2017. *Intersectional inequality: race, class, test scores, and poverty.* Chicago: University of Chicago Press.

Ravallion, M. 2016. *The economics of poverty: history, measurement, and policy.* Oxford: Oxford University Press.

Rawls, J. 1971. *A theory of justice.* Cambridge: Harvard University Press.

Rawls, J. 1982. Social unity and primary goods. In A. Sen and B. Williams (eds.) *Utilitarianism and beyond.* Cambridge: Cambridge University Press.

Richards, C., and M. O'Hara. 2014. *The Oxford handbook of depression and comorbidity.* Oxford: Oxford University Press.

Robeyns, I. 2017. *Wellbeing, freedom and social justice: the capability approach re-examined.* Cambridge: Open Book Publishers.

Rotberg, R. 2018. Good governance: measuring the performance of governments. In D. Malito et al. (eds.) *The Palgrave handbook of indicators in global governance.* London: Palgrave.

Rupp, A. 2013. Clustering and classification. In T. Little (ed.) *The Oxford handbook of quantitative methods, vol. 2: statistical analysis.* Oxford: Oxford University Press.

Sachs, J., et al. (2019). *Sustainable development report 2019.* New York: Bertelsmann Stiftung and Sustainable Development Solutions Network (SDSN).

Sambanis, N. 2004. What is civil war? Conceptual and empirical complexities of an operational definition. *Journal of Conflict Resolution* 48:814–58.

Sandler, T. 1992. *Collective action: theory and applications.* Ann Arbor: University of Michigan Press.

Sartori, G. 1970. Concept misformation in comparative politics. *American Political Science Review* 64:1033–53.

Schärlig, A. 1985. *Décider sur plusieurs critères.* Lausanne: Presses Polytechniques Romandes.

Schenoni, L., et al. 2020. Settling resistant disputes: the territorial boundary peace in Latin America. *International Studies Quarterly* 64:57–70.

Schmitter, P. 1974. Still the century of corporatism? *Review of Politics* 36:85–131.

Schmitter, P., and T. Karl. 1991. What democracy is … and is not. *Journal of Democracy* 2: 75–88.

Schumpeter, J. 1950. *Capitalism, socialism, and democracy*, 3rd edition. New York: Harper & Row.

Seawright, J., and J. Gerring. 2008. Case selection techniques in case study research: a menu of qualitative and quantitative options. *Political Research Quarterly* 61:294–308.

Sen, A. 1973. Behavior and the concept of preference. *Economica* 40:241–59.

Sen, A. 1992. *Inequality reexamined.* Cambridge: Harvard University Press.

Sen, A. 1999. *Development as freedom.* New York: Anchor Books.

Sen, A. 2009. *The idea of justice.* Cambridge: Harvard University Press.

Shugart, M. 2005. Semi-presidential systems: dual executive and mixed authority patterns. *French Politics* 3:323–51.

Siaroff, A. 2003. Comparative presidencies: the inadequacy of the presidential, semi-presidential and parliamentary distinction. *European Journal of Political Research* 42: 287–312.

Signorino, C., and J. Ritter. 1999. Tau-b or not tau-b: measuring the similarity of foreign policy positions. *International Studies Quarterly* 43:115–44.

Simon, H. 1996. *The sciences of the artificial*, 3rd edition. Cambridge: MIT Press.

Skocpol, T. 1979. *States and social revolutions: a comparative analysis of France, Russia, and China.* Cambridge: Cambridge University Press.

Stepan, A., and C. Skach. 1993. Constitutional frameworks and democratic consolidation: parliamentarism versus presidentialism. *World Politics* 46:1–22.

Stevens, S. 1946. On the theory of scales of measurement. *Science* 103:677–80.

Stevens, S. 1968. Measurement, statistics and the schemparic view. *Science* 161:849–56.

Stiglitz, J., et al. 2009. Report by the Commission on the Measurement of Economic Performance and Social Progress. https://www.ofce.sciences-po.fr/pdf/dtravail/WP2009-33 .pdf.

Stinchcombe, A. 1968. *Constructing social theories.* New York: Harcourt, Brace & World.

Suppes, P., and J. Zinnes. 1963. Basic measurement theory. In R. Luce et al. (eds.) *Handbook of mathematical psychology.* New York: John Wiley & Sons.

Swedberg, R. 2015. On the near disappearance of concepts in mainstream sociology. In H. Leiulfsrud and P. Sohlberg (eds.) *Concepts in action: applications and development of theory in the social sciences.* Leiden: Brill.

Swedberg, R. 2017. Theorizing in sociological research: a new perspective, a new departure? *American Sociological Review* 43:189–206.

Teorell, J., et al. 2019. Measuring polyarchy across the globe, 1900–2017. *Studies in Comparative International Development* 54:71–95.

Tiberius, V. 2004. Cultural differences and philosophical accounts of well-being. *Journal of Happiness Studies* 5:293–314.

Tir, J., and J. Karreth. 2017. *Incentivizing peace: how international organizations can help prevent civil wars in member countries.* Oxford: Oxford University Press.

Treier, S., and S. Jackman. 2008. Democracy as a latent variable. *American Journal of Political Science* 52:201–17.

Tsebelis, G. 2002. *Veto players: how political institutions work.* Princeton: Princeton University Press.

Tukey, J. 1969. Analyzing data: sanctification or detective work. *American Psychologist* 24: 83–91.

UNDP. 1994. *Human development report.* Oxford: Oxford University Press.

UNDP. 2018a. Human development indices and indicators: 2018 statistical update. New York: United Nations.

UNDP. 2018b. Human development indices and indicators 2018 statistical update; Technical notes. New York: United Nations.

United Nations Secretary General. 2010. *Guidance note of the Secretary-General: United Nations approach to transitional justice.* New York: United Nations.

Weber, M. 1949. *Max Weber on the methodology of the social sciences.* New York: Free Press.

Weede, E. 1976. Overwhelming preponderance as a pacifying condition among contiguous Asian dyads, 1950–1969. *Journal of Conflict Resolution* 20:395–411.

Weeks, J. 2014. *Dictators at war and peace.* Ithaca: Cornell University Press.

Wickham-Crowley, T. 1991. *Guerrillas and revolution in Latin America: a comparative study of insurgents and regimes since 1956.* Princeton: Princeton University Press.

Wintrobe, R. 1990. The tinpot and the totalitarian: an economic theory of dictatorship. *American Political Science Review* 84:849–72.

Wittgenstein, L. 1953. *Philosophical investigations.* London: Macmillan.

Wolff, J., and A. De-Shalit. 2007. *Disadvantage.* Oxford: Oxford University Press.

Wood, R., and M. Gibney. 2010. The Political Terror Scale (PTS): a re-introduction and a comparison to CIRI. *Human Rights Quarterly* 32:367–400.

Wuttke, A., C. Schimpf, and H. Schoen. 2020. When the whole is greater than the sum of its parts: on the conceptualization and measurement of populist attitudes and other multidimensional constructs. *American Political Science Review* 114(2): 356–74.

Ziaja, S., and M. Elff. 2015. An empirical typology of political regimes. Paper presented at the annual meeting of the American Political Science Association.

# INDEX

adjectives (in concepts), 70, 101, 113–114, 121–123, 134, 247, 262–269; fuzzy logic and, 30. *See also* hyphenated concepts; terminology

agenda-setting models, 174, 288–289

aggregation, 14–20, 28–29, 40, 93–94, 163–191, 194–195, 197–199, 201n, 214, 273; mathematics of, 26, 30–31, 147–148, 151, 166, 170–172, 177, 181, 183, 209, 254; weighting, 147, 171. *See also* best shot; concept structure; mean; substitutability; weakest link

Alexandrova, A., 12

Aristotle, 3, 35, 40, 55, 75, 167, 245, 253

asymmetry, 110, 112, 113, 127, 197, 206. *See also* concept pairs

average. *See* mean

authoritarianism, concept of, 21, 196, 209, 221; typology of, 218–219, 221–222, 231–232. *See also* autocracy, concept of; democracy, concept of; Geddes, B.

autocracy, concept of, 70, 153, 203n, 206–207, 208, 216–217, 221, 228, 268. *See also* authoritarianism, concept of

Ballung concepts, 245

basic framework, 3, 26–66, 163–166, 189, 196, 214, 280; aggregation in, 35, 40–41, 46, 48–51; basic level in, 27–29, 273–274, 275–277, 287, 292; data-indicator level in, 27–29, 46–51, 68, 69n3, 69n4, 98–135; 181, 189; fractal character of, 31, 98–99, 134, 136,

163–165; multidimensionality, 3, 25, 27, 137, 162, 292; multilevel, 3, 25, 27, 51–53, 137, 162, 166, 272–273; relation-ships in, 277–278; secondary/semantic level in, 27–29, 33, 37, 40–41, 43, 56, 62–63, 94, 176, 187, 244–271, 272–274, 277–279, 283–285, 287, 292, 298. *See also* aggregation; concept structure

basic-level dimensions. *See* basic framework

*Bell curve*, 104, 127–128, 153

Bernhard, M., 203

best shot, 16–17, 50, 165–166, 176–179, 246, 256–257; maximum and, 166, 176–177, 187–191; sum and, 176, 178, 179, 181, 261–262; union and, 177. *See also* aggregation; concept structure; necessary and sufficient conditions; substitutability

bipolar concepts. *See* concept pairs

Bipolarity-Incompleteness Guideline, 111–114. *See also* causal asymmetry

Borsboom, D., 61

Bowman, K., 7, 199–200

Bueno de Mesquita, B., 144–145, 148

calibration, 99n, 133, 134, 158. *See* fuzzy logic; semantic transformations

Cartwright, N., 23, 90–92, 245, 278

case selection, 75–76, 81, 192, 211–213, 272n; scope decisions and, 14, 75–76

categorization, 102, 109–111, 123–125, 125–129, 158–160; ordinal variables

A NOTE ON THE TYPE

This book has been composed in Arno, an Old-style serif typeface in the
classic Venetian tradition, designed by Robert Slimbach at Adobe.

GPSR Authorized Representative: Easy Access System Europe - Mustamäe tee
50, 10621 Tallinn, Estonia, gpsr.requests@easproject.com